Technical Analysis

4th Edition

by Barbara Rockefeller

A Wiley Brand

Technical Analysis For Dummies®, 4th Edition

Published by: **John Wiley & Sons, Inc.,** 111 River Street, Hoboken, NJ 07030-5774, www.wiley.com

Copyright © 2020 by John Wiley & Sons, Inc., Hoboken, New Jersey

Published simultaneously in Canada

For general information on our other products and services, please contact our Customer Care Department within the U.S. at 877-762-2974, outside the U.S. at 317-572-3993, or fax 317-572-4002. For technical support, please visit www.wiley.com/techsupport.

Wiley publishes in a variety of print and electronic formats and by print-on-demand. Some material included with standard print versions of this book may not be included in e-books or in print-on-demand. If this book refers to media such as a CD or DVD that is not included in the version you purchased, you may download this material at http://booksupport.wiley.com. For more information about Wiley products, visit www.wiley.com.

Library of Congress Control Number: 2019946701

ISBN: 978-1-119-59655-4

ISBN 978-1-119-59667-7 (ebk); ISBN 978-1-119-59670-7 (ebk)

Manufactured in the United States of America

SKY10025613_031121

Contents at a Glance

Table of Contents

Introduction

Timing can be everything.

Timing is critical in cooking, romance, music, politics, farming, and a hundred other aspects of life on this planet. Putting money into a securities market — and taking it out with a gain — is no different: You need good timing to get the best results.

Technical traders all over the world, amateur and professional alike, earn a living using technical analysis to time their trades in many different markets. And they're still standing after a market crash, unlike many so-called value investors. In this book, I try to explain how they do that and how you can do it, too.

About This Book

The technical analysis industry is expanding at an exponential pace. A few years ago, an Internet search for the term "technical analysis" returned 206 million responses. Now it returns *1.36 billion* responses. Even after weeding out duplicates and mismatches, it's still a huge amount of material. Don't be intimidated by the sheer size of the available material. In this fourth edition of *Technical Analysis For Dummies*, I cover the core concepts, most of which you could apply *today* with no further research. If you were to explore the most advanced entry in the 1.36 billion entries, most of it would be familiar to you from reading this book.

Technical ideas range from the super simple to the tremendously complex. I cover the core concepts that are the building blocks of all, or nearly all, of those tremendously complex systems. It's up to you to choose to stay with one of two simple ideas or forge onward to the complex. There is no single best technical idea or combination of ideas, for reasons I explain.

Technical analysis is not only a set of tools. It's also a mindset, a way of looking at securities prices and how they wag and what wags them. The first principle of the technical mindset is to throw conventional wisdom out the window and trade what you see on the chart. Technical analysis is an evidence-based method of making trading decisions, which means you won't be consulting earning per share, cash flow, management quality, or any of the other fundamentals that lead to an assessment of value. Technical analysis isn't value investing. *Value investing* would have you continue to hold a high-value security despite a big drop in price. The technical analysis trader will sell it, knowing he can always come back after the price bottoms and starts recovering.

Try to think like a 10-year-old as you read this book. In fact, go find a 10-year-old, if you have one handy, and ask him, "Which is better to hang on to: a thing that has already let you down (losses) or a different thing that's delivering exactly what you wanted (profits)?" See?

That doesn't mean you may not prefer to keep only high-value names in your portfolio and winnow the portfolio for changing value. It does mean your focus is not on the intrinsic value of the securities you're holding, but rather on the gain you expect to make in éach security.

Beating the system is fun and rewarding. The market doesn't know you, your age, gender, ethnicity, good looks or lack of them, singing talent, or anything else about you except whether you're a successful trader. The market is blind. In fact, the market is indifferent. It's the one place you can go to be judged solely on your merits. Use this book to help you find your way.

The good news is that *For Dummies* books are designed so that you can jump in anywhere and get the information you need. Don't feel that you have to read every chapter — or even the entire chapter. Take advantage of the table of contents and index to find what you're looking for, and check it out. Here are a few tidbits that may answer some questions before you jump in:

>> The point of technical analysis is to help you observe prices in a new way and to make trading decisions based on reasonable expectations about where the market is going to take the price.

>> Before you plunge into risking hard-earned cash on securities trading, you have to realize that it's not the security that counts; it's the trade. Each trade has two parts: the price analysis and you. Price analysis tools are called indicators, and you have to select the indicators that match your personality and preference for risk. But most people don't know their risk preference when they start out in securities trading (which changes over time, anyway), so you have a chicken-and-egg situation. By studying the kinds of profit-and-loss outcomes that each type of indicator delivers, you can figure out your risk preferences.

>> The price bar and its placement on the chart deliver a ton of information about market sentiment. It doesn't take much practice to start reading the mind of the market by looking at bars and small patterns. The payoff is cold, hard cash, but you have to be patient, imaginative, and thoughtful.

>> Indicators are the workhorses of technical analysis. They help you identify whether your price is trending, the strength of the trend, and when the trend is at a reversal point. Applying these indicators carefully and consistently is the key to trading success.

>> You don't have to be math-competent to do excellent technical analysis and make lovely profits. Technical analysis is mostly visual — what you see on the chart and how you interpret it.

>> Technical analysis is a form of quantitative analysis. Behind every fancy, complicated hedge fund system run by *quants* are the very core concepts I present here. It's how the quants put these factors together into a system, usually with automated buy/sell execution, that gives the hedge funds their edge. But you can get the same edge without building a system.

Foolish Assumptions

Every author must make assumptions about her audience, and I make a few assumptions that may apply to you:

>> You've dabbled in securities trading but without much luck. You want to become successful and make some money.

>> You're reasonably well versed in the trading game, but you're looking for new tools to become a more effective trader and improve your profits.

>> You're tired of the buy-and-hold approach in which your returns seem unrelated to the supposed quality of the security you bought.

>> You want to find out how to sell. You know how to buy, but timing your sales ties you up in knots.

>> You've experienced some setbacks in the market, and you need an approach to make that money back.

>> You want to know whether technical analysis has any basis in reason and logic — or whether all technical analysts are crackpots.

If any of these descriptions fits the bill, then you've picked up the right book.

Icons Used in This Book

Icons are small pictures in the margins of this book that flag certain material for you. The following icons highlight information you want to pay special attention to.

REMEMBER

When you see this icon, you don't want to forget the accompanying info — pretty subtle, huh?

TIP

This icon clues you in on hands-on time- and hassle-saving advice that you can put into practice. In many cases, this icon tells you directly how to conduct a trade on a technical principle, usually an indicator crossing something, breaking something, or dancing a jig.

WARNING

Ignore this information at your own financial peril. I use this icon to warn you about mistakes, missteps, and traps that can sink even the best trading professional.

TECHNICAL STUFF

This icon flags places where I get really technical about technical analysis. Although it's great info, you can skip it and not miss out on the subject at hand.

Where to Go from Here

If you're new to technical analysis, take a close look at Parts 1 and 2 for the scoop on the field. If you are already a good chart reader, what you probably need is help on managing the trade (Chapter 5). Applying indicators is better than willy-nilly trading decisions, but to get The Traders' Edge, you also need the discipline of a winner. How do you become a winner? The same way you get to Carnegie Hall — practice, practice, practice, and hanging out with other winners. Figuring out how to trade technically is a journey of self-discovery, corny as that sounds. Luckily, it's a journey with a lot of fellow travelers to keep you company. I hope you enjoy the road.

1
Getting Started with Technical Analysis

Find out what technical analysis is and isn't. Technical analysis bypasses fundamentals to make trading decisions on indicators that reveal market sentiment.

Understand supply and demand. Securities trading deals with two forms of supply and demand, the old-fashioned kind and also auction-style. You want to join the trading crowd to take advantage of momentum but very carefully, without going overboard.

Appreciate that indicators work most of the time because of the law of large numbers, but not always, and that's because the market is made up of humans who behave irrationally sometimes.

Check out sentiment indicators and some useful measurement methods to get an overview of the trading environment, especially volume as an indicator of what the crowd is doing — as contrasted with what they might be saying.

Protect your capital from random moves and from manias and panics by managing the trade from entry to exit, including exits that mean you'll be taking a loss. All trading involves taking losses and the secret of success lies in controlling them.

Chapter **1**

Introducing Technical Analysis

Technical analysis is the study of price behavior in financial markets in order to forecast the next price movement and to trade on that forecast with cold, hard cash. Focusing on price behavior gives you a window into the mind of the market — what the majority of key players are thinking — and helps you make better trading decisions. Technical analysis seeks to identify and measure market sentiment, described as optimistic (bullish), pessimistic (bearish), or uncertain about future prices (sideways range-trading).

To become a technical analyst, you need to figure out how to draw lines on your security price chart and work up the courage to place the buy and sell order with your broker. Each type of line is named an indicator, and I cover every major type of indicator in this book. You need to figure out whether the line/indicator embodies a bullish or bearish outlook (price rising or falling). Many lines/indicators contain a handy built-in buy-and-sell signal, but following those probably won't match your risk appetite given the amount of capital you have. In practice, you'll use a computer program to draw the lines (and to do whatever math underlies the lines). You'll also have many books and websites to guide you in deciding which lines to draw.

Knowing how to draw lines is relatively easy. Placing the trades is hard. This is because your technical-based buy/sell decisions don't come packaged with how much to trade, how long to hold, how much risk to take, or even how much risk is involved.

FINDING THE ORIGINS OF TECHNICAL ANALYSIS

Technical analysis isn't some newfangled flash in the pan. Observing prices and shutting out other noise has been in development for more than a century. Charles Dow, one of the founders of *The Wall Street Journal,* observed around the turn of the 20th century that the price of a security neatly cuts through all the clutter of words and is the one piece of hard information you can trust, no matter what the other facts about a security and what people are saying about it.

Here are some basic observations underlying technical analysis that are attributed to Dow himself:

- Securities prices move in trends much of the time.

- Trends can be identified with patterns that you see repeatedly (which I cover in Chapter 9) and with support and resistance trendlines (see Chapter 10).

- Primary trends (lasting months or years) are punctuated by secondary movements (lasting weeks or months) in the opposite direction of the primary trend. Secondary trends, today called retracements, are the very devil to deal with as a trader. (See Chapter 2 for more on retracements.)

- Trends remain in place until some major event comes along to stop them.

These ideas are part of what is called *Dow theory*, although Charles Dow himself never called it that and many ideas are called Dow theory that would surprise Dow. An Internet search of the phrase *Dow theory* yields 23 million hits. A key point is that traders were using technical ideas long before the advent of electronic communication and software programs — technical analysis is hardly a gimmicky fad that will have a short shelf life.

Building on Dow theory were Robert D. Edwards and John Magee, whose *Technical Analysis of Stock Trends* (St. Lucie Press) was the first major book to use the term "technical analysis" in the title. It was published in 1948 and has been in print ever since. Edwards and Magee expanded on Dow's observations, covering many of the core concepts of technical analysis such as support and resistance, breakouts, retracements, many patterns, and more. Edwards and Magee noted the universal pattern of a primary upmove followed by a shallower secondary pullback and then another upmove. You'll see this configuration repeatedly as you explore technical analysis. Edwards and Magee were the first to introduce the tools still in use today to evaluate the pattern and to trade it profitably.

What's different from Dow's day and Edwards and Magee's day is the advent of computers that take drawing lines and calculating indicators away from paper and colored pencils to a screen and cursors. Something else that differs from Dow's day is the continuous incursion of the scientific method into everyday life. At the turn of the last century, the scientific method was confined to scientists. Regular people would take a homemade folk remedy for a malady because their grandmother swore by it. Today the average person wants to know if that remedy was scientifically tested in double-blind tests and the results peer-reviewed. The comparable development in technical analysis is to take an observation about market prices and volume and to test what percentage of the time the observation results in a correct deduction.

To help you start, this chapter provides an overview to this book and what you can expect. Consider it your jumping board into this book and the world of technical analysis.

Stepping Up to Science

It may be hard to consider drawing lines on a chart as "scientific" in any sense of the word, but it's through the scientific method that scientists can forecast outcomes in the physical world and through the scientific method that you can forecast price outcomes in financial markets. Technical analysis of securities prices follows the scientific method in that it entails systematic observation of the subject with standard measurement methods to form a hypothesis and then testing the hypothesis many, many times to validate the theory. But there's a problem. In a hard science like fluid dynamics, the thing being observed and measured is an object — in this case, water. In technical analysis, the thing being measured isn't hard — it's market sentiment generated by human beings, who have far more variability than physical objects. Even given human variability, market sentiment tends to move in repetitive and predictable ways. Technical analysis gives you the tools to identify which sentiment the market has on display at any one time.

Today's technical analysis has a wider understanding and appreciation of statistics and probability, and thus the value and pitfalls of forecasting. The theory of probability originated in the 16th and 17th centuries, but dealt mostly with the outcome of games and thus the best way to bet on games. Not until the 1920s and 1930s did statistics and probability enter the general public mainstream. Today even ordinary people routinely ask health questions of their doctors in probability terms, such as what percentage of small children without the measles vaccination does it take for the rest of the school class to risk a measles outbreak?

Throughout this book I use words like "highly likely" and "forecast." I say, for example, technical analysts use lines and indicators to identify price moves that provide a fairly reliable forecast of upcoming future price moves. The word "forecast" makes everybody squeamish because everyone knows stories of catastrophically bad ones. History is full of them, like a top economist saying in 1929 that the stock market was in fine fettle — just before the crash.

But don't be misled. Although the word is riddled with negative implications, everyone makes forecasts all the time. They just don't think of them as forecasts. In fact, you make forecasts many times every day. You take this travel route over some other route because you forecast it will save time or aggravation. On a larger scale, when you move to a new city, take a new job, get married, have children, or buy a house, you're making a forecast about the outcome. Every life decision you make is a forecast — a bet — almost always made on incomplete or hidden information. Technical analysis entails forecasting, but don't let that scare you. You'll have plenty of data in dozens of formats to help you, and I describe nearly all of them in this book.

Unpacking Lingo

To get you started, most of the vocabulary associated with technical analysis that you need to know you learned in grade school. Here is a list of some of the important lingo to know:

>> **Chart:** The workspace of technical analysis is a *chart*. Much of the time the chart will show time along the horizontal axis and price along the vertical axis, but not always. (Some charts are formed differently, as I discuss in Chapter 15).

>> **Bar:** The price information on the chart is presented in several different formats, but usually you'll see each period's price as a standard *bar* showing the price open, high, low, and close. (Refer to Chapter 6 for more about bars.) Bars, or a series of bars, can be used alone to detect patterns that reveal how participants in that market feel about the security and therefore what might happen next to the price. (Chapters 7, 8, and 9 discuss how technical analysts use bars to forecast prices.)

>> **Candlesticks:** Another method of showing the same information that the bar does is the *candlestick bar* (see Chapter 8).

>> **Lines:** Drawing *lines* on the chart helps forecast future prices. For example, you may draw a line connecting a series of price lows and name it "support," meaning you expect the traders in this security will see the next low as a buying opportunity, raising the price again. (Chapters 10 and 11 provide more detail.)

>> **Indicators:** You want to enhance the information in the price data by arithmetic manipulation, creating *indicators.* Indicators comes in all shapes and sizes. For example, you see a price chart where the price jumps all over the place. You have no idea whether to buy it or at what price. Now take an average of the closing price over the past 20 days to smooth out the price jumps. Does that line of averages point up or down? Aha! You may have identified a tradeable trend. I describe a wide range of indicators in Chapters 12, 13, and 14.

Buy-and-Hold Is Bunk

You may think that active trading is too much work and too uncertain to spend the time on. Why not just buy-and-hold? *Buy-and-hold* is a philosophy that says most equities are best left unattended for long periods of time in your portfolio. They'll rise more or less in sync with the overall economy so that avoiding turnover saves you transactions costs and taxes. Besides, who are you to suggest a security is over or undervalued?

One reason to distrust buy-and-hold is that over really long periods, returns aren't very good at all. Stocks from 1950 to 2018 returned 11.1 percent annually. Bonds returned 5.8 percent. If you had a 50/50 stock and bond portfolio, you averaged 8.8 percent. The average return on the S&P 500 over the past 30 years is only about 8 percent. In order to get higher returns, you had to pick one of the periods when market was in a bull market phase. In the United States, from 1927 to 2018, the Standard & Poor's equity index has been in 25 bull market phases, meaning it rose more than 20 percent. Each one averaged about three years, and the average return of each of the bull markets was 127.36 percent. But the S&P also fell 20 percent or more, defined as a bear market, 25 times over that same period. Timing counts.

In other words, to buy and hold securities for a long period of time is a well-documented path to accumulating capital, but *only if you got in at the best time.* Otherwise, buy-and-hold is a path to the poorhouse. Consider the following:

>> If you had bought U.S. stocks at the price peak just ahead of the 1929 crash, it would've taken you more than 20 years to recover your initial capital.

>> Since the end of World War II, the Dow Jones Industrial Average has fallen by more than 20 percent on 14 occasions.

>> From January 2000 to October 2002, the S&P 500 fell by 50 percent. If you owned all the stocks in the S&P 500 and held them throughout the entire

period, you lost 50 percent of your stake, which means you'd now need to make a gain equivalent to 100 percent of your remaining capital to get your money back. Ask yourself how often anyone makes a 100 percent return on investment.

» During the Crash of 2018, the S&P fell 6.2 percent and the Dow 5.6 percent, the worst performance in a decade — during a year that saw the highest economic growth in a decade.

That covers the factual aspect of buy-and-hold — you need to get lucky in your entry. Now consider the underlying assumption that all information is already incorporated into the price, the so-called *efficient markets hypothesis.* Even in the "weak" form of the argument, the assumption is patently untrue.

For one thing, if markets were actually efficient, you shouldn't get bubbles and crashes, and yet undeniably they happen. Behavioral economists have found that prices are influenced by all kinds of bias, including overconfidence, wishful thinking, and the whole panoply of possible errors in both reasoning and in evaluating information that's not always unambiguous.

Can you beat the market using timing over buy-and-hold? Yes. *Timer Digest* has tracked dozens of timers in gold, bonds, and equities who publish newsletters over the past 35 years (www.timerdigest.com). In 2018 alone, the S&P ex-dividends fell 6.24 percent. The top ten timers had gains ranging from 12.86 percent to 40.32 percent. Over the past ten years, the S&P rose a cumulative 177 percent. The top timer had a return of 249 percent. The timers aren't getting one-time lucky. You see the same names over and over again.

REMEMBER

The emphasis in technical analysis is to make profits from trading, not to consider owning a security as some kind of savings vehicle. In buy-and-hold investing, you hardly ever sell, sometimes waiting until you have a catastrophic loss. In technical trading, when you sell is just as important as when you buy.

Before diving into technical analysis, first you have to appreciate that it's the chart that determines the trading decision, not the underlying fundamentals of the security. You don't have to follow earnings, management style, new inventions and designs, or any other qualitative aspect of an equity security. In commodities, that might be the weather in Brazil or Chinese demand for rare metals. In foreign exchange, you can ignore inflation, GDP, and central bank forward guidance.

You can still use fundamentals if you want to. Although technical analysis is the central factor in the trading decision, it doesn't have to be the *only* factor. Many technical analysts use programs to winnow out the best candidates in a list of securities based on fundamentals like earnings, dominance in its sector, sales forecasts, dividends, and so on, and then apply technical analysis to the select few that remain.

Fundamental analysis and technical analysis aren't enemies. They can be combined to complement one another.

Recognizing Who Uses Technical Analysis

Both traders and investors use technical analysis. So what's the difference between a trader and an investor? Most people consider that a *trader* is someone who holds securities for only a short period of time, anywhere from a minute to a year. An *investor* is someone who holds securities from many months to forever. You may also think of an investor as someone who seeks income from dividends or bond coupon payments.

Actually, the dividing line between trader and investor isn't fixed except for purposes of taxation. Be careful not to fall into the semantic trap of thinking that a trader is a wild-eyed speculator while an investor is a respectable guy in a pinstriped suit. I use the word *trader* in this book, but don't let it distract you. People who consider themselves *investors* use technical methods, too.

REMEMBER

You can use technical methods over any investment horizon, including the long term. If you're an expert in Blue Widget stock, for example, you can use technical analysis to add to your holdings when the price is relatively low, take some partial profit when the price is relatively high, and dump it all when it falls more than you can stomach, only to buy it back when it bottoms. Technical analysis has tools for identifying each of these situations. You can also use technical tools to rotate your capital among several securities, allocating more capital to the ones delivering the highest gains or the lowest risk. At the other end of the holding period spectrum, you can use technical analysis to spot a high-probability trade and execute the purchase and sale in one hour.

Remembering the Trend Is Your Friend

You can look at most charts and see that securities prices tend to move in trends, and trends often persist for long periods of time. Opinion varies as to how long any specific security remains in trending mode. It may be 20 percent or it may be 80 percent. A *trend* is a discernible directional bias in the price — upwards, downwards, or sideways. Many people don't consider sideways a trend in its own right, but rather a departure from an upward or downward direction.

And yet it can be useful to consider sideways a trend because when you widen the time frame to include more time, you often see that a sideways move is a transition phase from one direction to the other, often on a sudden breakout. You gain an edge when you can forecast a change in direction, even if you don't know yet which way. The secret to successful trading is to buy at a low price and sell at a higher price. The chart displays lows and highs, and your charting work should indicate where you can next buy low and sell high.

In these sections, I show a model for identifying trendedness and how technical analysts use the model to make money.

Charting your path

The price chart is the primary workspace of technical analysis. Many technical analysts work only with mathematical manipulation of prices in order to devise probabilistically optimum trades, but the chart is the starting point for nearly everyone and remains the main workspace for the majority. Figure 1-1 shows a classic uptrend following a downtrend.

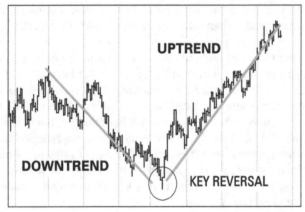

FIGURE 1-1:
Uptrend and downtrend.

© John Wiley & Sons, Inc.

REMEMBER

At the most basic level, your goal as a technical trader is to sit on your hands while the security is falling and wait to identify the *reversal point* — the best place to buy (shown in the circle) — as early as possible. Figure 1-1 is a good example of the kind of chart with which you'll spend most of your time. Unfortunately, most charts aren't as clear-cut as to the correct trading decision as this one.

Trendiness versus trendedness

To say that something is on a trend is to say that it's moving in a specific direction and exhibits evidence of a tendency to continue in that same direction. The use of social media like Twitter and Facebook is a trend. What's the difference between trendiness and trendedness?

>> *Trendiness* implies a fashion or fad that may wither and blow away, like skinny jeans.

>> *Trendedness* refers to a measurable directional bias. It's a more serious word reflecting a more serious and enduring phenomenon.

Skinny jeans may be out of fashion 30 years from now, but social media will probably still be around and securities charts will still be exhibiting price trendedness.

BECOMING A QUANT

You don't need to know any math at all in order to use technical analysis. If the word "algorithm" makes you feel faint, fear not. It's enough to know the difference between big and small, up and down, black and white.

Math is a shorthand method of expressing what nonmath types (me included) put into words. For example, I may say, "The price is moving upward at a faster pace than before." The math person measures the exact extent of the upmove in arithmetic terms such as momentum. He takes today's price and divides it by the price times number of days ago. He does this for five days in a row and gets a momentum indicator that is a higher number every day. Just because the math person has a number doesn't make his trading decision any better than yours without the number — the observation of the price event is equally valid however you express it.

You can use indicators that you put on the chart yourself from your charting program, broker platform, or website that lets you fool around with their indicators — without knowing or caring about the math behind the indicator. Your job as a student of technical analysis is not to know exactly how an indicator is calculated arithmetically. It's to know what the indicator is indicating and what decision the indicator is suggesting to you.

Don't worry about finding a user-friendly program to do the math work for you. Twenty years ago, both the data and the software were very expensive — now they're a given. Do a web search of "free charting software" and you get more than four million hits, including reviews of the programs.

Picking a time frame

You don't have to select a time frame right away. In fact, don't rush. You may fancy yourself a conservative person who would never want to join the ranks of those flibberty-gibbet day traders, but the fact remains that day trading is a deeply risk-averse form of trading when properly executed. And your position on life's timescale can be important, too. You can't day trade when you have a day job, but you can when you've retired or are temporarily out of work. I know of one auto company president (yes, president) who got through a rough patch (meaning unemployed) by day trading.

REMEMBER

Complicating your decision about what time frame to trade is the weird and wonderful aspect of market prices named their fractal property. *Fractal* refers to the odd fact that a price chart of a security on a one-hour time frame basis can't be told apart from the price chart on a four-hour time frame or daily time frame or even weekly. If the chart isn't labeled along the bottom horizontal *x*-axis to disclose its period, you can analyze it using any indicator and get the same outcome as you would get on any other time frame.

Viewing the Scope of Technical Analysis

Technical analysis focuses on prices and often on the accompanying volume. Analyzing prices can take many different forms — from drawing lines on a chart by hand to using high-powered computer software to calculate the most likely path of a price out of all possible paths. Technical analysis is sometimes called by other names, such as *charting, market timing,* and *trend-following.* The press, the public, and even technical-analysis authors all use these terms interchangeably. All technical analysis methods fall under the broad term *quantitative analysis* to set it apart from fundamental analysis.

TIP

When you see these terms in this book and elsewhere, don't fret over a strict interpretation — and don't accept or reject a technical idea because it has a particular label. You can put ten technical traders in a room and get ten definitions of each term. The following sections are my interpretation of these terms and their nuances.

Charting

Charting is probably the oldest generic term used for technical analysis. I cover charting techniques in Parts 3 and 4. *Charting* refers to reading supply and demand into bars and patterns. Some technical analysts reject the term charting because it harkens back to the days of colored pencils and rulers. They see charting as subjective, whereas statistics-based indicators (which I cover in Part 5) are objective. But many traders use charting conventions developed over decades because they *work*.

Market timing

Market timing is another term used in place of *technical analysis*. All technical trading involves timing, but this term refers to statistical analysis that goes beyond a single chart. It encompasses many techniques, such as sentiment indicators and calendar effects, that many self-described chartists say aren't charting, and at least some technical analysts say aren't technical analysis. I cover these and other tools in Chapter 3.

Trend-following

The very first question to ask when you look at any chart is, "Is the price trending?" Because so much emphasis is put on the presence or absence of a trend, technical analysis is sometimes named *trend-following*. Parts 4 and 5 contain techniques that are trend-following. Some analysts object to the term because you aren't always following, but often anticipating, a trend such as when you use momentum indicators (see Chapter 13).

Technical analysis

Technical analysis is the broadest of the terms. It's a term encompassing all techniques, but at heart technical analysis seeks to measure and quantify market sentiment.

Technical analysis isn't confined to just math-based techniques, as some folks may think. Using math is a breakthrough and a curse. Math may outperform human judgment and the human eye, as many an optical illusion has proved, but it's not true that numbers never lie. Numbers lie all the time in price analysis. You can have a textbook-perfect trend with ten confirming indicators, and it can still run into a brick wall — really bad news that trashes the price of the security overnight. Math can never overcome the inconvenient fact that a Shock, which no one can predict, may overwhelm any price trend. Shocks in capital letters are events like 9/11.

TIP

In your quest to define trendedness and formulate trading rules to maximize profits and reduce risk, don't run the risk of turning into an obsessed, nerdy number cruncher. Don't forget that behind the numbers are other human beings who often behave in irrational ways. Technical analysis (so far) remains an art, not a science, even when it uses scientific methods.

Algorithmic trading

Algorithmic trading, also referred to as *algo trading,* uses a specific set of conditions, including technical analysis indicators, to trigger a trade. After the computer identifies that all conditions are met, it automatically sends the trading order to the broker. Computer programs are faster than human brains or fingers, so ordering a trade as quickly as possible is one of the benefits of algo trading. Some algo trading companies pay for data collection sites a few seconds closer to the physical location of exchange data. Conditions can include time of day, volume, and other parameters as well as nuts-and-bolts technical analysis indicators. Algo trading, like technical analysis, removes emotion from the trading decision.

If you're a beginner in technical analysis, you won't much care about algo trading, but you should have at least an outline of what it is in order to know the lingo and be able to judge commentary and promotions.

Understanding how algo trading works

Here is algo trading in a nutshell: A modeler designs a set of indicators, all expressed mathematically, and devises a buy/sell program to execute the trades automatically with no human participation after the original design. As in all technical analysis, the design relies upon present price behavior repeating past price behavior. The modeler is using the very same indicators you'll be using after you get started in technical analysis.

Algo trading gone berserk has been blamed for a rise in volatility, especially in the U.S. stock markets, and for at least two flash crashes (a *flash crash* is an abrupt, unexpected, extreme drop in prices in minutes):

>> In 2010, the Dow fell 998.5 points in 36 minutes before recovering.

>> In June 2016, algo trading was blamed for the collapse of sterling after the Brexit vote. Sterling has yet to recover.

>> In 2018, the Dow fell 800 points in ten minutes before recovering.

Algo models often use a strategy of systematically placing *slices* of the total order at specific time intervals to conceal the trader's position from the rest of the market, such as 20 percent of the capital stake at ten-minute intervals as long as the price is moving favorably. When the model identifies the end of the price move, the algo system will dump all the slices, all at once.

Noting the benefits of algo trading

The primary benefits of algo trading are as follows:

>> It takes human decision-making out of the immediate trading decision.

>> It's much faster. The computer can do in nanoseconds what takes the normal person at least a minute or two.

Much algo trading is high frequency trading (HFT), meaning in and out again in seconds. This is "trading without emotion" in spades!

The predecessor of algo trading was HFT, which is now a feature of algo trading, too. HFT is based on the high speed of computerized trading. The value comes from being able to get in and out of a trade very, very fast, and generally with a large number of trades and small gains or losses per trade. You wouldn't buy and sell a stock for a one penny profit, but if you're doing it with $1 million and doing it dozens of times per day, if you get it right, you'll make hundreds of thousands.

Rocketing to the moon

What is the difference between algo trading and a robot? None. A robot performs the same functions — to find a defined set of conditions expected to deliver a gain and to place the orders with the broker without human action. Many brokers offer the capability of designing your own algo system, although transaction fees can be high. What they offer is special algo-building software and a trading platform that allows automated trades. Automation is the key to the speed, but you can also find programs that require manual approval before the trade is placed. You don't have to be a programmer to engage in algo trading; you can buy algo formulas online.

Or you can buy a *black box* algo trading systems from many different vendors, including brokers. They're named black box because the indicators dictating the trades are, usually, a secret. The trading rule for an entry may be something as simple as "buy if the open is higher than the close the day before." Some are undoubtedly far more complicated.

ALGO TRADING BECOMES AI

When an algo trading system gets the ability to think, otherwise known as *machine learning,* it becomes *AI* or *artificial intelligences.* The essence lies in the computer program being able to modify some aspects of its performance using feedback. Say you have a system that always buys a security when its price has fallen by *x* percent, based on the observation that an *x* percent drop is the most probable norm for a bottom over many instances in the price history. But now market volatility is higher — prices change direction faster and after lesser moves. The program records these lesser moves and, without human judgment, alters the buy rule to (say) 15 percent. At the minimum, AI makes a technical trading system more adaptive and does it far more quickly than a human can do.

The fancier AI story would be when the machine can observe dozens of nonprice factors, such as the overall index to which the security belongs, economic data, or news events like central bank policy changes, and can simulate the price change in this one security in a flurry of mock trials — in nanoseconds. It calculates the probability of each of those events and all combination of those events as a price influencer. As the actual information becomes available, like an economic data release, the program starts all over again with the new information and its now-known effect. This effect becomes an input in the next round of mock trials. And as I keep saying, the rules of probability hold that the more trials you can run, the more reliable your forecast.

This form of AI is growing by leaps and bounds in medical diagnosis and treatment as well as other fields, including the rapidly improving hurricane forecasting. There is now facial recognition, self-driving cars, Apple's Siri and Google's Alexa, and thermostats that track your habits to adjust the temperature in your house.

This form of AI will someday become the true pinnacle of technical analysis. It's possible that some fund managers are already there, or close to it. More than one big-shot fund manager has designed algo systems to mirror his own thinking in a way that is mathematically expressible and thus programmable, but going beyond technical analysis. In the U.S. equity market, JP Morgan estimated in early 2019 that various quant strategies manage at least $1.5 trillion. Another scary idea from JP Morgan is that traditional nonquant investors account for only about 10 percent of U.S. equity trading.

But note that somebody — a human — has to design the feedback protocol in the first place. A researcher can discover that a central bank rate decision affects a stock, bond, or currency price on *x* percent of the occasions and generates a *y* percent move. But if you get an *y* percent price change in the absence of the trigger event, the computer program is at a loss as to where to look for the cause in order to include it in the next iteration. The program can always go hunting for some data event that seems correlated and possibly causative, but the program won't know whether the data event makes sense. You could end up with the price of oranges in Marrakech as a determining factor in a buy signal for IBM. A computer program can beat a human at chess, but it can't invent chess in the first place. The point is that while employing technical analysis qualifies you as a quant, not all quants are technical analysts.

Why Technical Analysis Works and What Can Go Wrong

Technical analysis works because humans behave in repetitive ways in response to the same stimulus. Everyone jumps back and yells "ouch" when their hand touches too-hot water. People did that in 1000 BC, and they do it today.

In measuring market sentiment, history repeats. The traders facing the 1989 stock market crash and the 2018 crash reacted exactly the same way as the traders in the 1929 stock market crash; in all cases, market players exhibited both flight and fight, the classic response to a fearful event. Granted, technical analysis uses scientific measurement to measure an unscientific object, the market. Human behavior repeats, but not in as precise a known range as actual hard objects like metal or water.

Many indicators contain an implicit instruction as what to do — buy or sell the security — but no indicator will tell you how much money to place in this single trade or what to do if your indicator and therefore your forecast is wrong. Yes, indicators have a high probability of being right, but high isn't 100 percent certainty. That means there is some *risk* of loss when indicators are wrong. And indicators will be wrong some percentage of the time and you need to have a trading strategy to guide you through whatever pitfalls emerge.

REMEMBER

The ultimate tactic is to set a sell price that incorporates the worst loss you're willing to take. Some technical analysts have good indicators but fail to manage risk properly, meaning in line with the amount of capital they have and how much loss they can tolerate psychologically and financially. All securities trading entails taking losses, and technical analysis is no exception. One of the main contributions of technical analysis to the finance industry is forcing you to face head-on the potential gain and loss of every trade, that is, to quantify gain and loss in an unemotional, rational way.

Setting new rules

Get rid of the preconceived notion that because technical analysis entails an active trading style, or at least a more active style than buy-and-hold, you're about to embrace more risk. Exactly the opposite is true. Because you always know ahead of time where you'll sell, you always know your gain or loss before you buy. So, for example, to conduct a one-hour trade is inherently less risky than buying and holding a security indefinitely without an exit plan. The existence of an exit plan is what defines and limits the risk. Where does the exit plan come from? The indicators you choose — and you choose indicators based in part on how much gain and loss they are likely to entail in real-time trading. You can also choose your exit based on dollar amounts, either the hard number ($200 and not penny more) or as percentage of capital stake per trade. Or you can mix methods, always exiting a position if the loss is $200, but letting gains accumulate until an indicator tells you the party is over.

The one-hour trade entails risk management, whereas holding a security without an end in mind on some concept of hypothetical "value" is to take 100 percent risk. That supposedly "valuable" security can quickly tank and go to zero. Think of Enron, WorldCom, Lehman Brothers, or Bear Stearns — all failed companies whose stock price went to zero, even though "experts" said that these names were buying opportunities right up to the last minute.

In early 2019, Warren Buffett reported a $3 billion quarterly loss in one of his supposedly "high value" brand companies, Kraft Heinz, whose price fell from $96.65 in February 2017 to $34.95 by February 2019, losing nearly two-thirds. Maybe the stock will recover and maybe it won't, but no technical analyst would accept so large a loss and would have exited before it got so big, using the money from the sale to trade/invest in something that was going up instead of down.

Controlling losses to protect gains

Preventing and controlling losses is more important than outright profit seeking to practically every technical trader you meet. The technical analysis approach is inherently more risk averse than the value-investing approach.

To embrace technical analysis is to embrace a way of thinking that's always sensitive to risk. *Technical trading* means to trade with a plan that identifies the potential gain and the potential loss of every trade ahead of time. The technical trader devises rules for dealing with price developments as they occur in order to realize the plan. In fact, you select your technical tools specifically to match your trading style with your sensitivity to risk.

TIP

Using rules is the key feature of lasting success in trading. Anybody can get lucky once or twice. To make profits consistently requires that you not only identify the trading opportunity, but you also manage the risk of the trade over the lifetime of your ownership of the security. You never buy it and forget it. The technical analysis mindset is constantly aware that the gain needed to recover a loss rises in the most awful way, as Table 1-1 demonstrates. How can you know that a specific trade may result in a loss of (say) 20 percent? Although you can't know the outcome of any trade with 100 percent certainty, you *can* know with 100 percent certainty how much you could lose. That's because you'll set a worst-case loss limit at the same time you order the purchase. The worst-case exit price is usually set by your own dollar amount, say *x* percent of the capital stake in in the trade. You may or may not set a profit-target at the same time. Knowing the expected gain and loss ahead of time is the central feature of the technical mindset, which is referred to as managing the trade (check out Chapter 5).

TABLE 1-1   **Recovering a Loss**

Loss	Gain Needed to Recover Loss
10%	11.1%
20%	25.0%
30%	42.9%
40%	66.7%
50%	100.0%
60%	150.0%
75%	300.0%

Why Technical Analysis Gets a Bad Rap

Technical analysis works because people consistently repeat behaviors under similar circumstances. For example, I say in Chapter 10 that support and resistance lines are a simple and effective method to identify the limits of a trend, and when a price breaks a support or resistance line, it's called a *breakout*. Breakout is a powerful concept and used in many other indicators as well as support and resistance. Why does a breakout attract so much attention? Because over decades of analysts following prices, a breakout reliably signaled the end of a trend many, many times.

TIP

Even though the term "breakout" is powerful, it isn't always correct. You'll run into situations where a breakout isn't respected, and the price resumes the direction it was headed in the first place. In short, some breakouts are false — they lead you to the wrong deduction.

The biggest mistake that beginning technical traders make is attributing too much reliability and accuracy to technical methods. I talk about this issue in Chapter 3. Experienced technical traders know that no technique works all the time. In fact, many techniques work only when the majority of market participants believe that they'll work, forming a self-fulfilling prophecy. You needn't care whether the theory is valid. Your goal is to make money, not to be scientifically pure.

Understanding that no technique works all the time helps you overcome doubts raised by critics who say that the whole field of technical analysis isn't worthwhile when techniques aren't 100 percent reliable. Because a method doesn't work all the time isn't the right criterion for evaluating it. Just because the meteorologist is wrong 50 percent of the time doesn't mean you should take off in your Cessna when he's forecasting a violent thunderstorm in the next hour.

REMEMBER

In financial markets, the value of an analytical method is determined by whether it helps you to consistently make more money than you lose. Notice that this statement has two components: The method, and you. The "you" variable is why two traders — whether newcomers or grizzled old hands — can use the same method but achieve very different results.

Beating the market is hard, hard work

Every day, hundreds of thousands of traders all over the world beat the market. To *beat the market* means to earn a return higher than the benchmark in that market, such as making more from trading a single stock included in the Dow Industrial Average than the Dow Industrial Average index returned in the same period. Beating the market can also mean to earn a return greater than the return on the return on a risk-free investment, usually defined as the three-month U.S. Treasury bill.

Technical analysis is about making extraordinary gains — beating the market — and if you think that isn't possible, you haven't looked hard enough. Many people try to beat the market and fail. Consider the story of the hapless day-traders of the 1990s who deluded themselves into thinking that they possessed trading secrets when all they had was a roaring bull market. A few survived — because they adapted their trading techniques to the changing market. To trade well is a skill that takes training, practice, and benefiting from mistakes, just like any other business. You wouldn't open a restaurant without knowing how to cook, but somehow people think they can trade securities without understanding how and why prices move.

Current thinking has it that it takes 10,000 hours of practice to become skilled at any endeavor, and trading is no different than any other skill. You may be disappointed to discover that technical analysis doesn't offer a single, coherent path to market wisdom. You'd think that after 100 years of development, traders would have a rule book with a single set of steps to take and processes to go through, and one that takes a whole lot less than 10,000 hours. But they don't.

Why not? No one can name the single best way to trade a particular price situation. Each trader sees a different amount of risk on any particular chart, chooses one set of indicators over another, and has a taste for taking a certain amount of profit (or loss) for the capital at stake. Theoretically, you could say that the best way is the way that makes the most money, but that fails to account for the trader — his personality, goals, and experience — and how much money he has to risk.

REMEMBER

To blend technical methods with your own personal risk profile isn't the work of one day. It's a lengthy and difficult process that requires some soul-searching. To keep the process manageable, confine your conclusions to what you can observe and verify — the empirical approach. Be careful to avoid the error of composition, like reading that one set of technical traders believes in magic numbers and concluding that all technical analysis involves magic numbers. (It doesn't.) It's astonishing how many otherwise smart people misjudge technical analysis in exactly this manner, based on an incomplete understanding of the field. Many critics take one technical idea, fail to integrate it with their personal risk profile, and then blame all technical analysis for their losses.

The truly random — one-time Shocks

Technical analysis is of no use when the world serves up one-time Shocks, such as 9/11. Depending on the time frame of your charts, you could get false sell signals on prices crashing on events both real and imagined. To be fair, fundamental analysis is of no use, either. The following are a few examples:

>> In May 2010 the Dow fell 1,000 points, attributed to high-frequency algorithmic traders.

>> Exchanges (in Tokyo, London, Frankfurt, and New York) experienced data problems during which data was delayed or missing, or the exchange was closed. A subset of data problems is new rules, usually temporary, forbidding the shorting of certain stocks, such as banks.

>> The Shanghai stock index fell 5 percent in a single day in July 2019 and set off declines in equity indices worldwide.

>> The Associated Press Twitter feed was hacked in April 2013 with the message that the White House was bombed. The Dow fell 100 points.

>> By February 2018, the S&P was down 10 percent from January 1 and by December, the losses were the most in more than a decade, even though the economy had the best growth in more a decade.

Finding Order

Much of the time you can see order in the way securities prices evolve, even though they develop in an infinite variety of configurations. Technical traders attribute that orderliness to the swings of market sentiment. Prices form patterns because the traders in the market behave in regular and repetitive ways. You can identify, measure, and project prices because you can identify, measure, and project — forecast — human behavior. Most people can do it only imperfectly, but you and I can both do it.

REMEMBER

Probably the most intriguing thing about technical analysis is that ideas and insights about price behavior from 1900 are as fresh and valuable today as they were then. Technical analysis never discards an idea — it just finds more efficient ways to capture price moves. After the PC came along, technical analysis has become more math oriented, but the essence of technical analysis is still to grasp the underlying human behavior that makes prices move.

What do analysts know for certain?

>> No technique works all the time.

>> No technique works on every security.

>> Something mysterious is going on that traders don't yet understand. A famous trader named Bernard Baruch said:

Have you ever seen, in some wood, on a sunny quiet day, a cloud of flying midges — thousands of them — hovering, apparently motionless, in a sunbeam? . . . Yes? . . . Well, did you ever see the whole flight — each mite apparently preserving its distance from all others — suddenly move, say three feet, to one side or the other? Well, what made them do that? A breeze? I said a quiet day. But try to recall — did you ever see them move directly back again in the same unison? Well, what made them do that? Great human mass movements are slower in inception but much more effective.

This phenomenon is what technical analysis seeks to explain.

What You Need to Get Started

If you don't already know trading basics, you need to get a few things under your belt to get the most out of this book — things like what a securities exchange is, exchange hours, what trades in after hours, what brokers do (and don't do), trading conventions like "bid and offer" and order types, how to read a brokerage statement, and oh yes, what securities you plan to trade.

After that, all you really need is a newspaper or website that publishes securities prices, a sheet of graph paper, and a pencil. Fortunes have been made with nothing more than that. But these days, a computer, an Internet connection, and at least one piece of software that allows you to collect data and draw charts are standard issue. You can also do charting directly on broker and technical analysis websites without buying software.

Don't skimp on tools to put in your technical analysis tool belt. Buy the data, books, magazines, and software you need. Be careful about paying for seminars and trading coaches, most of which are overpriced and promote only a few favored ideas that can be easily discovered much less expensively in books and online. Do an Internet search for specific terms, and you'll often find yourself landing at www.stockcharts.com, which is sane and reasonable.

You wouldn't try to make a cordon bleu dinner on a camp stove with three eggs and a basil leaf, so don't try to make money in the market by using inadequate tools. Your first task when you're ready to take your technical knowledge out for a trial run is to earn back the seed capital you put into the business, the business of technical trading.

WARNING

Technical analysis has its fair share of fruitcakes, ideologues, cranks, and scamsters as in any industry. Be careful.

Chapter **2**

Tapping into the Wisdom of the Crowd

Technical analysis focuses on the price of a security rather than its fundamentals. The collective behavior of buyers and sellers, also known as *the crowd* or *the market*, sets the prices. The market may be rational or irrational, but the market is always right in the sense that it sets the price of a security. You and I, as minor members of the trading crowd, don't get to set the price, no matter how intelligent our analyses and piercing our judgments.

In this chapter, I suggest one way of looking at the supply-and-demand dynamics of crowd behavior that's consistent with the technical approach — the auction model of supply and demand. Next, an outcome of crowd behavior is the tendency of prices to cluster around the average, even when the average is trending. It's useful to identify clustering, in part to know when to heed the prices that stray from the cluster. Finally, price extremes that seem to make no sense are another aspect of crowd behavior. You have to accept that prices not only refuse to move in a tidy straight line, but also deliver excessive moves far from what your eye tells you is normal. Understanding extremes first requires understanding "normal."

Comprehending the Conventional Supply/ Demand Model

In the everyday world of physical goods and human services, *demand* is a function of price. You'll buy more ice cream if the price falls from $5 to 50 cents, but no price will induce you to buy gallons and gallons of the stuff every week. People buy more when price falls, but with a limit. The same is true about price increases. If your barber raises his price from $20 to $120, you'll schedule fewer appointments. At some price, like $250, if everyone has that price, you'll demand no services at all.

Supply is relatively fixed at any one point in time, but manufacturers and service providers respond vigorously to price. Rising prices induce suppliers to make more of the product or offer more of the service. Retired barbers come out of the woodwork when the price of a cut goes to $250. New supply, whether of ice cream or barbers, forces the price back down, at least a little. The opposite is true, too. Falling prices send manufacturers and service providers out of business or into different businesses that don't have falling demand.

The constant shifting of prices as supply and demand adjust to one another is referred to as *price discovery* — the price point where supply and demand meet. It's a constantly changing number. Price discovery is dynamic, which means it's constantly adjusting to new conditions.

Securities prices behave in response to supply and demand like any other good. When a tool company started using lithium batteries in handheld drills, revolutionizing the drill business, another company quickly acquired it, and that company's price nearly tripled the following year. Demand for the stock mirrored demand for the product.

At any one time, securities traders have a good idea of the price range within which a security should trade — in the absence of a new factor like the lithium battery example. In other words, they can estimate demand for the stock based on a number of factors, including how the broad indices are behaving, economic growth or slowdown, and so on.

And because humans just love to draw lines, traders define the normal, no-surprises trading range with lines on a price chart. To start with, those lines are straight lines. I discuss more dynamic (non-straight) lines in Chapter 12.

Thus was born support and resistance. *Support* can be described as the lower limit of a security's price at which traders in this security think demand for the security will re-emerge. If people were willing to buy the security at $10 on many other occasions, they should be willing to buy it at $10 again. At $10, the stock is cheap.

Similarly, traders can see that in the past, holders of the security were sellers at $18. The highest prices form *resistance*, meaning demand falls off as traders resist paying that high a price and existing holders sell to take profit, lowering the price again.

Again, assuming no revolutionary discoveries (or the opposite, a product failure or management scandal), I can draw an $8 trading range on the chart. Right away a pair of lines on a chart is delivering guidance on the trading decision. In Figure 2-1, see how the price falls back after hitting (and slightly surpassing) resistance at the highs. Similarly, when the price falls below support, traders see it as cheap and deliver more demand, raising the price back into the trading range.

FIGURE 2-1:
Resistance.

Figure 2-2 shows a downward trending price range with support and resistance lines, indicating that traders will still buy at support but lose confidence near lesser highs. The security is in the process of falling out of favor. As price meets resistance, sellers get out.

REMEMBER

Support and resistance may show on the page as hard lines, but in practice they're more like support and resistance *areas*. The lines are really just approximations, not hard and fast limits, and they get broken by a little all the time without invalidating the support and resistance concept. For more on support and resistance, see Chapter 10.

The eBay Model of Supply and Demand

Securities aren't regular goods, and to apply orthodox supply-and-demand economics to securities trading in every instance can result in some silly conclusions. As a practical matter, the *auction model* of supply and demand, also referred to as the *eBay model,* is often more useful. This section explains the reasons behind wild price moves in securities prices like breakouts, spikes, and gaps (for breakouts, see below and for spikes and gaps, see Chapter 7). You don't see breakouts, spikes, and gaps in the pricing for ordinary goods, but you'll see them in securities prices. So, sometimes securities prices are set by plain old supply and demand as taught in Econ 101, and sometimes a different model is needed.

Securities aren't socks: The demand effect

Securities are different from cars, bread, and socks. You don't buy a security for the joy of owning it and using it. You can't drive it, eat it, wear it, or impress the neighbors with it. Aside from getting a dividend or coupon payment, the only reason to buy a security is to sell it again, preferably for more than you paid for it. Unless you're a merchant, you never buy anything with the idea of selling it again — except securities.

In an auction, what gets your blood running is that someone else also wants to buy the item in question. Visible demand begets more demand. Auction economics are contrary to what traditional economics teaches — that demand will *decrease* as the price rises. In the auction situation, demand *increases* as the price rises, sometimes to ridiculous levels. The item may or may not be actually scarce in the real world. It doesn't matter.

The auction pricing process features *momentum* (which is why auctioneers talk so fast; refer to Chapter 13 for more on momentum). Auction prices change rapidly, unlike the pricing of cars, bread, and socks, which don't change every few minutes. The pace of the price discovery process influences the buyers by generating excitement and even agitation. Excitement generates brain and other chemicals (such as dopamine and adrenaline) that actually promote more emotion and less reasoning.

Demand rises as the price rises because the thing being auctioned looks progressively more valuable. If you like to visit eBay, you've seen demand for an object rise as the price rises. If you ever bought something on eBay, you probably paid more for something than you should have. Every time someone else outbids you, you want the item more than ever and become determined to be the winner. The intrinsic value of the item doesn't matter. You may even have an object or two in the hall closet you're ashamed of having bought at an auction. I certainly do. The immediacy of the auction is what skews prices, sometimes to absurd levels. Later, when suppliers see the high prices, they may indeed be able to find or produce more of the item — but by then, the specific demand dynamic of that one auction is gone.

Shoving emotion to the back of your head is easier when market prices are slow-moving within an identified normal range than when a price makes a giant breakout outside that range. Then you might become victim to mania — buy more! buy more! — or panic — (sell all! sell all!). That's why trading according to strict technical rules as I outline in this book will save you from yourself.

Creating demand from scratch

When you're wearing your trader hat, you buy a security solely because you think the price will rise. You decide to sell because you have a profit that meets your needs or because you're taking a loss that is near intolerability. For-profit trading is purely opportunistic. You seldom think about the true supply of the security.

Technically, the supply of any security is limited by the number of shares outstanding and the like, but supply may be considered infinite for all practical purposes. For instance, at one point during the 2010s, the amount of oil in the world was less than the amount of oil embedded in oil futures contracts. And consider your own situation. A price exists at which you can be induced to sell the stock for which you paid $10. It might be $20, or $200, or $10,000 — but rest assured, some price will force you to part with it, and *right now*.

REMEMBER

In technical trading, think of demand for a security as rising on rising prices, not falling ones. Similarly, the supply of a security dries up on rising prices, at least in the short run. (Later, when the long-term security holder sees how high the price has gone while he wasn't looking, he may say "Holy Toledo!" and call his broker to sell, making more supply available.)

Identifying Crowd Behavior

Technical analysis is the art of identifying crowd behavior, also called the *bandwagon effect*, in order to join the crowd and take advantage of its momentum. (A subset of the bandwagon effect is named *momentum investing*, which I talk about in Chapter 13). Crowd behavior is also referred to as the *herd effect*, a somewhat insulting term considering that a herd stampedes when its leader spots a lion in the tall grass ahead and sends out a warning cry. In other words, it's not such a bad thing to be a member of a herd.

Here's how a bandwagon works: A fresh piece of news comes out. Traders interpret the news as favorable to the security, and a flood of bids allows sellers to raise their prices. You see the price going up and decide to join the crowd. Now the price has surpassed the upside resistance line and by a lot. Your crowd is like a horse with the bit in his teeth. It's a form of mania. People become reckless and irrational in a mania.

A *mania* is a situation in which traders buy an object or security without regard for its intrinsic value or even whether they'll be able to sell it again later at a higher price. They fear being left out of an opportunity. They're caught up in the moment and temporarily irrational. A *panic* is the opposite — people can't sell the thing fast enough and will accept ever-lower prices just to get any money back at all. They become overly cautious after a bubble bursts.

REMEMBER

In economic history, a mania or a panic comes along only a few times in a century. However, in securities markets, mania and panic happen far more often, if in miniature. Emotional extremes lead to price extremes in the context of the hour, day, or week — mini-manias and mini-panics occur all the time. Those words aren't used in technical trading lingo, but the emotion and the price effects are the same as in big-picture manias and panics.

In the following sections, I discuss normal pricing that follows the conventional supply/demand dynamics. When prices are moving normally, you can identify support and resistance and make note of minor excursions away from a central average. A price that is moving calmly seems to be governed by rational players.

But sometimes a normal price series suddenly erupts into a flurry of abnormal-looking price events on the chart. A price breaks support for a day or two but then falls aback into its support/resistance channel only to fly up to break resistance. Maybe it's that irrational auction pricing mode appearing out of nowhere. I explain some of the ways you can deal with those price changes later in this chapter.

Defining Normal

In trading, the crowd that trades a specific security has a firm grip on the normal daily high-low trading range and can quickly spot any big price move beyond that normal range. (I cover the high and the low in Chapter 6 and the average range in Chapter 7.)

Instead of looking to the outer edges (support and resistance), one school of thought in trading holds that a minor break of support or resistance is a normal price adjustment reflecting new conditions and nothing to freak out over. Instead look to the center of the trading range, the *norm* or average, for guidance on how to trade. This section describes how to identify what is normal and outlines a trading technique that some traders use. Alas, I have to throw in a few math terms, but fear not. You can easily wrestle the concepts to the ground.

Reverting to the mean

The phrase *reversion to the mean* refers to a statistical concept that accepts as its core assumption that high and low prices are temporary and a price will tend to go back to its average over time. The first step is to identify the normal trading range of the security, say $5 per day. (For more on the trading range, see Chapter 7.) You can observe that the price varies by about $5 every day around an average price of (let's say) $20 over the past week. Therefore, if the current price is $17.50, that's half of the normal trading range below the average price and a buying opportunity. If the price is $22.50, that's half of the average trading range above the average and a selling opportunity. If prices are normally distributed, you can buy at $17.50 and sell at $22.50 for a $5 profit. In other words, deviations from the average price are expected to revert to the average.

The concept of *deviation* (and its cousin, standard deviation) isn't as hard as it sounds. When discussing the idea of normal distribution and deviation from normal distribution, textbooks use the height of a group of people in a room. The average height is (say) 5 feet 8 inches, with some short people distributed on the left side at 4 feet 10 inches and some tall people on the right side at 6 feet 4 inches. The height measurement of the majority of people, about 67 percent, falls near the center, whereas the very short and very tall cases are out near the edges, called the *tails*. In this example, the mean height is 5 feet 8 inches — it's the average, and the normal range is 4 feet 10 inches to 6 feet 4 inches. In this crowd, you would instantly spot someone who was 3 feet 2 inches or someone who was 7 feet 10 inches.

REMEMBER

Prices clustered around the average are normal and represent the market consensus of the rough equilibrium price for that day — supply and demand are in balance. The prices farther away from the normal price tend to deviate by only one unit from the average in each direction: higher or lower. This unit is named a *standard deviation*. Frankly, that's all you need to know about the standard deviation — it's a unit of measurement that describes how far away from the average any new higher or lower prices are likely to land, based on the past distribution of highs and lows against a past average.

If your price normally averaging $20 goes beyond its average daily trading range and is now priced at $5, something happened to cause traders to dump it and you've just experienced *tail risk.* If your security frequently delivers extreme prices beyond the standard deviation, it has *fat tails.* It's still called tail risk when the price runs up to $50 and what you have is a giant gain. Risk is a two-sided coin.

The one standard deviation region is symmetrical. When you use the normal distribution concept, you assume that an equal number of prices will fall on each side of the average. This assumption isn't always true, of course. Prices are trended at least some of the time, and so if the price is on a generally rising trend, expect to see the distribution curve skewed to one side, toward the higher prices.

Trading mean reversion

To trade the concept of *mean reversion* means that you find an average price over some past period, figure out the high-low range, and simply buy when the price has deviated to the low side of the range and sell when it gets to the high side. Studying reversion to the mean is useful and effective during periods when the price is going sideways and not exhibiting a directional bias to the upside or downside, but can be useful in a trend, too, as long as you're willing to adjust the mean every so often. Does this sound too good to be true? Well, it is. Mean-reversion trading faces obstacles, such as:

>> The trading range can widen and narrow, like a pig in a python — with the average daily range expanding and contracting. Your mean is still an anchor, but what is the normal range? Suddenly you're uncertain of the right place to buy and sell.

>> What is the ideal look-back period to determine the average? Say, for example, that Blue Widget stock over the past two years averaged $20 — but that $20 average incorporates a few abnormal prices like $1 and $40. An average can disguise multiple deviations that have already occurred.

>> Is it true that securities prices are normally distributed? Statisticians say that securities prices aren't actually normally distributed — they just look that way sometimes. In technical analysis, your primary goal is to determine whether your security exhibits a price trend. You also want to know how strong the trend is and whether it may end soon. To accept the assumption that the distribution of prices will be normal is the same thing as saying that you know in advance where the price trend will end — at or near the price represented by the average plus one standard deviation. If the price goes higher than the price that one standard deviation dictates, the trading rule embedded in the mean-reversion trading technique would have you sell, perhaps right when a gigantic rally is starting.

WARNING

Mean-reversion trading techniques are beguilingly tempting, but may involve more risk than trend-following because you're using a high number of assumptions, many of which can be wrong.

Breaking Normal

Figures 2-1 and 2-2 illustrate support and resistance as measurements of supply and demand that is developing in a normal way. Support and resistance become inaccurate when markets get excited about big news, a revolutionary discovery, or a geopolitical event. Demand gets disrupted, sometimes irrationally, and prices soar or tank.

This disruption is called a *breakout,* and you never know whether it will persist and become a lasting uptrend (or downtrend as the case may be). Breakouts are a clear warning sign that something happened to change market sentiment toward the security and thus demand for it. Breakouts must always be respected, but beware — they're often *false,* meaning short-lived. No new trend emerges. The price slumps back into something resembling its former range; only support and resistance are wider apart now to accommodate that one breakout. I discuss breakouts in greater detail in Chapter 11, but remember that prices are reflecting human behavior and much of it is emotional, like the eBay bidder.

Here's the hard part to swallow — even the most sedate of price trends will deliver a breakout once in a while. The breakout can be caused by something as simple as a rumor that turns out not to be true or some big players deciding to unload some inventory in order to buy something more interesting.

When an oddball price move comes along and you can't identify the trigger for it, you might be forgetting another supply and demand factor — the financial condition of the rest of the crowd. This is named *positioning,* and it can be a powerful factor that moves prices substantially and seemingly without a reason.

There is a reason, but it's confidential information kept secret by the big players. Each of the big players in every market has a *position limit* dictated by top management. For example, the guy in charge of high-tech stocks at your pension fund can invest no more than $500 million in that sector at any one time. Say the high-tech names have rallied substantially and now his position is $600 million. He has to sell $100 million, no matter what the chart or gurus say about likely gains still to come.

Position squaring is the closing of positions. Position squaring doesn't necessarily imply that market participants think a move is over. They may plan to reenter the security in the same direction later on.

Position squaring occurs for many reasons, including the following:

>> Traders think that the move is exhausted for the moment.

>> Traders have met a price objective — whether profit or loss.

>> Traders have met a time limit, such as the end of the day, week, month, or tax period.

>> Traders want to withdraw money from the security to trade a different security, or for a nontrading purpose.

Position squaring occurs when a large number of traders have big losses, too. Say, for example, a high percentage of traders believe in a particular price-move scenario that then fails to develop in the expected way. A few traders throw in the towel. The resulting lowering of the price causes bigger losses for the remaining traders, and they, in turn, give up. You get a cascade of stop-loss orders being hit that turns into a down-market rout, or even a panic. A *stop-loss order* is an order you give to your broker to sell your position if it goes against you too far and reaches the maximum loss you're prepared to accept. (I talk about stop-loss orders in Chapter 5.)

Going against the grain: Retracements

Repositioning by big players, whether they want to or not, can sometimes be the secret reason you'll see get *retracements,* defined as minor moves in the opposite direction of a trend. Retracements can also occur because a majority of players just think a price move has gone too far. For either reason, prices seldom move in one direction for long. A retracement is also called a *correction,* which explicitly recognizes that the security had gone too far and is now correcting course, like a ship. A retracement may also be termed a *pullback* or *throwback*.

Retracements don't really come out of the blue. Usually a retracement is a function of traders seeing too much of a one-way street — all buyers and no sellers, or the other way around. When a position is *crowded*, at some point prices just stops moving. There is no fresh news to change market sentiment, just a kind of temporary exhaustion.

Sometimes the price just stops and hovers in a narrow range around a particular level, but just as often the price moves in the opposite direction for a while as traders take profits or cut losses as the case may be.

Recognizing why retracements happen

When the market runs out of cash, traders have to close positions to get their cash back so they can put on new trades. If they've been buyers, they need to sell. If they've been sellers (shorting the security), they need to buy. Therefore, at the extreme outside limit of a price move, you should expect a temporary, minor reversal of the previous price move. In an uptrend, a retracement is always a drop in price. In a downtrend, a retracement is always a rise in price.

You can sometimes see a retracement coming. When a price has reached or surpassed a normal limit defined by support and resistance or an indicator, that price is at an extreme. In an upmove, everyone who wanted to buy has already bought. In this case, you can say that the market is *overbought*, a term specific to securities trading, or *extended*. In a downmove, when everyone who wanted to sell has already sold, the security is called *oversold*. Several indicators help identify extended positions, including something frighteningly named a stochastic oscillator, which I discuss more in Chapter 13.

Notice that the terms *overbought* and *oversold* are applied to the security, but what the terms secretly refer to is how much money the traders in that security have available at the moment. By the time most of the market participants have jumped on the bandwagon, they are tapped out. All their money is in a position. Traders have to exit their positions just to get the cash or credit to conduct additional trades. One excellent way to detect an extended position and imminent correction is volume. This is logical. When you get more traders crowding into a position (rising volume) but hardly any price increase, the move is ending.

Using fundamentals to gauge retracements

Retracements can get out of hand and transform themselves into trend reversals, too. At the time a retracement starts, you don't know for sure that it is a retracement. For all you know, it could be a full reversal, with the price switching directions. In this situation, you do well to check the *fundamentals* — the news and events pertaining to the security. An ordinary retracement caused by normal position squaring can suddenly turn into a full-fledged rout in the opposite direction if fresh news comes out that seems to support a reversal. Figure 2-3 shows a primary trend with several retracements, each outlined by an ellipse. In this instance, the retracements last only a day or two, but retracements can last a lot longer, even several weeks on a daily chart, for example.

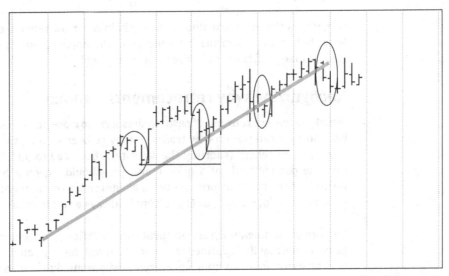

FIGURE 2-3:
Trend with four
retracements.

REMEMBER

The press often asserts that every retracement is a profit-taking correction. This assumption isn't accurate. If traders took profit on every correction, they'd all be rich. Remember, somebody bought at the high. If the correction goes too far against him, he must get out of the position at a loss. From this observation you should deduce that to stick to a position when it's correcting against you requires the courage of your convictions — and capital. (I talk more about managing money during retracements in Chapter 5.)

Catching a falling knife: Estimating where and when a retracement will stop

To try to estimate where a retracement will stop is called "to catch a falling knife." In other words, no reliable rules exist to tell you *where* a trend correction will end or *when* the primary trend will resume, or even that it will resume. One of the chief uses of indicators and combined indicators, described in Chapter 16, is to get guidance on where and when a retracement will stop. Remember that the indicators only indicate; they don't dictate.

TIP

Your tolerance for retracements is the key to deciding in what time frame you want to trade. If the security you want to trade regularly retraces 50 percent and the prospect of losing 51 percent turns you into a nervous wreck, you need to trade it in a different time frame — or find another security.

Acknowledging that no one can forecast a retracement hasn't stopped technical traders from trying to establish forecast rules. The following rules are generally helpful, but no one can offer reliable statistics to back them up, so take them with a grain of salt:

>> **Look for the previous significant high or low.** In Figure 2-3, for example, the second retracement doesn't challenge the lowest low of the first dip, and the third retracement doesn't challenge the second. Alas, knowing where it *won't* go doesn't help you figure out where it *will* go.

>> **Look for round numbers.** Research shows that support and resistance levels (see Chapter 10) actually do occur more often at round numbers than chance would allow.

>> **Remember the 30 percent rule.** Measure the percentage change and assume that a majority of traders will place stops to avoid losing more than *x* percent, such as 30 percent. The problem with this idea, and it's a chilling one, is that you're measuring from a peak and you don't know the price level where the majority of traders entered. Logically, you should assume that they're protecting 70 percent of their personal cash gain from their entry, not from the peak. To measure from the peak would be to say that traders make decisions based on opportunity loss rather than cash loss, and although this contains a germ of truth, it's not a reliable assumption about crowd behavior.

>> **Use magic numbers.** Some traders believe that retracements always end at a specific ratio to the preceding move, such as 38 percent or 62 percent. I cover these ideas in Chapter 17.

REMEMBER

Breakouts and retracements each occur in sedate normal trends as well as more choppy price moves. A great many breakouts are false, meaning they seem to signal a pending change in direction but they're in reality just exceptionally loud noise. Similarly, a great many retracements are just normal adjustments to changes in supply and demand conditions. All securities exhibit both breakouts and retracements. You can't avoid them. One of the biggest challenges in technical trading is figuring out how to cope with breakouts and retracements by using indicators carefully.

Accepting When the Crowd Is Extreme

You'll experience occasions when the crowd gets out of control and prices go haywire, moving by huge amounts and breaking support and resistance left and right. Your indicators are literally off the chart.

REMEMBER

Indicators like support and resistance work because of *the law of large numbers.* This law states that when thousands or maybe millions of observations of a breakout resulted in a reversal (say) 90 percent of the time, you should attribute a 90 percent probability to the next breakout, too. The law of large numbers applies to all indicators, all the time, not just support and resistance.

That is, except when the market runs off the rails and the crowd goes to extremes. This is the 10 percent of the time when market behavior isn't hewing to its customary norms such as a price bouncing off support to the upside. At these times, acknowledge some of the strange characteristics of the crowd you have just joined by trading the same securities alongside it. Famous investor George Soros called it "reflexivity," meaning a two-way feedback loop in which mania or panic causes prices to move abnormally and those moves are then accepted by the very same creators of the mania or panic as vindications of their initial impulse.

Soros contributed mightily to the understanding of crowd behavior by noting that no matter how hard you try, your knowledge of all the factors affecting securities prices is always incomplete. That makes you — and everyone else — fallible to a distorted view of reality that can get an iron grip on the imagination of the crowd. Every piece of new information has to be fitted into that distorted view and anything that doesn't fit is discarded.

Big rallies that lead to bubbles — severe overpricing divorced from reality — develop because a series of news events is forced to fit the rally model. If countervailing events are recognized but not heeded, the rally and bubble are only reinforced. The same thing happens in a panic. Traders sell a large amount, see others following so that prices really do fall, and say "See? I predicted prices would fall." That trader then sells some more. The trader creates an environment and is then influenced by the very environment he created.

Avoiding stampedes

You need to accept that people behave differently as individuals from the way they act when they're part of a crowd. Crowd behavior encompasses fraternities, sports teams, political parties, gangs, religious sects, mobs, people attending an auction — the list goes on. A crowd is more than the sum of its parts. Otherwise sensible individuals can behave in the most extraordinary ways when they become part of a crowd. One famous case is how people in 17th-century Holland saw tulip-mania, the trading of tulip bulbs for sums like $250,000, deflate overnight when someone mistakenly ate one, revealing how ridiculously far prices had diverged from any reasonable concept of value.

At the opera, regular people don't shove others aside on their way to the exit. But if someone shouts, "Fire!" in a crowded theater, people will trample each other to get out of the building. In markets, you see the same thing in the price of a security when bad news about it is released. The bad news may not be actual news at all. It may be a single seller dumping such a large amount of the security that the price falls by a large amount, making other traders imagine that there must be bad news even though they haven't heard it.

In contrast, if someone shouts, "Free ice cream!" people will throw elbows to be first in line. The same thing happens to securities prices as they reach new highs, especially if an authority figure pronounces the security a gem and a bargain. But you don't need actual good news to get a rally. All you really need is a large purchase that drives the price up past what seems normal, the trading range earlier determined by support and resistance lines.

TIP

Don't be surprised when traders invent rumors to try to create a stampede — in either direction. As a technical trader, you want to be sensitive to what the crowd is doing without succumbing to the ruling passions of the crowd itself. Technical traders work hard at not listening to chatter about securities, even from experts. You may get information overload — and you may get *disinformation* (deliberately misleading information). All the information you need to make a trading decision is embedded in the price. The price incorporates the crowd reaction to information, and it's more practical to look at prices than to guess what the crowd might be thinking. When you check the news for the cause of a price action, do it with a healthy dose of skepticism.

Lesser devilry — playing games with traders' heads

Each security has its own crowd, and you'll get a payoff if you can figure out what pushes the buttons of the crowd that trades your security. One crowd may always respect a support line, for example, whereas others enjoy breaking the support line by just a little to induce selling so they can buy at a cheaper price. (For more on support lines, see Chapter 10.) In foreign exchange (FX), the Fibonacci number sequence has a grip on many traders' imaginations. You may not respect the theory but still want to know the retracement level that many in the FX crowd expect. See Chapter 17 for more information.

Whether you're facing a mini-mania or mini-panic or the real thing — a giant mania or panic — you need to accept that your indicators are going to stop working. All or nearly all of the standard measurements will lose their usefulness. It's up to you to decide whether you can safely follow the crowd or it's wiser to get out of Dodge.

The market is self-regarding; in other words, it watches itself. One behavior begets another in a dynamic way. For example, many advisors recommend a rule that if a price falls by x percent from a peak, it's prudent to exit the trade. This is a money management rule rather than a technical one based on historical evidence. William O'Neil of *Investor's Business Daily* made the 8 percent rule popular. Famous investor Gerald Loeb and others used the 10 percent rule. Other advisors recommend a 25 percent rule.

Because these rules are so well known, many traders use them and cause the rule to be self-fulfilling. Traders know that others will exit at a level of (say) 8 to 10 percent or 25 percent under the peak and will sell the security specifically to get everyone else to exit, whereupon they're able to buy the security at a cheaper price. Game playing can become incredibly complex, replete with bluffing, cheating, feinting, and double crossing. Note that many top traders are also top competitors in fencing, chess, backgammon, bridge, and poker. Each security or class of securities has a different degree of crowd complexity. The crowd that trades the S&P e-mini futures contract is different from the crowd that trades the soybeans futures contract, and in turn, that crowd is different from the one that trades the Swiss franc and the one that trades Apple stock.

Chapter **3**
Trade What You See: Market Sentiment

Your goal as a technical trader is to identify what the crowd is doing and take advantage of it — without falling prey to the market's emotions. The primary technical tools for identifying sentiment are patterns and indicators, and the discussion of these tools forms the core of technical analysis (and this book). However, you have two other methods of measuring sentiment:

» Sentiment indicators describe the market as a whole.

» Volume directly represents the extent of trader participation. Volume is a powerful indicator in its own right and adds confirmation to price indicators.

REMEMBER

Sentiment and volume indicators operate on the principle that "The trend is your friend — until the end," meaning that the crowd is wrong at price extremes and simply clueless when markets are nontrending. Sentiment indicators, also called *market indicators*, describe the overall environment in which your specific securities are being priced and can be helpful to evaluate your securities in context and when markets are nontrending.

TIP

You want to know whether your security is going up because its own qualities are inspiring demand or because the whole market is going up and your security is getting a free ride. The old saw has it that "A rising tide lifts all boats." Knowing your security's place in the overall market can be handy when the market turns down because a falling tide lowers all boats, too.

Sentiment indicators that pertain to the entire market are like any other indicator — they're designed to forecast the upcoming behavior of the price. But remember, indicators only indicate; they don't dictate.

In this chapter, I discuss a few of the 100 or so sentiment and volume indicators commonly used. Later in the chapter, I describe some of the characteristics of the way the human mind works to sabotage good trading decisions, and I propose using simple probability measures to overcome your own personal sentiment that arises from your thinking habits.

Where Market Sentiment Comes from and What It's Good For

Charles Dow invented the very first market sentiment indicator in the early 20th century. Dow observed that rising transportation stocks, chiefly railroads, reflected robust economic conditions, also called *market fundamentals,* even though they're actually economic fundamentals. When transportation stocks were rising, it was because sales and earnings were rising. The price of industrial company shares would follow for the same reason — rising earnings. The transportation stocks were thus a leading indicator of overall market sentiment.

The Dow Jones Company continues to track the transportation sector today in the form of the Dow Jones Transportation Average, although now it contains more than railroad companies. Other indices include the Baltic Dry Index that tracks shipping costs of major raw materials, and indeed, both the DJTA and the Baltic Dry index are highly correlated with major market indices like the Dow Industrial Average and S&P 500. In currencies, the dollar index is a proxy for all currencies against the U.S. dollar.

I can summarize market fundamentals as the assessment of economic growth, the sustainability of economic growth, and confidence in government and central banks to keep the economy on a sustainable growth path. This is different than the fundamentals of a single security, which is a function of earnings, management, product excellence, competition, and so on.

When market fundamentals line up well, you get bullish market sentiment. Just as with an individual security, sentiment is *bullish* when prices are moving upward in a steady and consistent way. The same thing is true of *bearish* sentiment, only prices are moving downward in a steady and consistent way.

TIP

Sentiment indicators are useful to confirm a trend in your security that is starting or already in place. If market sentiment indicators point to an upmove and your security is also in an upmove, your confidence in your trade goes up. Conversely, if market indicators point to an upmove but your security isn't going along, you should consider whether your security is exceptional and whether it's worth "fighting the tape" (trading contrary to what market sentiment indicators are saying).

Sentiment indicator may offer guidance when trendedness collapses into non-trendedness or sideways, range-trading mode. This occurs during the confusing transition phases between up and down, and also between up and higher, or between down and lower.

Securities aren't always trending. Experts can't agree on what proportion of the time they are trending. The consensus seems to be that most securities are trended up or down about 30 to 40 percent of the time. The tendency for trends to collapse into lack of visible, obvious trendedness is very pronounced. The untrended transition phase is sometimes called *trader's nightmare* because all trend-following indicators fail, and many other indicators, including bar-reading and patterns (see Chapters 7 through 9) deliver false signals. The absence of trendedness reflects uncertainty about either the fundamentals or whether the security's price accurately reflects the fundamentals (or might be overbought or oversold — see Chapter 2).

The resulting sideways move in prices, called *congestion* (see Chapter 10), is a frustrating condition for traders. You literally don't know what the next move will be. You might as well toss a coin, which clearly violates the technical mindset of action based on reasonable expectations of gain/loss.

TIP

Consulting market sentiment indicators might ride to the rescue and deliver valuable clues as to the next move in your own security. At the least, market sentiment indicators provide other factors to plug into your estimation of reasonable expectations and may well be a deciding tipping-point factor between taking action or twiddling your thumbs until the sideways move switches into a trend.

Thinking Outside the Chart: Gauging Sentiment

You may have the inside scoop on the best stock ever, but if the entire market has a case of the collywobbles, your best-ever stock is likely to fall, too. Conversely, when the market is in a manic phase, even the worst of stocks gets a boost. This ebb and flow isn't only because of individuals, but also because money flows into and out of mutual funds and other institutional players, like insurance companies and pension funds. All these institutions have latitude about how much to keep in cash. In a mania, they get more fully invested, and in a panic, they pull funds out of the market and into cash.

REMEMBER

Nobody knows for sure, but some percentage of any security's price move is attributable to changes in the market environment. Factors include not only the index to which it belongs, but also its size (large-cap or small-cap, for example) and sector (biotech, high-tech, no-tech). A guess is that about 25 percent of a price move in any single issue should be considered a function of what is going on in its index (or other benchmark to which the issue belongs). That's in normal conditions. In a mania or panic, the price of your security will be far more closely related to the overall index move.

Most sentiment indicators look outside the price dynamics of a particular security or index of securities for information about whether the trading crowd is humming along with expectations of normalcy or is willing to jump ship. Market indicators aren't technical indicators in the strict sense but are consistent with the technical principle that you want to study what people *do*, not what they *say*.

There are at least 30 indicators such as "percentage of stocks above their 200-day moving average" (see Chapter 12 on moving averages) and "number of stocks above the 52-week high." These indicators have their own symbols and can be charted just like the price history of individual issues. In the following sections, I review some of the more prominent sentiment indicators.

Monitoring investors: The bull/bear ratio

Meaningful reversals come when the majority of advisors are bullish or bearish. In other words, when everyone recognizes the trend bandwagon and has hopped on board, it's over. Investors Intelligence Service (started more than 60 years ago) measures the balance of bullish sentiment against bearish sentiment (called the *bull/bear ratio*) and claims an excellent track record in predicting turning points.

Note that other services have sprung up to measure bull and bear sentiment in general, in specialized sectors, and in mutual funds. You can find the bull/bear ratio in various forms on hundreds of websites and TV. Both CNBC and Bloomberg TV channels have their own versions. Rising equities are shown in green and falling ones are shown in red. It can be mesmerizing to watch the colors change as news comes out, especially important news like a central bank rate change.

Following the money: Breadth indicators

Breadth indicators measure the degree of participation by traders in the overall market represented by an index, such as the Dow or S&P 500. You can track the breadth indicators to get a feel for market sentiment.

Breadth indicators include

>> **Ratio of advancing to declining issues:** This indicator measures the mood of the market.

- **Advancing issues:** Stocks that are reaching a higher price today than yesterday.

- **Declining issues:** Stocks that are reaching lower prices.

When advancers outnumber decliners, money is flowing into the market. Bulls are beating bears. Sentiment is favorable. When the rally starts getting tired, the number of advancing issues declines while the number of falling issues rises.

If you subtract declining issues from advancing ones, you get the *advance/decline line.* In the same vein, if you divide advancing issues by declining issues, you get the *advance/decline ratio,* abbreviated A/D.

>> **Difference between issues making new highs and new lows:** The logic is the same as in the advance/decline indicator. If more stocks in an index are closing at higher prices than the period before, bullishness is on the rise. When a higher number are putting in new lows, supply is overwhelming demand and the mood must be bearish.

Following the betting: The put/call ratio

The Chicago Board Options Exchange (CBOE) publishes the ratio of puts to calls, where a *put* is the right to sell at a specific price in the future and traders who buy puts are bears (pessimists) who think the index will fall below their set price. A *call* is the right to buy at a set price in the future, and traders who buy calls are bulls (optimists) who think they'll profit when the market rises to and beyond their set price.

Accordingly, the *put/call ratio* is an indicator of whether sentiment is bearish or bullish. A high put/call ratio means bears are winning. Recognize that an extreme of emotion like this is usually wrong, and marks a turning point. You should start planning to do the opposite. The same line of thinking holds true for a low put/call ratio: When emotions are running strongly optimistic, watch out for an opportunity to take advantage of a change.

Viewing volatility: The VIX

The volatility index (VIX) is among the most popular breadth indicators today. Theoretically, you can create a volatility index for any security in which options are traded, although it takes computational expertise. Its calculation is too complicated to get into here, but for information about volatility, see Chapter 14. For your purposes, know that when the crowd is jumpy and nervous, it projects that anxiety into the future and assumes that prices will be abnormal.

In other words, the crowd believes volatility will be high. When the price of VIX is high, options traders have been buying puts and selling calls on the index — they're bearish and think the market may fall. What they really think is that the *risk* of a fall is high and worth spending some insurance money on. When VIX is low, the market is relaxed and confident — overly confident.

REMEMBER

VIX is generally used as a contrary indicator. When VIX is either abnormally high or abnormally low, you know it's getting to the right time to trade against the crowd. A high VIX value means exactly the opposite of what it seems to mean — the bottom isn't coming, it's already in! If VIX is low, the crowd is girding its loins for a big move. When VIX is low, traders are complacent. They're projecting the same price levels, or nearly the same levels, into the immediate future with little variation and therefore little risk.

New and improved sentiment indicators

In recent years, many new sentiment indicators have been devised. An alternative to VIX is the *stress index* devised by the Kansas City and Cleveland Federal Reserve Banks. The Cleveland index contains 16 indicators from all corners of the economy and financial sector, including bonds, real estate, currencies, and so on. When the stress index is high, you can expect fear to take over and market indices are at risk of a big fat sell-off.

Another is from Stockcharts.com, a nifty hybrid indicator named StockCharts Technical Rank that places the performance of a stock within the context of the performance of the group to which it belongs on a technical basis, not a fundamental basis. Six technical indicators are used, like how far the stock price is from the 200-day moving average. The S&P 500 is broken up into groups of 50 stocks each, and thus you can see instantly whether your security is a leader or a laggard in the context of its technical performance against a similar group, an original and advanced way of looking at market sentiment. Notice that sector (energy, pharmaceutical, and so on) isn't the grouping principle, but technical considerations.

Getting the Lowdown on Volume

You're more confident that a price move has staying power if you know that many traders are involved in a price move and not just one or two. (Chapter 2 addresses the concept of demand in greater detail.)

Volume is the term for the number of shares or contracts of a security traded in a period. Volume is the most powerful confirming indicator of a price move, and *confirmation* is a key concept in technical analysis. (See Chapter 16 for more on the confirmation concept.) When you look at price changes, you imagine buyers demanding more of the security at ever-higher prices or sellers offering a greater supply at ever-lower prices. But a price can move on a single large purchase or sale, especially if the market happens not to have many participants at that exact moment, a condition named *illiquidity*. (See Chapter 6 for a more-detailed description of liquidity.)

REMEMBER

In technical trading, you use volume to measure the extent of trader participation. When a price rise is accompanied by rising volume, you have confirmation that the direction is associated with participation. Volume is outright, direct evidence of demand. Similarly, if you see a price fall by a large amount but the change isn't accompanied by a proportional change in volume, you can deduce that the price change was an aberration. Volume tells you only the number of shares or contracts traded, not the number of participants. Obviously you can get a jump in volume that is due to only a handful of participants, and then you'll be drawing the wrong inference from high volume.

REMEMBER

You're welcome to ignore market sentiment indicators and stick to looking at your own charts. But don't ignore volume, the only nonprice factor that genuinely contributes to enhancing the probability that your technical analysis is correct. Despite the occasional mishap, volume is the single best indicator to give higher probability to your identification of a trend.

In this section, you can turn up your use of volume in technical analysis by considering a few top-drawer indicators. These indicators tend to be among the most reliable in technical analysis.

Tracking on-balance volume

On-balance volume (OBV) is a single number representing cumulative volume. A market technician named Joe Granville devised the OBV indicator to display volume adjusted as follows: To calculate OBV, you add volume on days that the close is higher than the day before and subtract the volume on days that the price is lower than the day before. You're assuming that when the price closes higher than the day before, demand was greater than supply at each price level. Buyers had to offer higher prices to get holders to part with their shares.

In OBV, you're attributing *all* the volume on a higher-close day to net buying and *all* the volume on a lower-close day to net selling. This assumption isn't realistic, but hang in there for another minute. See Figure 3-1, which shows Apple stock. Daily prices are in the top part, volume (in hundreds of thousands of shares) is the center of the chart, and the OBV indicator is in the bottom window of the chart.

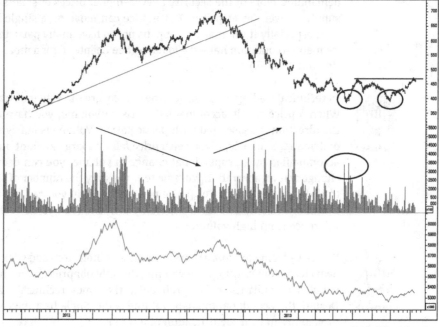

FIGURE 3-1:
On-balance volume.

TIP

OBV doesn't work all the time, but a change in the indicator often precedes a change in the price. You can see how to use the OBV indicator in two instances on the chart in Figure 3-1. Follow along:

>> **The downmove:** On the left side of the chart, the price is rising, as shown by the support line (see Chapter 10), but notice that volume is falling. The OBV indicator in the bottom window is falling, too. This is a warning that the move is running out of participants, even though it's very early; OBV peaks in April and the true final reversal doesn't come until October.

If you waited to sell until you got confirmation from the price breaking the support line to the downside in October, you would have sold at $646.88 and covered your short sale at $385.10 in April (circle) for a gain of $261.78 or 41 percent. How do you know to cover in April? First, you see a spike in volume as the last of the diehards sell. Then you see another volume spike that suggests buyers are back, and this time price rises. The rout is over. Not everyone can sell short, of course. Just consider that if you are a long-time fan of Apple stock, you could have saved yourself from a nerve-wracking 41 percent drop by selling at the confirmed point. **You can always buy it back.**

>> **The upmove:** Apple puts in a double bottom (see Chapter 9). Volume and OBV are falling. But at the right side of the chart, price and OBV are rising while volume is falling. When price rises on falling volume, it means the bulls in Apple stock are persisting. The price has surpassed the previous high (horizontal line). You should keep an eye peeled for a spike in volume that will be reflected in OBV, accompanied by a further rise in price, to determine a new entry point.

TIP

The divergence of price and an indicator that normally move in tandem is a wake-up call. A change in volume often predicts a change in price. The indicator is telling you something you can't see with the naked eye — in the Apple case, prices are putting in new highs but not yet on higher volume and with OBV not yet confirming new participation. Get ready to buy, but not quite yet.

The term *smart money* refers to traders who see an opportunity forming, as in the Apple case, or the exhaustion of a price move ahead of the other traders. They're alert to the moment when the crowd suddenly realizes that it has taken a price too far — and reacts violently in the other direction.

Truth to tell, though, no indicator works all the time, and this one doesn't, either. The OBV indicator was way early in calling the price drop and isn't actually leading as this chart ends. Even OBV inventor Granville famously missed a major bull market that started in 1982, and then persisted in saying it was a false bull for the next 14 years. However, periodically you can find an article online or in the magazine *Technical Analysis of Stocks and Commodities* in which the author tests the OBV principle on real cases in real time and it worked spectacularly well to direct good timing.

Refining volume indicators

As I note in the section "Tracking on-balance volume" earlier in the chapter, the OBV indicator attributes *all* the day's volume to buying. However, doing so isn't realistic. It makes more sense to attribute only a portion of the volume to the price rise rather than the whole kit and caboodle.

A technical analyst named Marc Chaikin figured that a more representative amount would be the percentage equivalent of the price that is above the midpoint of the day. You calculate a *midpoint* as the high of the day plus the low of the day divided by two. Chaikin's version of accumulation and distribution is more refined than OBV.

If a security closes above its daily midpoint, bullish sentiment ruled. The close over the midpoint defines *accumulation*, revealing that investors are buying shares. The closer the closing price is to the high, the more bullish it was. If the price closed right at the high, then you say that 100 percent of the volume can be attributed to bullish sentiment.

Conversely, *distribution* is the term for sellers willing to accept lower prices in order to induce buyers to buy. Lower prices imply bearish sentiment. Distribution is calculated the same way as accumulation — a close below the price midpoint means distribution. The closer the closing price is to the low, the more distribution prevailed. If the close is exactly at the midpoint, then the indicator has the same value as yesterday — and you have no reason to add or subtract volume from the running total.

If you need any more convincing, consider that Mark Liebovit, author of the definitive *The Traders Book of Volume* (McGraw-Hill) and website VRTrader.com, is one of those who consistently beats the market and is often in the newsletter *Timer Digest* top ten.

Leading the way with spikes

Volume sometimes leads price. The most obvious situations are when volume spikes. A *spike* is a volume number that is double or more the size of volume on the preceding days but with volume returning to normal average levels the following day. Say volume has been running at 100,000 shares per day for several days or weeks and suddenly it explodes to 500,000 shares. If the price had been in a downtrend, this wild increase in volume means that the crowd is throwing in the towel and exiting en masse.

REMEMBER

When everyone has jumped off the bandwagon, get ready to jump back on. Nobody's left to propel the price lower. Conversely, the same advice is usually correct when you see a volume spike as the price is making new highs. The underlying principle is the same — the crowd has exhausted its supply of cash. Think about taking profit if you own the security. If you're considering a new position in a rising security that just had a volume spike, think again. Look at other indicators. Try to understand why so many people suddenly jumped on the bandwagon — does fresh news justify the increase in demand for the security, or is it just animal spirits?

A volume spike is one of the occasions when fundamental information is complementary to a technical observation. Beware a price making new highs coupled with a volume spike when there is no fresh news or fundamental information that attracted new buyers. Chances are that the price has gone as high as it will go — the top is in. If the security has new, legitimately exciting news and you can reasonably deduce that it attracted new buyers, you have a nontechnical reason to ignore the usual spike interpretation.

Getting a two-for-the price-of-one coupon

Another sentiment indicator is the relative price of the options for a specific security. The more costly a call option (the right to buy), the more you project that traders expect a price move upward. In addition, volume in options at increasing higher strike prices is a crystal-clear indication the traders in this security expect it to rise. Because each option for a particular date, you also get to see the time frame over which the price change is forecast.

Options are far beyond the scope of this book, but if you like the idea of confirming sentiment, go find a copy of *Stock Options For Dummies* by Alan R. Simon and *Trading Options For Dummies* by Joe Duarte (John Wiley & Sons, Inc.). A terrific source is schaeffersresearch.com, published by Bernie Schaeffer, author of *The Option Advisor* (John Wiley & Sons), and his team. The site uses futures and options as well as technical price analysis to identify and to forecast sentiment in the indices as well as individual securities.

Blindsiding Yourself

You may look at a price falling and volume confirming that you should exit the position to protect your capital — and then not do it. Seems ridiculous, right? But it happens all the time. It even has a name, *hyperbolic discounting,* meaning you see the chop coming but want to believe it will come later, not now.

Behavioral economists have devised a series of terms like hyperbolic discounting to identify the myriad factors that influence an individual's decisions. The factors arise from existing cultural bias (for example, the idea that selling a company's stock short is to wish doom on it whereas the American way is ever hopeful for upward progress, so shorting is anti-American). Other factors are psychological and cognitive, meaning humans have some peculiar ways of thinking. Some of these ways of thinking have the power to create in your mind a kind of baseline personal sentiment that is a mishmash of contributing factors. A chief purpose of technical analysis is to remove emotion from the trading decision, but technical analysis is fighting an uphill battle against your own personal sentiment and ways of thinking.

The psychologist Daniel Kahneman, who won the Nobel Prize in economics in 2002, writes in his book *Thinking, Fast and Slow* (Farrar, Straus and Giroux) that humans have two modes of thinking and decision-making. The first is based almost entirely on "cognitive biases," unconscious preconceptions that bypass rationality and shove a decision out the mental door quickly.

In this fast-thinking mode, humans give undue weight to information that is already familiar, easily available, and memorable or vivid. For example, a trend-line running abnormally steeply and for an abnormally long time is very rare — the trend must be nearing an end. An experienced trader may recognize from his thousands of hours of observation of previous long-running, steep trends that the probability is high of a pending reversal. But it's still jumping to a conclusion to predict a reversal without hard evidence. That doesn't mean the experienced trader is wrong. The long-running, steep trend may indeed be due for a reversal. But the absence of evidence makes the trading decision to bet on a reversal an intuitive one, rather than a rational one.

The second, slow mode of thinking is supposedly the rational, take-your-time mode of decision-making. But it, too, often violates the assumption of maximization of self-interest. For example, experiment after experiment shows that avoiding loss is a bigger preference than making a gain. In other words, the pain perceived on making a loss is greater than the pleasure of making a profit. Traders will get jittery and exit a winning position before the charts shows any sign of a reversal — solely to avoid taking a reduction in the new (and so far hypothetical) gain.

In addition, who you are counts. A rich person will always prefer to keep his stake than bet on a low gain at high odds, while a poor person will always take the low gain/high odds. Millionaires don't play the lottery.

Understanding confirmation bias and anchoring

Technical traders like to think that technical analysis is the antidote to the threat of emotions pushing you to make bad trading decisions. And yet rational "slow" thinking is still contaminated by bias. In technical analysis, the minute you put support and resistance lines on your chart, you're *framing* your perception of the price move. The lines themselves are like a frame around a picture and you can't see outside the frame. You can't avoid looking at how far away the current price is from support (in a falling price situation). In reality, outside the frame is a previous low that the current price trend may be targeting — your support line can be easily broken. Looking at only the immediate support line may be a form of confirmation bias — seeing what you expect to see. Consider the following:

» *Confirmation bias* arises from belief in a hypothesis and expecting it to deliver the theoretical outcome without fail. It's actually a form of wishful thinking, like the police who see some evidence the suspect is the murderer and never look elsewhere for other suspects. Confirmation bias has a dangerous side effect: You stop gathering information, especially information that might jolt you out of the desired confirmation. Confirmation bias is probably the single biggest shortcoming of the technical trader. The lines and indicators on your chart lead you to a deduction about where the price should go, and you forget that other lines and indicators — or a chart on a different time frame — would lead you to a different conclusion and a different decision. Another form of confirmation bias might be seeing that the overall market index is rising and the market sentiment indicators described above are all in fine shape, and failing to notice that your own specific security is circling the drain.

» Another bit of bias is *anchoring,* where a person would rather retain something for which the original price was high even as its price falls. Anchoring affects lookback periods in charting. When you paid $100 for a stock and now it's priced at $50, you can't help imagining it should be $100. It's a slam against your identity and worth for the darn thing to have fallen so far. And instead of selling the security that just cost you a 50 percent loss, you hang on to it because if it was worth $100 when you bought it, it's supposed to be worth $100 again. Another example is when the pound sterling falls from an average of $1.6500 for a decade to $1.3000, it's hard to reset the anchor in your mind. That $1.6500 remains the benchmark and $1.3000 is low. If you believe in reversion to the mean, you can't avoid imagining the pound must rise. This is just one of many reasons why the choice of time frame to display on any particular chart is critical.

Being aware of potential errors

When conducting chart-based trading, you're under time pressure. Seconds count. Nearly all traders are fast thinking and become at risk of Kahneman's "severe and systematic error."

Fast thinking is intuitive and based on first impressions. It's fast and takes seconds. And when the fast thinker is an expert, having put in many long hours of study, fast thinking is often right, although it risks jumping to conclusions.

Expert insights are a wonder of the human brain, but a practice of intuitive fast thinking can close a person's mind to ridiculously obvious facts or alternative solutions to problems. In the invisible gorilla experiment, a group of subjects watched a video of two teams passing a basketball around and were tasked to count the number of passes by one team. During the video, a gorilla comes into the middle of the scene, thumps his chest, and leaves after 9 seconds. *Half the subjects failed to see the gorilla.* Clearly human perception can be distracted to the point of blindness.

Another error is becoming so overjoyed at identifying a trend that you leap to the fast-thinking mode of making the trade without calculating how much money you'll lose if the pattern fails. Even if you're right and the trade makes money, it was still an irrational decision. And if the trade loses money, you'll gloss over the loss in your memory until it fades to nothing.

What's left is more of that confirmation bias; you saw what you expected to see and the trade did, in fact, make money. But you think you have made a friend, the crowd, when all that happened was you got lucky. In fact, you're now a victim of groupthink. A great many other people saw the same indicators you were using and executed the same trade. Because it was a profitable trade this time doesn't mean it will work next time — in part because of all the indications you didn't see on the same chart.

You may find it comforting to think that you can find regularity and orderliness in charts, using the technical methods that take up most of this book, or the sentiment statistics pertaining to the market at large described in this chapter. But don't get too comfortable.

Thinking Scientifically

Technical analysis is a form of data science. But making a good trading decision takes more than just data, especially when your eyes are going to betray you with confirmation bias and other pitfalls. So you may consider technical analysis more of a decision science, meaning it combines data with other disciplines, especially some amount of behavioral science insight and risk management.

Even the best indicator fails to work all the time. In fact, some of the best indicators work less than 50 percent of the time, and that's when conditions are normal! The following sections introduce some probability concepts to keep in mind to prevent your own errors of thinking from sabotaging your trading decisions. The goal is to acquire some new thinking habits that will help overcome cognitive errors like confirmation bias.

Humility: Conditions and contingencies

When you hear someone say, "Blue Widget has a 75 percent chance of rising," you can assume that three out of the last four times the technical method was applied, the security rose. The unspoken assumption is that conditions didn't change. But the market isn't a laboratory. Of course conditions changed!

The forecast needs to be qualified because of the thousands of factors that may come along and influence the price. *Contingencies* are things that are possible but not expected or not expected in any great number at the same time. You know what a contingency is — like hitting every red streetlight on the way to the train station to catch the 6:09. If you hit the average number of red lights, you can make it on time to catch the train. If they're all red and you also have to slow down for construction, you miss your train.

REMEMBER

When you hear a promoter predict a price change with a 75 percent probability, chances are he's talking through his hat. He may have failed to incorporate all the reasonable contingencies, or he may have attributed too small a probability to any of them (or to all of them). Read financial history, and you find the ground littered with the corpses of traders who failed to include a key contingency in their calculations.

Unlike promoters, most technical traders hate to attach a probability to a particular outcome, like "Blue Widget has a 75 percent chance of rising." Reluctance to apply the term *probability* is due to a realistic assessment of the contingencies. In statistics, when you want to calculate the probability of two events happening simultaneously (called *joint probability*), you multiply their probabilities. If you have two remotely possible contingencies, each with a probability of 10 percent, the chances of both happening simultaneously is 10 percent times 10 percent, or 1 percent.

Returning to the 75 percent chance Blue Widget will rise, assume a single 10 percent contingency. To calculate the effect of a 10 percent probability contingency on your trade, you take the reciprocal of the probability, or 90 percent, as the amount to modify the 75 percent. In arithmetic notation, it looks like this:

$$75 \text{ percent} \times 90 \text{ percent} = 67.50 \text{ percent}$$

In other words, introducing just *one* contingency reduced the probability of your outcome from 75 percent to 67.5 percent. Wait, it gets worse. If you have four contingencies and you attribute a 10 percent chance to each of them, the same process reduces your 75 percent odds to a mere 49.21 percent, which is less than 50-50.

Joint probabilities are a real bummer and are the real reason honest technical traders hate to declare a forecast. The more contingencies you admit, the lower the probability of the outcome.

Sample size

Statisticians say you need a minimum of 30 cases before you can say anything valid about the probability of history repeating itself. Scientists who do really serious science, like missiles and moon shots, demand a minimum of 200 cases. In setting up the Blue Widget example in the preceding section, I attributed a 75 percent chance of the price rising because three out of the last four times that conditions looked the same, that's what happened. But a sample size of four instances is hardly sufficient.

Your price data seldom presents you with 30 identical cases, let alone 200. Why should you accept less? The answer is that you're using a technical analysis method that works across a wide range of securities and time frames, even if you don't have enough cases in this specific security.

For example, when you have a support line and your price breaks it to the downside, that's a sell signal. Over the past 100 years, technical analysts have used the break of a support line millions of times, and it worked in a majority of cases. Using this method was the correct trading decision, although using the break of a support line as a signal doesn't work every time. A support line break is an example of a technical forecast that has a high probability in the context of many different contingencies and over many sets of conditions.

Other techniques are less reliable. You may think it would be wonderful to have a list of techniques with their *reliability quotient,* or a ranking of how often they're right. Some writers and software vendors claim that their techniques are "95 percent correct." This lofty proclamation is never true. For one thing, the vendors aren't considering new contingencies and conditions. Markets are dynamic. Something that worked 95 percent of the time in the past may have worked because a rising tide lifted all boats, and may work only 65 percent of the time in the future. In fact, it may not work at all in a true mania or panic.

Chapter **4**

Gaining Critical Advantage from Indicators

I ndicators are a shorthand way to identify and measure market sentiment. They give you a platform for making rational trading decisions, bypassing greed, fear, and the other emotions that accompany trading. That's the first advantage of using indicators — getting rid of emotion in trading.

Technical traders believe that systematic trading has a sporting chance of making significant profits. That's the second advantage of indicators: They identify conditions based on data and by having realistic expectations about how well indicators work as forecasting tools, you're led to having trading rules that offset indicator shortcomings.

And indicators have shortcomings! They don't always work, and I explain why in this chapter. To overcome the unreliability of indicators, a money management plan is necessary, which I cover in Chapter 5.

REMEMBER

Trading is about money, and money arouses emotion. The shorthand description is "greed and fear," but those terms aren't enough. Trading is also about personal success and failure. You'll be able to fend off the emotional roller coaster that trading can set in motion after you figure out how to attribute gains and losses to your tools — the indicators — rather than to your own identity, brainpower, and character. After you become proficient at technical analysis, you'll feel chagrin at losses instead of screaming anguish and falling into the slough of despond. Your mind will be clear enough to judge whether the indicator failed or the market was abnormally weird and whether you may perhaps need to tweak your indicator set. Likewise, when your indicators deliver winning trades, you can credit having found a successful methodology, not imagine you have super powers.

You'll see promotions for indicators and trading systems that never fail and will make you a fast fortune. These promotions are never true. The promoter got lucky on a small number of securities over a short period of time, and his ego got too big for his britches. Indicators are notoriously unreliable. The true secret to successful trading is to accept indicator unreliability and to take steps to offset that unreliability with good trade management practices.

The purpose of indicators is to separate the signal from the noise. Indicators are based on price and volume data, and data can be noisy. To get a grip on noisy data, check out Nate Silver's book, *The Signal and the Noise, Why So Many Prediction Fail — but Some Don't* (Penguin). Silver writes about polling data, including political polls, economic forecasting, and business data like sales forecasting, but the principles are the same as for the predictive value of indicators. Data is data, and all data is dirty.

Indicators are a substitute for that miraculous ability some few persons have of being able to get in sync with the market. To be *in sync* means you know intuitively exactly what's going on and where prices will go next — you're on the same wavelength as the other market participants. Such unquantifiable insight is more art than skill. Leo Tolstoy, when answering the question "What is art?" said it's "a means of union among men, joining them together in the same feelings." This is exactly what you have, a form of union with other traders, when you are in Zenlike harmony with the market. You might be lucky enough to get in sync with the market sometimes, but don't count on it. Count on indicators, despite their shortcomings. This chapter gives you the lowdown on indicators, including what indicators are, how they work, and what you need to know when choosing which indicators to use.

Overcoming Noise

Every price series, trending or not, has a certain amount of noise. *Noise* refers to price changes that arise from unforeseen quarters, can't be forecasted, and tend not to last. The causes of noise vary from security to security and over time. Noise seldom changes a trend already in place, but it can mess with your indicators enough that you'll get false signals. Technical analysts likes to draw a difference between noise and a market-moving *Event*, which I like to emphasize with a capital E. An Event is generally more than just another bit of news in a series of news — it's a game-changer.

Distinguishing between noise and an Event

To differentiate between noise and a genuine price Event, consider that in the foreign exchange market, you sometimes get a 1,000-point move in a single day when the average daily range is 120 points. A move of this magnitude isn't noise because noise implies a minor price move with rapidly diminishing reverberations. The 1,000-point shocker is an authentic price Event and almost always signals a major change in trend (or starts a trend from a state of untrendedness). In equities, ordinary noise can be an earnings announcement that is different from the earnings guidance the company or analysts told the market to expect ahead of time. An Event would be an unexpected massive loss. In foreign exchange, ordinary noise is the release of the payrolls report. An Event is the United Kingdom deciding by referendum to leave the European Union.

Note that a barrage of noises, however, can become an Event even though no single component is more than noise. Famous economist Fischer Black said noise is when a large number of small events has a more powerful effect on prices than a small number of large events. In other words, be wary of dismissing an inexplicable price move as "only noise." Noise can rule the roost. You may still want to try to distinguish between Events and noise, because Events change prices for sure, and with noise, you never know.

One useful clue that ordinary noise is actually an Event is to compare the news release with what had been expected by experts, which is named a *surprise index* and can be found in various formats. Comparing actual to expected takes you back into the realm of fundamentals, but may give you an edge when you see prices on the chart behaving abnormally.

Knowing where noise comes from

Noise arises from news and can be big or small. Big news includes a stunning reversal in an economic trend, a revolutionary product discovery, or a meaningful change in sales and earnings from the previous guidance. Smaller news is a smaller change in an economic trend, the appearance of a long-awaited product development (think Apple), or a minor change in sales and earnings. Some analysts think noise is always external to the security whereas others think noise can just as easily be inherent in the security's core conditions. An example is a change in a company's dividend policy or a plan to execute buy-backs. Noise also comes from big market players changing positions, as a supply and demand factor (refer to Chapter 2) you may sometimes neglect to consider.

Perry Kaufman, author of the encyclopedic *Trading Systems and Methods* (John Wiley & Sons, Inc.), now in the 6th edition, says that noise is a difficult concept. He pictures noise as raindrops falling on a pond, causing what looks like random ripples. The interesting thing about market ripples is that markets adapt to them, and they stop being Shocks and become normal, losing their power to change prices.

What's the relationship of noise to randomness? A lot of what is considered noise isn't really a surprise and not really unforecastable. For example, you get the U.S. nonfarm payrolls report on the first Friday of every month. You know it affects many market prices disproportionately. What you don't know is in what direction. Often you know payrolls will likely cause price spikes in *both* directions but the spikes aren't forecastable as to extent or duration, let alone which direction comes first. The spikes are noise and certainly reflect Shock, but they aren't random.

Some noise, however, is truly random. Uncle Fred decides to sell 100,000 shares of Blue Widget to buy a yacht, and his decision has nothing to do with the valuation of Blue Widget. Imagine that 100,000 shares is a relatively large amount for Blue Widget. Other traders assume there is a story behind the price drop and jump on the selling bandwagon, inflating the volume and taking the price far lower than the original 100,000 shares would have done. This is why it's not wise to couple the word *random* with *noise* in all cases.

Noise from inside the market

Noise can arise from traders trying out a bizarrely off-trend price, which is mischievous and at the far boundary of the price-discovery process. One subset of noise traders are the high-frequency model-driven traders whose computers spew out thousands of bids and offers, virtually none of which get filled, trying to get a rise out of the unwary. Another subset of mischievous traders is named *noise traders* by academic economists, a class that includes traders driven by ideology rather than information. Noise traders, also called *uninformed traders,* are often contrarian, and academic studies find they tend to lose money in both noisy and non-noisy market conditions.

From the view of a single security, what the overall market is doing is an external factor. But as Chapter 3 shows, as much as 25 percent of a price move in a specific security may be due to the effect of changes in the index or class of securities to which it belongs. The fundamentals that move the index may or may not affect the security, but it gets saddled with the effect anyway.

A nontrending price series is especially vulnerable to random inputs that move the price disproportionately to what rational analysis would say real cause-and-effect ought to be. The shorter the time frame you're looking at, the more influence noise has on your indicators. Noise, random and otherwise, is one of the main reasons why untrended price moves are susceptible to false breakouts, but trended price moves aren't immune either.

Indicators Give You the Edge

If you had inside information about a company's earnings ahead of time, market players would say you had an edge (or advantage) that allowed you to trade profitably on that information. A poker player who can read the other players' hands from their facial expressions has an edge, as does the blackjack player who can count cards. Technical analysts perceive indicators as like the inside information edge — indicators give you an advantage by identifying upcoming price moves that not everyone can see.

Indicators are the technical analyst's tools. For a formal definition, an *indicator* is a line or set of lines that you put on a chart to identify chart events, chiefly whether the price is trending, the degree of trendedness, and whether a trend turning point is being reached. The purpose of indicators is to clarify and enhance your perception of the price move.

Every trader wants to buy low and sell high. You use indicators to gain an edge in doing exactly that. As I note in Chapter 1, the technical approach has two key components — a rational forecast based on probability and a trading plan that always contains the price point at which you'll exit with the most tolerable loss, avoiding the risk of ruin, if your trade goes against you.

Classifying indicators

Analysts like to categorize indicators in many different, but equally valid, ways. Some like to put indicators into one of two buckets, such as accumulation (bullish) or distribution (bearish). Another classification method is indicators for trendedness, indicators for trend momentum, and indicators for volatility. Although you can classify indicators a dozen different ways, I prefer to boil it down to the following:

>> **Judgment-based indicators:** This group includes visual pattern-recognition methods such as bar, line, pattern, and cycle analysis, as well as candlesticks. These indicators can be time consuming to master and to use, although nowadays software will do the interpretation for you.

>> **Math-based indicators:** The math group includes moving averages, regression, momentum, and other types of calculations. Expressing chart events in mathematical terms allows you to backtest the event over historical data to discover how well it predicts the next price action.

WARNING

You may prefer to jump straight to math-based indicators because they're faster, cleaner, and scientific. But math-based indicators do the same job as judgment indicators — they display price data in a specific format to assist you in making a trading decision. Just because they're based on math doesn't mean that they aren't subjective. *You* determine the specifications of math-based indicators in the first place (such as how many days are in a moving average). Visual recognition and math-based techniques are equally valid and useful. Some traders use only visual-recognition techniques, some use only math-based indicators, and some use both. Remember, the use of math doesn't confer a crown of authenticity on any technique. And you may discover that visual recognition can work just as well as fancy indicators.

REMEMBER

If math isn't your cup of tea, don't worry. The math involved in most technical analysis isn't all that difficult. You can apply math-based techniques without understanding the math behind them as long as you understand the crowd behavior that the indicator is identifying and how to apply the indicator. Think of it as knowing how to drive a car without being able to rebuild the carburetor.

Understanding what indicators identify

In Chapters 1 and 2, I point out that securities prices are sometimes *trending* — they have a strong directional bias — and that trends are punctuated by *retracements,* or small moves in the opposite direction before the trend resumes. At other times, prices go sideways, called *range-trading.* Finally, trends end, and after they end, they may reverse to the opposite direction. So indicators identify five conditions; note that in this list, I put some suggestions next to each condition, but someone else could name other, equally valid, indicators:

>> A trend is beginning (moving average crossover or pattern breakout).

>> A trend is strong or weak (momentum, slope of linear regression).

>> A trend is retracing but will likely resume (relative strength index).

>> A trend is ending and may reverse (momentum, moving average crossover, or pattern breakout).

>> A price is range-trading (slope of linear regression or moving average).

Each indicator works best in one situation and less well in others. Technical traders argue the merits and drawbacks of indicators in each situation, and if you ask ten technical traders to list their top indicator for each task, you'll get ten entirely different lists. Most traders use a fixed set of indicators and try to remember that Indicator 1 is pretty good at validating rising prices (like the moving average) while not so hot at identifying an impending reversal. For that they may prefer Indicator 2, the MACD. Traders don't identify conditions and then apply an indicator; they leave the indicators on every chart and expect to remember how to rank reliability under changing conditions.

Choosing your trading style

Identifying trendedness is always your first task. Ah, but which trend over what time period? Take a good hard look at Figure 4-1, which depicts a downtrend that consists of four legs down punctuated by four legs up. If you knew at the beginning of this chart how it was going to look three months later, how many trades would you take?

FIGURE 4-1:
Count the trends.

There's no single right answer. If you sold at the first high and bought back on the last bar, you'd have one outcome. Instead if you sold at every peak and bought at every bottom for a total of eight trades, you'd have a different outcome. In fact, your total gain would be higher than the one-trade version, assuming you could buy at the lowest low and sell at each tippy-top (something you should *never* assume in technical analysis because it's unrealistic).

Calling the one-trade person a trend-follower and the eight-trade person a swing trader has gone out of fashion. In practice, both are trading trends — they just have different durations. Both trading styles may or may not entail going short. To *go short* is to sell a security you don't actually own — you borrow it from someone else through your broker — with the intent to buy it back more cheaply. If the security is priced at $10 and your indicators tell you it's likely to fall to $5, that $5 gain from the short trade is just as green as the gain you get from the long trade, that is, buying at $5 and selling at $10.

In commodities and foreign exchange, shorter-term swing trading is the norm. In equities, getting broker permission to go short can be hard (and expensive) for most traders. Most retail equity traders can go in only one direction — long. They can buy, but they can't go short. This removes half of the trading opportunities your indicators will deliver, and when you get to the point of backtesting your indicators, you need to specify whether you can trade in both directions. If Figure 4-1 represents your security and you can only buy, you have four trades.

Which type of trader are you, the longer term or the shorter term? If you're a beginner, don't decide just yet. Let your indicators choose for you. As you begin to apply indicators to the charts of the securities you like, some will appeal more than others. They'll make sense to you, and you'll be comfortable using them. And your chosen indicators will work better in some time frames than in others.

And after you have a small set of preferred indicators, you can employ a scan, available in many software programs, to find other securities on which your indicators work well, expanding your universe of securities.

How about being a trend-follower in some securities and a swing trader in some other securities in your portfolio? Chances are good doing so could end up becoming confusing, but there's nothing wrong with it in theory.

FADING THE TREND

Prices often move two steps forward and one step back. Sometimes you see a pause in an uptrend arriving, and you know that early buyers are about to take profit, setting off a domino effect of falling prices. You know that the uptrend is well established, but instead of waiting for the trend to end, you sell your position and also go short today with the intention of exploiting just this one small downmove retracement. Selling into an uptrend sounds counterintuitive. But in practice, retracements are fairly reliable. Trading the retracement is called *fading the trend,* and it is standard operating procedure, especially in futures. Fading the trend works best if the countertrend trade is very short term (such as hours or days).

When you fade the trend, you break a cardinal rule of technical trading — to trade with the trend, which is based on the Dow principle that once a trend is established, the probability is high that it will continue. Therefore, to fade the trend is a purely opportunistic action based on an understanding of crowd psychology. Fading the trend also illustrates that the frame of reference of technical trading isn't the security and its fundamentals, but crowd behavior. Just remember, swing trading against the trend requires lightning speed, total concentration, and nerves of steel.

REMEMBER

If you choose longer-term trend-following, you choose to suffer through the downward bounce in an uptrend. Figure 4-1 shows four downward moves. Whether you can sit them out is a function of personal patience combined with confidence in your indicators.

Examining How Indicators Work

Indicators can't be easily categorized as belonging to trend trading or to swing trading, although it's obvious that if you're using a long-term moving average like the 50-day (see Chapter 12), it won't be appropriate to a shorter-term swing trade on a daily chart.

That doesn't mean you can't use a 50-*period* (or a 200-period) moving average on an intraday chart. In intraday analysis, the period isn't a day, but some number of minutes. For example, the 240-minute bar (4 hours) is popular in foreign exchange. That makes the 50-period moving average consist of 8.33 days, fairly long-term when your analysis window is 4 hours and your holding period is 24 to 48 hours. Likewise, a 200-period moving average is 33.33 days, which in swing trading is definitely a long-term period. In the sections that follow, I describe the general way indicators work, but be aware that technical traders are sometimes mavericks and use indicators in an infinite variety of ways.

Finding relevant time frames

Most indicators measure price and volume changes relative to previous prices and volume over a specific *lookback* period, such as 12 days or 21 days.

REMEMBER

Most indicators have a range of time in which research shows they work best. Most charting software incorporates this information as standard default parameters. A default parameter is only a starting point, and if 12 periods doesn't work on your chart, you're welcome to use a different number of periods. Twelve periods is the default because researchers found it the best number over many thousands of price series. Be sure to differentiate between the lookback period, such as the number of days of past data you're putting in the indicator, and your trading frequency. Using a 12-day momentum indicator, say, doesn't mean you'll trade every 12 days. It means simply that for this security, a 12-day lookback period was effective. Most indicators and patterns can stretch from a few minutes to several days or even many months, with a few exceptions. You wouldn't use momentum, for example, on a monthly chart, but you could use it on weekly and more frequent intervals. Support and resistance lines can be drawn on a chart of any time frame, and you can often see patterns like head-and-shoulders on 60-minute bars as well as a chart containing a year of data. Technology offers the ability to put an indicator on the screen that traditionally used (say) 12 days — but today it can be

12 periods, and the period could be 15-minute bars. Many traders just leave the default parameters of their indicators in their chart-drawing system and use them on every time frame.

REMEMBER

The ability to apply an indicator over any time frame reflects the *fractal* quality of prices — the weird and wonderful fact that without a label, a price series of 15-minute bars can't be distinguished from a month's worth of daily bars. Intraday bars are like microcosms of daily bars, and daily bars are like microcosms of weekly or monthly bars. Traders respond to price changes in regular, consistent, and repetitive ways no matter the time frame.

TIP

You should discard the idea that you already know your time frame. You may think you're a long-term trader but then discover a real affinity for an indicator that works stunningly on your favorite securities but entails trading 10 to 20 times per year when you started thinking you would trade twice a year at most. You don't want to miss an indicator that seems to "belong" to a different time frame just because you've already boxed yourself in. The indicator may be more flexible than you first think. You can use short-term indicators to make long-term trades and the other way around.

Heeding indicator signals

Indicators are designed to give buy-and-sell signals, although in many instances, the signal is more like a warning and doesn't have a black-and-white embedded decision rule. Indicators generate signals in three ways as I describe in the sections that follow — crossovers, meeting a range limit, and convergence and divergence.

Crossovers

The term *crossover* refers to one line crossing another line. They include

>> **The price crossing a fixed historic benchmark:** (See the "Establishing Benchmark Levels" section later in this chapter.)

>> **The indicator crossing the price or the price crossing the indicator:** (See Chapter 10 for support and resistance and Chapter 12 for moving averages.)

>> **One line of a two-line indicator crossing the other:** (See information on the moving average convergence/divergence indicator in Chapter 13.)

REMEMBER

In most instances, the price crossing an indicator is named a *breakout,* one of the most important concepts in technical analysis. When a price rises above a long-standing resistance line, for example, technical traders say it "broke out" of its previous trading range and now the sky's the limit — until the new range is established. Usually, you want to scrupulously observe and measure a breakout. If the resistance line is at 10 and the price goes to 12, it's a breakout. If the price goes to 10.05, it's also a breakout.

The word *breakout* itself tells you the crowd psychology behind the price move. In an upside breakout, bullish sentiment triumphed. The bulls broke out of the enclosure and are cavorting in the pasture. When bearish sentiment wins, the bears have broken down the fence and are eating your prize roses. A breakout doesn't necessarily imply a trend reversal, though; sometimes a breakout is a confirming factor that the existing trend is gathering new momentum or passing new benchmarks.

Range limits

Oscillators describe where today's price stands relative to its recent trading range, as I describe in Chapter 13. Oscillators are usually based on 100, so they range from zero to 100, or minus 100 to plus 100, or some other variation using the number 100.

In practice, traders find that usually the scope of the price range falls well under the outer limits and doesn't vary by more than 20 percent to 80 percent of the total possible range, so they draw a line at 20 percent of the maximum range and another at 80 percent (or 10 percent and 90 percent, or some other variation). When the indicator approaches one of the lines, the price is nearing an extreme of its recent range. This is a warning of an overbought or oversold condition and thus a potential retracement or reversal.

Convergence and divergence

Convergence refers to two indicator lines coming closer to one another, such as when a support line and a resistance line converge to form a triangle (see Chapter 9) or two moving averages get closer together (see Chapter 13), indicating less difference between their numerical values. Convergence generally means that the price action is starting to go sideways or has a narrower high-low range, or both. A sideways move, in turn, generally leads to a breakout, although it can take a painfully long time. Convergence doesn't have an embedded trading rule and is more often used as a warning that a change in direction or the strength of a trend is changing.

Divergence refers to two indicator lines moving farther apart, such as when the spread between two moving averages widens. Divergence also refers to an indicator and the price going in different directions, which is the most common and useful application of the observation. Momentum indicators, in particular, reshuffle the components of the price bar to come up with a price's rate of change, so that the slope of the indicator is a sophisticated measure of the strength of a trend.

When the price is still rising (making new highs) but the momentum indicator starts to fall (making progressively lower highs), the price and indicator are diverging. This divergence is almost always a warning that the rising price is going to stop rising sometime very soon.

REMEMBER

Divergence is one of the few leading indicators in technical analysis and something you should note as a warning of a possible trend change, although it, like convergence, doesn't have an embedded trading rule. Volume is a notable instance of divergence that assists tremendously in making a trading decision. Chapter 3 discusses volume in greater detail.

Establishing Benchmark Levels

Some price chart characteristics are inherent to the chart and independent of your indicators. Every price series has historic highs and lows that aren't indicators, and yet they may serve to indicate future price action, like the 52-week high or all-time high (or low). In some instances, years can pass before the benchmark is matched again. Historic levels are magnetic — they attract some traders to try to break them — but they're also barriers. Hesitation ahead of the breach of a benchmark price can be prolonged, demonstrating that traders are fully aware of "historic levels." In addition to historic highs and lows, some analysts like to check out the high or low over the past three or five days. Most analysts consider the long-term moving averages (20-, 50-, and 200-day) as benchmarks.

TIP

Historic levels are a cause and an effect of strange indicator behavior. If an uptrending indicator like the moving average flattens mysteriously, widen the time frame on your chart to see whether the price is near a historic level. The market is going to test the old high. If the test fails, expect a retracement and maybe a reversal. If the price passes the test and makes a new high, you expect the price to accelerate with high momentum and deliver a juicy profit.

Choosing Indicators

The good news is that everything works, at least some of the time. Moving average indicators work. Channel breakouts work. Trading in a three-to-five-day time frame with candlestick analysis works. But indicators only *indicate*. They don't *dictate* the next price move. For one thing, there's that monster, noise. For another, fresh news and perceptions of news arrive on the scene.

REMEMBER

All newcomers to technical analysis (and many old hands as well) tend to lose sight of the limitations of indicators. Folklore says that technical traders are always seeking the Holy Grail, or the perfect indicator or combination of indicators that is right 100 percent of the time. It doesn't exist. One of the reasons it doesn't exist is that *you* are different from the next guy or gal. Equally important, *you* change over time. The ideal indicator that delivered great profits 10 years ago is one that you now avoid as carrying too much risk. In other words, an indicator is only what you make of it.

The old joke has it, "Give 12 technical traders a new indicator, and a year later you have 12 different track records." How you use an indicator isn't set by the indicator itself, but by the trading rules you use. Indicators and trading rules have a chicken-and-egg relationship. The process of selecting and using indicators involves not only the characteristics of the indicator, but also a consideration of the trading rules you must employ to make the indicator work properly for you.

For example, you may like an indicator but find it generates too many trades in a fixed period, so you don't execute every single signal. This is called *cherry-picking,* and you should avoid letting it become a habit. It will bite you in the rear someday because indicators work on the law of large numbers. Indicators don't work every time, but you don't know ahead of time when those instances will occur. You also don't know when the indicator will surprise with a gigantic profitable breakout. In other words, you have to trust your indicators, and if you don't, don't override them — just get new ones. Or instead of overriding indicator signals with personal judgment, modify the exact timing of trades by using a second indicator. Chapter 16 discusses combining indicators.

TIP

Modifying indicators with trading rules is *always* better than overriding them. To override your indicator haphazardly is self-defeating. You're letting emotion back in. Plus, you won't get the expected result from the indicator — and then you'll blame the indicator. Fortunately, most indicators are fairly flexible. They can be adapted to fit the trading style you prefer, such as the frequency of your trades. Indicators are about price-move measurement. Trading rules are about you and your tolerance for risk. Trading rules must be appropriate to the indicators you choose. In short, don't pick indicators that you can't follow, like a momentum indicator that gives 50 trading signals per month when you don't have the time or inclination to trade that often.

Examining Indicators in Detail

The first step in seeing whether a given indicator can work for you is to test how it would have worked in the past. You expect price patterns to repeat, because crowd psychology doesn't change much. *Optimization* is the process of testing a hypothesis on historical data, named *backtesting,* to discover which parameter would've worked the best. In practice, the terms *backtesting* and *optimization* are used interchangeably.

Backtesting is a necessary evil because when you're starting out to trade a new security, you don't know which indicators to use or which parameters to put into the indicators. In keeping with the empirical approach, try various indicators and different parameters in the indicators to see what works.

I say that backtesting is evil because common sense tells you that conditions are never exactly the same and what worked on historical data may not work in the future. Backtests to find good indicators and optimum parameters give you a sense of accuracy and reliability that may be misleading. To perform backtesting and obtain all the data you want about indicator performance, you need your own technical analysis software. Websites and most broker platforms don't offer back-testing capabilities.

Constructing a backtest

Backtesting is a valuable exercise that delivers a measure of how well an indicator parameter might work — in a situation where you have no other evidence that the indicator will work at all. Backtesting using computer software is better than eye-balling multiple versions of the indicator on a chart because good software can give you all the metrics you need whereas eyeballing gives you none. I name the four top metrics here.

A popular place to start backtesting indicators on your security is the simple moving average crossover. The goal of the backtest is to find *x*, which is the number of days in the moving average that would generate the best profit by using a crossover rule (refer to Chapter 12). Here's the formal hypothesis: "If you buy XYZ stock every time the price crosses above the *x*-day moving average and sell it every time the price crosses below the *x*-day moving average, it'll consistently and reliably be a profitable trading rule."

Just about every software package allows you to search for the optimum moving average and will deliver the results in minutes. In this case, I ordered the software to test every moving average from 10 to 50 days over the past 1,000 days to see which moving average would have delivered the most profit on XYZ stock (the name is withheld to protect the innocent). I also ordered a buy-only strategy, although you can also test for additional gains from going short, if you're able to do so. Table 4-1 shows the three best results.

TABLE 4-1 **Results of Simple Moving Average Crossover Backtest on XYZ Stock**

Number of Days in Moving Average	Average Profit/Loss	Percent Gain	Number of Trades
10	$1.56	68.60%	178
31	$3.02	59.34%	32
35	$3.32	61.69%	47

If you'd been willing to trade 178 times in 1,000 days, or roughly every two weeks, you'd have made 68.6 percent by using a 10-day moving average crossover of the price. Is that a good number? One way to judge is to compare it to buy-and-hold; in other words, buying on Day 1 and selling on Day 1,000. In this case, the software calculated the buy-and-hold return as 43.4 percent, so for all that trading work, you made an additional 25.2 percent. On a $10,000 starting capital stake, that's $2,520. Or did you? No. To get a realistic net gain, you need to subtract brokerage and other costs.

WARNING

It's common sense to look at backtest results *after* slippage, which is the cost of brokerage fees plus the broker not giving you the exact price on your screen. Checking the indicator's performance after slippage can make all the difference between a profitable trading rule and an unprofitable one. Subtracting a $10-per-trade brokerage and slippage cost to the results in Table 4-1 changes everything! That's because the high number of trades in the best outcome carried with it a high dollar per-trade brokerage cost. Now the optimum moving average is 31 days (from 10), the number of trades is 32 (from 178), and the profit is 49.3 percent (from 68.6 percent). This is only 5.9 percent more than buy-and-hold. You're swapping a very high number of trades for less profit. Quick, which one would you choose?

The other top metrics

In the simple moving average crossover test, I used a single criterion for selecting the optimum moving average — percent gain. But percent gain isn't the only goal. If percent gain were the only goal, you could find yourself accepting a trading regime that delivers 100 losing trades for every 10 winning trades. The ten winners each had to be a home run to make up for all those losses. But you're looking for systematic trading, not a few home runs that may not repeat in the next 1,000 days. Therefore, you also care about the number of winning trades versus losing trades and the average win-loss ratio. You want as few losing trades as possible, and you want to get more profit from the average winning trade than you lose on the average losing trade. Eek! That's a total of four more criteria you need to measure in your backtest to choose the best parameters.

WARNING

Backtesting never delivers a single, no-brainer parameter. Even after factoring in brokerage and slippage costs, you still have to choose between the parameter that calls for more trades over one that calls for fewer trades, between one that delivers more winning trades than losing trades, and the one that delivers a better win-loss ratio. You hardly ever find a parameter for your indicator that meets all the criteria. A compromise is in your future.

Fixing the indicator

Assume that percent gain is your priority. What comes second? Most people choose reducing the number of losing trades, which is the correct choice. The single best way to reduce your losing trades is to add a confirmation requirement, such as one of the momentum or relative strength indicators. Requiring a second indicator to confirm a buy/sell signal will reduce the number of trades by 30 to 50 percent without sacrificing much profit. And because the trades being eliminated by momentum confirmation are generally losing trades, the gain-loss ratio improves, too.

After choosing your indicator parameter, your job isn't finished. Backtests are hypothetical. You didn't actually make those trades. To get a more realistic idea of how an indicator-based trading rule works, backtest the rule on historical price data and then apply it to out-of-sample data. In the case in Table 4-1, for example, I backtested on 1,000 days of data. Now I should backtest it on the next 500 days of data, named a *walk-forward test.* If the results are about the same on the fresh data, you consider your rule to be *robust,* meaning it works across a wide range of conditions.

Evaluating the risks of backtesting

The flaw in backtesting is that the ideal parameter for an indicator is ideal only for the past, which is referred to as *rearview-mirror criticism.* Although it's accurate, it's not terribly useful. Critics of backtesting point out that even if your indicator is robust on the next 500 days of out-of-sample data, after you actually add that 500 days to the backtest, the perfect parameter is now some other number. You can go mad backtesting until you're blue in the face, and you'll never find the optimum parameter that stays the same over time.

The unreliability factor gets worse if you fiddle with the indicator with filters. This is named *curve-fitting,* or making the indicator perfect for the past. The probability of that indicator being perfect for the future is low, because the market is dynamic and changes.

Bottom line: Don't count on finding a magic number to put into your indicators. Now you know why many traders just use the default parameters supplied with software and on websites. I recommend backtesting anyway because it's a tremendously educational experience. You discover not only about the inner workings of indicators, but also about yourself and your own risk preferences. For example, you may start out thinking you care most about total percent gain and are willing to disregard big losses as long as you get a high gain in the end. But when you see that a favored indicator can cost you 20 percent of your capital stake several times a year, you may suddenly start preferring a less aggressive indicator that tends to cost you only 5 percent in each losing trade. Choosing indicators via backtesting is a journey of self-discovery as well as a scientific exploration.

Backtesting has fallen out of favor in recent years, probably because it's a massive amount of work that takes a vast amount of time and ideally should be refreshed repeatedly. At a minimum you're trying to get the best combination of percent gain, highest gain-to-loss ratio, more winning than losing trades, and an indicator that is robust across a range of conditions. That's a tall order, and the trade-offs are sometimes peculiar. Adding additional indicators to get confirmation increases the workload exponentially. If you're computationally competent and clever with numbers, you can modify the parameters of multiple indicators to generate a trading system having exceptional profitability. While you're doing that, though, you're not doing other things, like watching prices move to get a feel for the rhythm of the market. I've known math whizzes who devise devilishly intricate sets of indicators and revise them obsessively — and never execute any trades at all.

IN THIS CHAPTER

» **Creating trading rules: The five-step plan**

» **Blending trading rules with indicators yields trading style**

» **Knowing when to take the money and run**

» **Keeping losses under control**

» **Finding out how to adjust positions**

» **Nailing down the best trade management tool**

Chapter **5**

Managing the Trade

Indicators are notoriously unreliable. The true secret to successful trading is to accept indicator unreliability and to take steps to offset that unreliability with disciplined trade management practices.

The indicator system doesn't exist that always results in gains and never results in losses. *You will take losses.* Indicators are like the raw materials for baking a pie — the oven, the pie plate, the flour, the filling. Indicators are about price changes, or *things*. Trading rules are about the *process* of trading, involving you and your money. Managing the trade is like becoming a skilled baker; you need to massage the pie dough but not too much, thicken the filling, and bake the pie for the right amount of time at the right temperature. Some trade management skills are mechanical (set the oven temperature at 450 degrees), and some involve more judgment and nuance (the right amount of water to add is a function of the humidity in your kitchen).

In this chapter, I talk about developing trading rules that reflect your risk appetite. The emphasis is on the stop-loss rule — don't leave home without one.

REMEMBER

Talking about managing the trade before I talk about indicators may seem a little strange, but I have a good reason for it. After you find a few indicators you like and you're fairly well convinced you can do trade on technical signals, you'll be champing at the bit to get going. Don't take the plunge just yet! You're only halfway there.

Building Trading Rules

A *trading rule* is the specific action you take when certain conditions are met. At the most basic, a trading rule instructs you to buy or sell when an indicator meets a preset criterion (like the moving average crossover in the case in Chapter 4). Many indicators have a buy/sell trading rule already embedded in them, as I describe in each of the chapters about indicators.

But technical trading is a mindset that goes beyond using indicators. Trading rules improve your trading performance by refining the buy/sell signals you get from indicators. Trading rules tend to be more complex and contain more conditions than raw indicators, such as "buy after the first 45 minutes if x and y also occur" or "sell half the position when z occurs."

Finding your risk profile . . . not yet

Every trade you take needs to meet a simple goal: Your expectation of gain is higher than your expectations of a loss. This is a fancy way of saying you want to get the highest return for the lowest risk. In this context, risk refers to the risk of loss. And that's as far as you need to go right now in determining your own personal risk profile. How much are you willing to lose in order to have the opportunity to make how big a gain? You may think today that you're willing to risk losing $500 for the chance to win $10,000. However, this trade-off is unrealistic. How about being willing to risk losing $500 for the chance to make $1,500? This trade-off is more realistic in real-world conditions, but you have no way of knowing upfront if the indicators you come to like will deliver that win-loss ratio.

REMEMBER

In a nutshell, you need to develop your indicators and your trading rules dynamically with constant feedback from one to the other in a process of self-discovery as to your risk profile. You don't set your risk preferences first and then choose your indicators. Risk preference emerges organically from the process of developing indicators and trading rules. And it may surprise you. You can start out imagining you're a buttoned-down, ultra-conservative type with a low tolerance for risk, but you discover you're darn good at using quick-time, short-term indicators that have you in and out of trades far more often than you expected upfront and that deliver a high gain/loss ratio that arises more from hewing to disciplined trading rules than the indicators themselves.

Adhering to the no-guru rule

Trading rules are intimately intertwined with indicators. You can easily find the "trader's top secrets," "magic indicators," and the "trade of the day" on websites. Many promoters even explain their techniques. But you aren't doing yourself any favors adopting somebody else's indicators — because those indicators embed that guru's trading rules. He may be willing to swing at every pitch and able to accept big losses that will freeze your soul. Instead you need to tailor the indicator to your risk appetite and not the risk appetite of the guru selling the trade or the program. The fault lies not in the indicator but in the execution of the entry and exit that suits your risk appetite. Good trading isn't about the securities you trade or about indicators. It's about planning the trade ahead of time to suit your personal risk tolerance, and following the plan. Managing the trade isn't exclusive to technical analysis. But all successful technical traders manage their trades.

REMEMBER

The no-gurus rule does have one exception. If the guru discloses all his indicators and has a long-term (more than five years) track record of completed trades that you can verify, you may find his style suits you just fine. But remember, the absence of indicator disclosure is a fatal flaw. The absence of a long-term real-time track record is a fatal flaw. Hardly any guru can meet these criteria, however charming and seductive his presentations.

Creating your trading plan with five easy rules

At each step you have to decide which indicators or combinations of indicators to follow, and your exact specifications for them.

REMEMBER

Each rule has its place. You shouldn't follow just one or two of the rules. You need to follow them all. Here's what your rules need to do:

1. **Determine whether a trend exists.**

    This rule may seem obvious, but keep in mind that trend-following indicators are going to fail when the security isn't trending.

2. **Establish the rules for opening a position.**

    Some advisors say this rule is the most important. Like buying real estate, getting the house at the lowest possible price is the benchmark for ending profit, given average price ranges in the neighborhood. Greg Morris describes this principle in *Investing with the Trend: A Rule-Based Approach to Money Management* (John Wiley & Sons, Inc.).

3. **Manage the money at risk by scaling up or down (adding or subtracting the amount of money in the trade).**

    This rule is the most important step named by professional futures fund managers, which is logical. It's more profitable to increase funds in the currently winning trades and to withdraw funds from the laggards.

4. **Establish the rules for closing a position — set stops and targets.**

Professionals always observe this rule. For the individual whose mind may still hold vestiges of value-investing and buy-and-hold ideas, this rule is the most important. The paramount rule in technical trading is to control losses.

5. **Establish a reentry rule after being stopped or after the target is hit.**

This rule is my own contribution. Most technical analysts consider each buy/sell situation as a stand-alone case. After you've exited a position, you need to start all over again at the top and determine whether the security is trending. They say a reentry is the same as an entry and takes all the same amount of work. But when you're looking at trading *within* a big macro trend, the reentry is a different process.

Say your security has been in an uptrend for many months. As in every uptrend, it corrects downward from time to time, exactly as Edwards and Magee described decades ago. You want to take profit at the first sign of a pullback and reenter at a relative low (refer to Chapter 4). You want to be the swing trader who takes the eight trades in the overall move, or four if you're unable to take the short side. You already know the security is trending. Your reentry rules are inherently different from entering from scratch and will most likely involve additional indicators.

The technical trader plans the trade from entry to exit. This is the opposite of traditional investing, where you buy a security for an indefinite period of time without a stop or profit target. But if you want to increase your stake or preserve capital, it's when you sell that counts. You sell for one of three reasons — you met a profit target, you met a loss limit, or you chose to increase or decrease the risk of the trade.

You can pick so-so securities and apply so-so indicators to them, and if you're trading systematically, you can still make a decent net gain if you only control losses.

Combining indicators with trading rules

The key to technical trading success is being doubly systematic — systematic in identifying what are for you tradable trends and conditions and systematic in applying your trading rules.

Trends can be defined by dozens of different criteria, as I show you in Part 2. A trend defined by a simple measure, such as two or more touches of a support line, gains credibility when you can add confirmation from a second indicator, such as volume, momentum, or relative strength. All indicators fail sometimes, so a trend can be deemed more reliable if it's confirmed. By the time you add a third confirming indicator, your confidence level should be pretty high that this will be a winning trade.

But price series seldom cooperate and deliver confirmation after confirmation from multiple indicators. In fact, by the time everything lines up perfectly, the trend is probably ending! It drives some people nuts to have three indicators saying buy and one saying sell, but trust me on this, that's exactly what you'll face, almost all the time. Depending on what indicators you choose and how well they tend to perform on your securities, you should rank trendedness by your own measures of reliability from real-life experience. You can take guidance from statistical work on reliability by analysts like Bulkowski (see Chapter 9), but you need to remember that even though history repeats, it never repeats exactly.

This is why book authors and other gurus who claim to have ideal indicators for their securities aren't necessarily lying — maybe they did, for their securities and in the time frame they were working. That doesn't mean their magic formula will work for you on your securities going forward and with your risk preferences. It's therefore better to master the principles behind many different indicators and understand why they work so that you can be flexible in choosing the ones that work for you. It took me 20 years of looking at it every blessed day to get the Fibonacci retracement concept. It's now on my list of must-haves, and I still look at it ahead of every trading decision.

REMEMBER

Ranking your indicators as to their value in meeting your trading rule criteria is a personal job. Not all indicators are created equal. The zippy indicator that yields good gains for the high-frequency trader may entail too much risk for you. The reliable slow-poke indicator that's hardly ever wrong may get only minor gains as well as put you to sleep.

Trading styles

There are as many trading styles as there are individual traders in the world. I propose a way of looking at trading styles that aims to blend indicators with rules, but it's very general.

System-mechanical trading

Truly systematic traders take every trade that their indicator system dictates. Indicators are selected because they deliver the desired risk metrics, but after the design phase, the indicators rule. The actual trading is not only mechanical but also literally can be done by a computer. Two major system designers are Keith Fitschen and Perry Kaufman, each of whom has written an excellent book on building trading systems. See the Appendix for additional resources. If you're a computer whiz, you absolutely, positively need both books.

System design that blends indicator choices with risk management rules is very advanced stuff. But after the system is built and tested, you can sit back and let 'er rip. In the system-mechanical world, especially if indicators are adaptive to changing conditions, you apply no judgment after the design phase. You don't sit around contemplating noise versus Event (see Chapter 4) or worry about contingencies. A successful system should be robust across all conditions.

System-guided trading

Say that you've developed a set of indicators that delivers the mix of percent gain, gain/loss, and so on, that you prefer, but sometimes it fails to live up to expectations. This generally occurs during retracements but also when trendedness collapses into lack of trendedness — the dreaded sideways movement. It's very hard to modify indicators to be adaptive in both trending and nontrending situations, and it's equally hard to identify precisely when trendedness is giving way to nontrendedness so that you can change to a different set of indicators.

Not all trends are created equal.

In system-guided trading, you want to apply additional techniques, usually from the nonmathematical collection (like candlesticks and other patterns) to help you modify your trading style to preserve your trading rule goals. In other words, your trading rules are more important than your indicators to lasting success. You don't discard your indicators, but you have a healthy skepticism about their usefulness in untrended conditions.

How does this work, exactly? You have three tactics to consider:

>> **Embrace the idea that you don't have to take every trade.** When your chart is a mishmash with no obvious directional bias, your indicators are still pumping out buy/sell signals that are mostly wrong. Don't hate your indicators — it's not their fault. Just accept that they aren't reliable under these conditions and because your priority is to preserve capital, don't trade. This doesn't include cherry-picking, meaning taking some trades and not others. Doing so is almost always self-defeating and causes confusion to boot; you start thinking your intuitive feel for the security is better than the indicators. It's not. Once in a blue moon it may be, but don't count on it. Just stop trading until you see trendedness return.

>> **Change your time frame.** Say you consider yourself a position trader with a holding period of months, but along comes a choppy chart with high volatility, meaning a wide high-low range. Instead of sitting it out twiddling your thumbs until a trend emerges, trade the choppiness on a swing basis using patterns or other techniques. This proposition is also iffy. It entails changing horses in midstream. Again, you can easily get confused.

>> **Adapt your risk management rules — stops and targets and perhaps scaling in and out — to the new conditions.** If you've been setting profit targets as a function of average range and stops just below support levels, but support levels are broken or can't be found in the new environment, devise new stops that still preserve your gain/loss ratio.

Guerrilla trading

The term *guerrilla trading* is mostly used by one school of analysts that specializes in sideways-market, special set-up situations, but it can be used in other contexts. In military terms, a guerrilla engages in irregular fighting, meaning he is the one to choose his time and place, not the enemy.

Guerilla trading is the least systematic method of trading and relies on special pattern setups and/or an astute eye or intuitive feel for crowd psychology. An example is stipulating a buy-entry order below the current level (but still within the normal range) because the desired target would be outside the normal range and therefore not likely to get hit. In other words, the market isn't offering you a profit opportunity at current levels but could easily go to your preferred levels while you aren't watching. If the price falls to the guerrilla entry, you have a fighting chance to hit the target, but the trade isn't otherwise worth doing on a gain/loss basis.

A parallel guerrilla tactic is seeing with blinding clarity where a stop should be placed and determining the entry as a function of the stop. Again, if the entry isn't hit, the guerrilla trader doesn't care. The trade was worth doing only on *his* terms. Individuals can't tell markets what to do, of course; you and I are always price-takers. But if a better entry is possible using average range or other concepts, why not try? In nonsystem trading, you don't have to take every trade.

Guerrilla trading comes in at least two flavors:

>> Guerrilla trading can take the form of entering and exiting an existing trend multiple times, each with a deliberately short time frame (like a few minutes) but staying out of the market or reducing the stake (scaling out) when the trendedness ranking is low or medium. It may also entail tactics like specifying nonmarket entries as I describe earlier in this chapter. To a certain extent, using a trailing stop (see the following) is a guerrilla tactic, although trailing stops can be system-mechanical, too.

>> A subset of guerilla trading is setup trading, in which trades are inspired by a Shock that results in specific bar configurations, especially in candlestick form or patterns like gaps. The Shock, especially if it's noise (see Chapter 4), is expected to be short-lived and so the exit depends on time, usually a very short holding period, or dollar gain/loss, rather than an indicator.

Knowing How Much Is Enough

When you have a gain in a trade, how do you know when to take profits? Unfortunately, few experts offer guidance on how to design a take-profit rule. You never know at the beginning of a trend how long it will last or how far it will go. The central issue in managing the trade is that you can have control over the size of your losses (via stop losses), but very little control over the size of the gains. You can buy a stock at $5 and make sure that you only lose $2, but you can't force the stock to go to $9.

In practice, each individual trader develops his own technique that is a combination of risk analysis and indicator readings. The optimum way to take profit is, in fact, one of the great, unexplored frontiers of technical trading. Here are some choices for selecting a profit target:

>> **Name a dollar amount.** Logically, you want a gain that is a multiple of the risk you're taking. Say your security costs $8 and you want to lose no more than 25 percent, or $2. You can place your stop at $6 ($8 minus $2) or a smaller amount, like $1.50. Your profit target is double initial risk, or $4. This is a 50 percent return, which may or may not be realistic depending on your holding period, changes in volatility, and other factors. After you have made the 50 percent, however, you obey the target and exit the trade when it reaches $12. The problem with this approach, of course, is that the price may keep on rising and then you have an opportunity loss if it reaches (say) $20.

>> **Set a true-range amount.** Your security, historically, has an average high-low range of $10 over 20 periods, your expected holding period. You want to capture 75 percent of the range, or $7.50. Because you use indicators to time your entry, you assume that you're entering at the low end of the range; therefore, 75 percent is realistic. When the price reaches your target, you take profit.

  The problem with this approach is twofold:

  • The range can widen or narrow. If it widens, you aimed too low, and if it narrows, your original target is too ambitious.

  • A pullback can wreck your expectations. You may have met the goal of entering at a low only to have an aberrant pullback take the price down 30 percent rather than up 75 percent. This movement wasn't enough to hit your stop, but now your profit target is $10.50 away from the current price. Because you know the average range is $10, the probability of meeting your $7.50 target within your holding period just went out the window.

>> **Rely on indicators.** Instead of formulating take-profit rules, most technical traders rely on indicators to signal when a move has ended — the signal is the *de facto* take-profit rule. Relying on indicators is likely to result in the biggest

gains, but doing so requires more market monitoring than the fixed dollar amount or average true-range methods.

>> **Consider the measured move concept.** Some patterns and theories about price movements contain a forecast of how far the price should go (see Chapter 9). Some evidence shows certain measured moves can be trusted to appear *x* percent of the time but not every time. You're welcome to test the measured move concept on the price history of your securities and rank measured move as an indicator, just as you should rank your other indicators for reliability.

Controlling Losses

Your level of risk-seeking or risk-aversion is personal. Therefore, nobody can design rules for you. You must do it for yourself. Ask yourself whether you'd faithfully follow every buy/sell signal of a given indicator when history suggests you'll have some trades that entail a loss of 50 percent. No? Well, how much of your trading capital *are* you prepared to lose? This isn't an idle question. Your answer is critical to whether you succeed in technical trading. If you say you can accept no losses at all, forget technical trading. You *will* take losses in all trading, even well-designed and planned technical trading. If you say that you're willing to lose 50 percent in a single trade — whoa, Nellie! That's too much. Three or four losing trades in a row and you wouldn't have enough capital left to do any trades. I offer some help in deducing your personal number in the following sections.

WARNING

Experienced traders ask themselves, "How much will I lose today?" when they wake up every morning. They expect loss on some level. In contrast, beginners find losses almost impossible to contemplate. Yet if you don't control losses, the question is not whether you go broke, but *when* you go broke (as a famous trader named W.D. Gann wrote on the very first page of one of his books).

Exiting a losing trade is heart-breaking. For one thing, it means your indicator let you down. Accept that your indicators have shortcomings and that your job is to overcome those shortcomings by using money-management rules.

A bigger problem may be your bruised ego. To sell a losing position means that you failed, and the standard response to a loss is denial. "It will come back!" you cry. In the long run, maybe it will come back. But by then, you may be broke and unable to take advantage of it. As I show in Chapter 1, the percentage gain that you need to recover a loss can be shocking. To recover a 50 percent loss, you need to make a 100 percent gain.

Every top trader admits to taking bigger losses than they planned. Many go out of business for a period of time, only to come back later with essentially the same indicators — and better ways to manage the trade. In fact, some investors say that the best time to place money with a professional trader is right after she has taken a fat loss — because then he's a better trader. Note that such investors aren't predicting he'll be a better indicator analyst, but a better *trader.* You can find good lessons on this subject in the Jack Schwager books *Market Wizards* and *The New Market Wizards* (both published by John Wiley & Sons, Inc.). Often the secret ingredient the wizards discovered to gain lasting success is the mindset and discipline to control losses.

Using the First Line of Defense: Stop-Loss Orders

You use a stop-loss order to overcome the unreliability of indicators as well as your own emotional response to losses. A *stop-loss order* is an order you give your broker to exit a trade if it goes against you by some amount. For a buyer, the stop-loss order is a sell order below the current market price. For a short-seller, it's a buy order above the current market price.

If market conditions are choppy (high volatility), you may want to widen your stop even though your own particular security is behaving nicely. In this instance, you fear an overflow effect from the general market to your particular security. You may switch from a money-based trailing stop like the 2 percent rule to a volatility or pattern type of stop.

Here is an overview of the main types of stops and how they work. Don't skip over this section. More than likely it can save your bacon from a catastrophic loss.

Mental stops are hogwash

You should enter your stop-loss order at the same time you enter the position. In fact, you need to know the stop in order to calculate how big a position to take in the first place, if you're using any risk-management rule. Why some traders don't do this is a mystery. Many traders say they keep a mental stop in their heads, but this method is a delusion. It's self-delusion to think you'll be watching the price every minute the market is open and you'll have the gumption to sell at a loss if the limit is reached. But no one can watch the market every minute, and in practice, most traders with mental stops sit hopelessly by as the trade goes further and further against them.

Other traders say that their security isn't suitable for stops because it's too volatile. Or the trader is so big that the market would find out where his stops are and maliciously target them. Another rationalization is that the trader's stops get hit, and often, only for the price to move back in the original direction right afterward. This excuse isn't a reason to avoid using stop losses. It's a reason to reset the stop to a better level.

WARNING

To pretend that you have a mental stop or to refuse to place stops is to avoid accepting the reality of trading — it's a business, and setbacks happen in business. Setting a stop-loss order is like buying insurance in case the house burns down. Not to take out insurance is to treat trading as a hobby and view the amount at stake as play money rather than as risk capital.

Sorting out the types of stops

Technical traders have developed many stop-loss principles. Each concept is either a fixed trading rule or a self-adjusting one. Stops relate to indicators, to money, or to time, and often these three don't line up neatly to give you an easy decision. You have to choose the type of stop that works best for you.

The 2 percent stop rule

Probably the most famous stop-loss rule is the fixed 2 percent rule that was employed by a trading group named the Turtles. (To find out more about how complete amateurs were taught to trade successfully on trading rule discipline alone, check out *The Way of the Turtle* [McGraw-Hill] by Curtis Faith.) The *2 percent rule* states that you should stop a loss when it reaches 2 percent of starting equity. If you're trading risk capital of $10,000, you can afford to lose no more than $200 on any single trade if you expect to stay in business for a long period of time. The 2 percent rule is an example of a *money stop,* which names the amount of money you're willing to lose in a single trade.

Two hundred dollars may sound like a tiny number to you, but in the context of active trading, this figure is quite large. You need only 50 losing trades in a row to go broke. And 50 trades may sound like a lot of trades, but you find that many valid indicators have you trading that often, depending on your time frame. If you're trading 15-minute or 60-minute bars, you could easily have more than 100 trades in a month. If you're trading five securities, for example, you go broke after ten consecutive losses per security.

Risk-reward money stops

The *risk-reward ratio* puts the amount of expected gain in direct relationship to the amount of expected loss. The higher the risk-reward ratio, the more desirable the trade. Say, for example, that you're buying Blue Widget stock at $5 and your indicators tell you that the potential gain is $10, which means that the stock could go to $15. You could set your initial stop at $2.50, or 50 percent of your capital stake, for the chance to make $10. That gives you a risk-reward ratio of 10:2.5, or 4:1. (Strangely, the amount of the gain, the *reward*, is always placed first in the ratio, even though it comes second in the name.)

But consider the premise from this example — your ending capital triples your initial stake. But gee, expecting a 300 percent return is going a bit far, isn't it? Well, it depends on your skills. If you consistently forecast and get 300 percent gains, good for you. You may be able to accept a higher initial stop-loss level than other mere mortals.

REMEMBER

To apply the risk-reward ratio in a conservative and prudent manner, turn it upside down. Instead of calculating it with your best-case expected gain, use a realistic worst-case estimate of the loss. Your worst-case gain should be higher than your worst-case loss. For example, say you're prepared to lose $2 for the chance to make $4. Your risk-reward ratio is 4:2, or 2:1. If you practice this exercise on every trade, the risk-reward ratio becomes a filter that winnows out trades that may be high probability but with excessive risk.

WARNING

Calculating the risk-reward ratio and using it to set a stop has its own dangers. In the earlier Blue Widget case, you're willing to lose 50 percent of your capital. If you lose, you can take only a few such trades before you run out of money. Moreover, you can start out with a fixed risk-reward money stop but then change it to an adjustable stop as you modify your idea of how much the trade could potentially gain. Say the price falls from $5, your original entry, to $3.50. But the average range is widening and still telling you the potential high price is $15. If you buy more at $3.50 and the $15 is indeed reached, your gain is even bigger in percentage terms. Using the risk-reward ratio this way is how traders trick themselves into adding to losing positions, the blackest of cardinal sins in trading.

Analyzing risk-reward ratios can quickly become a complex task requiring knowledge of statistics and probability. But you can take a stab at it using simple arithmetic as in the examples in this chapter. Any estimation of risk-reward is better than none, and surprisingly, after it becomes second nature, your comfort level with trading will rise. The central idea is that in technical trading, the general rule is to take small losses and aim for bigger gains, not to take big losses and aim for gigantic gains.

Maximum adverse excursion

John Sweeney developed the concept of *maximum adverse excursion*, which is the statistically determined worst-case loss that may occur during the course of your trade. Using this method, you calculate the biggest change in the high-low range over a fixed period (say 30 days) that's equivalent to your usual holding period. Actually, you need to calculate the maximum range from the entry levels you would've used. Because you know your entry rules, you can backtest to find the maximum range that was prevalent at each entry.

For example, if the security never changes from high to low by more than $10 over the period, you could set your stop at $11. You should see a regular pattern between the maximum adverse excursion and your winning and losing trades over time. In fact, you can use the inverse of the adverse excursion, the *maximum favorable excursion*, to select trades in the first place. See Chapter 14 on volatility.

Trailing stops

Trailing stops use a dynamic process that follows the price: You raise the stop as the trade makes profits. A trailing stop is set on a money basis — you maintain the loss you can tolerate at a constant dollar amount or percentage basis. You could, for example, say that you want to keep 20 percent of each day's gain, so every day you'd raise the stop day to include 80 percent of the day's gain. This method means calling the broker or reentering the stop electronically every day. The important point is to keep the stop updated to protect gains and guard against losses at the same time.

WARNING

Trailing stops are highly protective, but you risk being stopped out on a noisy price event that isn't really related to the overall price trend, like calendar events or the payrolls report the first Friday of every month. The normal average daily trading range encompasses the trailing stop level on most occasions, but you can still get stopped out on a random event causing an abnormal, off-trend spike.

Indicator-based stops

Indicator-based stops depend on the price action and the indicators you use to capture it. Indicator stops can be either fixed or self-adjusting. I mention them at various places throughout the book. Here are some important ones:

>> **Last-three-days rule:** The most basic of stop-loss rules is to exit the position if the price surpasses the lowest low (or highest high if you're going short) of the preceding three days. This idea sounds a little corny. However, it jibes well with another piece of trading lore that says a trade should turn profitable right away if you've done the analysis right and you're actually buying right after a low or selling right after a peak. If the price first rises for a day or two but can't hold on to the gain, the upmove that you think you've identified is probably a false one. Consider the crowd dynamics (see Chapter 2) and how they play out on the price bar (refer to Chapter 6). You need a series of higher highs *and* higher lows to name an uptrend. If you get a lower low in the first three days, the probability is good that the trade is going south.

>> **Pattern stops:** Pattern stops relate directly to market sentiment and are very handy. Most are of the fixed variety. I list a few here:

 • The break of a support or resistance line is a powerful stop level, chiefly because so many other traders are drawing the same lines.

- The last notable high or low (the *historic* level; see Chapter 4) or the high or low of an important time period, like a year, are noteworthy.

- You can infer stops from other pattern indicators, such as the center confirmation point of the W in a double bottom or the M in a double top (check out Chapter 9). When the confirmation point is surpassed, the probability is high that the move will continue in the expected direction. If you're positioned the wrong way when the pattern appears, the pattern confirmation is also your stop level.

» **Moving-average stop:** You can also use a separate indicator that isn't part of your buy/sell repertoire to set a stop, such as a moving average (see Chapter 12). Many traders use a breakout beyond the 10-day moving average as a warning to reduce a position and the 20-day moving average as a stop. You may find it interesting how often a retracement will penetrate a 10-day moving average but halt just short of crossing the 20-day moving average. A moving-average stop is clearly of the self-adjusting variety.

Volatility stops are the most complex of the indicator-based, self-adjusting stops to figure out and to apply, but they're also the most in tune with market action. Many variations are available. Here are three of particular interest:

» **Parabolic stop-and-reverse model:** Invented by Welles Wilder, the parabolic concept is easy to illustrate and hard to describe. The principle is to create an indicator that rises by a factor of the average true range (see Chapter 7) as new highs are being recorded, so that the indicator accelerates as ever-higher highs are met and decelerates as less-high highs come in. In an uptrend, the indicator is plotted just below the price line. It diverges from the price line in a hot rally and converges to the price line as the rally loses speed as in Figure 5-1. The parabolic stop is both self-adjusting *and* trailing — a rare combination.

» **Average true-range stop:** This stop is set just beyond the maximum normal range limits. I describe the average true-range channel in greater detail in Chapter 14. With this stop, you take the average daily high-low range of the price bars, adjusted for gaps, and expand it by adding on a constant, like 25 percent of the range. Say your average daily trading range is $3. If the price goes more than 25 percent beyond the $3 high-low range, you consider it an extreme price and the signal to exit. The average true-range stop has the virtue of being self-adjusting, but it also has the drawback of setting a stop that has nothing to do with your entry.

» **Chandelier exit:** This stop solves the entry-level issue. Invented by Chuck LeBeau, the chandelier exit sets the stop at a level below the highest high or the highest close *since your entry*. You set the level as a function of the average true range. The logic is that you're willing to lose only one range worth (or two or three) from the best price that occurred since you put on the trade. Like the parabolic stop, the chandelier is both self-adjusting and trailing.

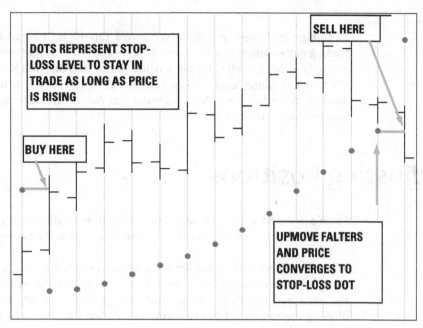

Inside the figure:

DOTS REPRESENT STOP-LOSS LEVEL TO STAY IN TRADE AS LONG AS PRICE IS RISING

SELL HERE

BUY HERE

UPMOVE FALTERS AND PRICE CONVERGES TO STOP-LOSS DOT

FIGURE 5-1:
Parabolic stop.

© *John Wiley & Sons, Inc.*

REMEMBER

Indicator stops usually entail taking a loss greater than the Turtle 2 percent benchmark rule. This factor hands you a hard decision. If you take the 2 percent rule, you have to live with the remorse of exiting trades only to see the price move your way later on. If you take an indicator rule that entails losses greater than 2 percent of capital, but have a series of losing trades early in your trading career, you could lose a lot of money before you figure out how to adapt your indicators.

Time stops

Time stops acknowledge that money tied up in a trade that's going nowhere can be put to better use in a different trade (or a savings account). Say you're holding a position that starts going sideways. It's reasonable to exit the trade and find a different security that is moving. Remember, the purpose of trading is to make money.

Clock and calendar stops

Clock and calendar stops pertain to a price event happening (or not happening) considering the time of day, week, month, or year. Clock-based rules abound. Some technical traders advise against trading during the first hour in the U.S. stock market, because buy- or sell-on-open orders are being executed then (see Chapter 6). Others say that more gain can be had from the first hour than any other hour of the trading day if you can figure out which way the crowd is trading. As I describe in Chapter 16, one setup technique is to buy or sell the direction of an opening gap — and be done in an hour.

In foreign exchange, you often see prices retrace at the end of the European trading day — about 11 a.m. in New York — because traders there close positions. Not only is this a swell entry place when you're sure that you know the trend, but it's also a benchmark for the U.S. trading day. If the price fails to close higher or lower than the European close, it means that American traders are having second thoughts about the trend.

Adjusting Positions

Stops are the first line of defense against indicator failure and market catastrophes. But a stop is a blunt instrument when more delicacy can be employed.

Most indicators are black and white. You should either buy or sell. But when you're using multiple indicators, you don't always get a clear-cut trading decision, or as the trade progresses, one of your confirming indicators weakens and is no longer offering the comfort of full confirmation. Perhaps a pattern spells doom to your position. You don't normally use patterns, but you can't avoid seeing the darn thing and it nags at you. Maybe you should scale out.

To increase the size of a position is called *scaling in,* and to reduce the amount you have at risk is *scaling out.* In the sections that follow, I go into more detail on these concepts.

REMEMBER

Position sizing can add or subtract from your bottom line by as much or more than your choice of securities or indicators.

When you get an itch to change position size, consider whether it's the security's price behavior that has changed — or your risk appetite. Your security makes a giant breakout, and the trend gathers steam in a straight line for an abnormally long period of time. Risk is (temporarily) lower. This is a good reason to scale in. Or, you just got a big bonus and are putting it all into your trading account and are newly willing to take a bigger loss per trade. This is an okay reason to scale in as long as you allocate capital among securities according to potential loss as a percentage of total capital.

Reducing positions

The safest way to reduce the risk of loss is to reduce exposure to it — scaling out. If you've bought on an indicator-based signal but if another indicator or a new fundamental suggests it's not going to be a good trade, get out of part of the position. Similarly, you may have a nicely trending security and get a surprise stop hit that you don't trust because you think you can identify the cause as an anomalous bit of noise. Instead of being paralyzed or not trading at all, you have options:

>> Delay following the indicator signal until the nontechnical event risk is past. Some traders advise reducing positions ahead of known event risks, such as central bank meetings, earnings announcements, and elections.

>> Stay in the trade, but reduce the amount of money you allocate to it (and perhaps tighten the stop). You can also hedge the risk in the options market or take the opposite position in a correlated security, but on the whole, scaling out is the most direct and efficient method.

Adding to positions

You can add to a position, or scale in, when your existing position is highly profitable. Statisticians disagree on adding to winning positions by using unrealized profits from the existing trade, called *pyramiding*. To *pyramid* is to use hypothetical profits to enlarge your position. Say you started with $1,000 and the trade has now generated another $1,000 in hypothetical mark-to-market paper profits, meaning the amount of gain you would get if you closed the position right now.

WARNING

Why not borrow against that extra $1,000 to buy some more of this high-performing security? The answer is that if a catastrophe strikes and the trade goes against you, your risk of loss can become huge — more than your original stake if your stop fails (or, heaven forbid, you didn't place one). Be aware that if you engage in pyramiding, you're taking a higher risk than if you don't. Pyramiding without proper stops has probably caused more traders to go broke than any other cause.

Scaling in and out 2.0

Other techniques for scaling in and out include the following:

>> If you're using a Turtles 2 percent stop rule, when the existing position has gained a profit that is greater than the 2 percent of starting capital you would have lost if the stop had been triggered, you add the amount of the surplus profit to the position with its own 2 percent stop. The problem, of course, is that it's awkward to trade in odd lots, and odd lots don't even exist in futures.

>> If you're using *margin* (where the trader puts down only a fraction of the value of the contract being traded), one general rule is to add to the position when the existing trade has earned the cost of the minimum initial margin of a second position. If you're trading on a 50 percent margin, you add to the

position when the existing position has racked up enough paper gain to fund the new position.

This rule is especially valuable in the futures market, in which the trader puts down only a small fraction of the value of the contract being traded. For example, if the initial margin required by the exchange and your broker is $2,500, you don't add a second contract to your position until the first contract has a profit of $2,500. By then, you figure that the move is well in place. But remember, you have to have one stop-loss order on the first contract and a different one on the second trade.

Applying stops to adjusted positions

If you're using an indicator stop and it signals that the price rise is over, doesn't that mean you want to exit all positions at the same level as soon as possible? The answer from statisticians is maybe. It depends on whether you're thinking in chart terms or money-management terms. If you're using a breakout concept to set your stop, for example, the price crossing a support line (as in Chapter 10) is a sell signal that would apply equally to all positions.

If you're using a 2 percent or other rule (like the chandelier exit I mention in this chapter) that is calculated specifically with reference to your starting point, you exit each trade according to the rule. This method has benefits and drawbacks. The benefit is that you're still in the trade if the stop was triggered for one trade but the price retracement is only a minor, temporary one. You still have other positions left and if the price makes a big jump your way, you're correctly positioned to take advantage of it. The drawback is that a well-set stop may really identify a change in overall price behavior. If it's a catastrophic price move, you may not get good execution of your stops and may end up losing more than the amount you planned.

Managing Your Trades Like a Pro

Every indicator and set of indicators generates a gain/loss profile. The next task in becoming a fully qualified technical trader is to apply the gain/loss profile of your indicator or indicator set to your own specific circumstances, namely how much capital you're going to put into trading and how many trades you can execute. These sections help you perform that task.

Introducing positive expectancy

The only reason to make a trade is that you have a *positive expectancy* of making money from it. *Expectancy* is a mathematical construct that can get very difficult very fast if you let it. But the basic concept is easy enough: You add up the possible outcomes and average them.

Here is an example. Pretend your indicator set would result in a 90 percent chance of a 50 percent gain and a 10 percent chance of a 100 percent gain. To put that in a formula, it looks like this:

$$\text{Expected Return} = (0.10 \times 1) + (0.9 \times 0.50) = 0.10 + 0.45 = 0.55 = 55 \text{ percent}$$

Where did those percentages come from? They come from your having looked at your indicator or indicator set over some past lookback period and written down every gain and every loss and calculated the percentage of times you got each outcome. You've read up on all the indicators and selected the ones you like and feel you can handle. You have either eyeballed those indicators on a chart of your favorite security or backtested them to verify the number of gains and the ratio of gains to losses.

The important point is that the expectancy is positive. It would be foolish to make a trade that you expect would result in a loss. And yet people do that all the time on the grounds that the stock is sure to be a winner in the long run because of its fundamentals (tech or pot stocks, for example).

Measuring the trade

Measuring your gain/loss numbers correctly isn't all that hard, although it can be time-consuming. Don't worry about applying formulas. The following formulas are logical and use only the arithmetic you learned in grade school.

To get to the numbers to fill in the formula, follow the steps below. Notice that it doesn't matter which indicators you put into your indicator set. It can be one indicator or any number of combinations of indicators. To see a discussion of combining indicators, see Chapter 16. This section isn't about indicators; it's about measuring the trades that result from the indicators.

1. **Calculate your win/loss ratio by adding up every winning trade and every losing trade over the past year, whether from your real-life trading or from your backtests, and then divide the winners by the losers.**

   Six months might be okay, but not less. Remember, you need a sufficient number of experimental trials to be able to deduce anything, as I describe in

Chapter 2. Say your trading, either real or hypothetical from the backtest, generates a win/loss ratio of 2:1, meaning a $2 gain for every $1 lost. This is pretty good, right?

Yes, but it doesn't go far enough. The win/loss ratio doesn't link the gains and losses to the amount of capital you put at risk and doesn't help you figure out the *expectancy* for the next trade. Maybe you made one trade in the year that netted $200 on a capital stake of $10,000 and one that lost $100 in the same year on the same $10,000. You still have a 2:1 win/loss ratio, but the rate of return on capital is tiny and the frequency of trading isn't high enough to deduce expectancy for the next trade.

2. Measure the expectancy.

You need to figure out whether you can have positive expectancy about the next trade using your indicators. Use this formula:

Average Profit per Winning Trade × Winning Trades as a Percentage of Total Trades − Average Loss per Losing Trade × Losing Trades as a Percentage of Total Trades

Say you find a set of indicators that would have generated this profile:

Expectancy on Indicator Set 1

$$(\$800 \times 35 \text{ percent}) - (\$400 \times 65 \text{ percent}) = \$280 - \$260 = \$20$$

In other words, the indicators deliver a home run of $800 on 35 percent of the trades but big losses on a majority of trades, so your expected gain per trade on the next trade is a mere $20.

Back to the drawing board. That set of indicators isn't good enough.

Here's the outcome from a different and better set of indicators, which I name Indicator Set 2. This new set of indicators generated 55 percent of winning trades and 45 percent of losing trades, but the average winning trade gained $400 and the losing trades lost half that, or an average of $200 each.

Expectancy on Indicator Set 2

$$(\$400 \times 55 \text{ percent}) - (\$200 \times 45 \text{ percent}) = \$220 - \$90 = \$130$$

Using this new Indicator Set 2, your expectancy for the next trade is a net $130, which is a whole lot better than $20, but $130 on how much capital and over how many trades?

Considering your stake

The word "stake" refers to how much money you're placing on each trade. You need to add that in to the expectancy formula because the amount per trade affects the outcomes over time. To get a handle on this idea, consider you have $10,000 to put into securities trading, but you're busy with a job and family, so you want to trade only four times a year, or once a quarter. Here's the question: Given these constraints, how much money can you expect to make by the end of the first year?

If you use the expectancy from the preceding Indicator Set 2 — that each trade has a high probability of making $130 — and you're trading only four times per year, you have a high probability of making 4 × $130 = $520. Given a starting capital stake of $10,000, this plan doesn't pass the so-what test. The so-what test asks how much money you want to make as a multiple of starting capital. This outcome is a 5.2 percent gain, more than a bank savings account but not worth the time and trouble of all that trading work.

Back to the drawing board again, but you'll keep Indicator Set 2. What you want to change is the percentage gain on your $10,000 that makes the trading effort worthwhile. Say you want to double your stake to $20,000. How many trades would you have to make to get that outcome? Here's the formula:

$$\text{Capital Goal} = \text{Starting Capital} + \left(\frac{\text{Expectancy} \times \text{Capital Stake per Trade} \times}{\text{Total Number of Trades}} \right)$$

Here's how to fiddle with the arithmetic:

$$\$20,000 = \text{Starting Capital} + \left(\$130 \times \text{Number of Trades} \right)$$

If you traded the full amount of $10,000 on every trade (and the expectancy remains stable at $130 per trade), you'd have to make 76.9 trades per year to double your money:

$$\$20,010 = \$10,000 + 10,010 \left(\$130 \times 77 \right)$$

Trading only four times a year won't double your money to $20,000. Given the expectancy of Indicator Set 2 — $130 per trade — you'd need to execute 77 trades per year, which is a little more than one trade per week. The only way around this deduction is to devise a new Indicator Set 3 that delivers more than $130 per trade.

And that's not the only issue. Notice that I haven't incorporated an initial losing trade in this example. But you know that in Indicator Set 2, 45 percent of the trades are losing trades and each losing trade costs $200. What if the first trade is one of the losers and you know you can expect to lose 45 percent on any losing trade? Your capital take is now $10,000 − $4,500 = $6,500. Now you're no longer seeking to double your stake but to more than triple it. Right off the bat you know it won't be 77 trades per year. You'll have to make more trades to restore the total capital stake to $10,000.

You should never put your entire capital stake on the first trade. Experts differ on how much you should put into the first trade, but a general rule is 10 to 20 percent.

Calculating expectancy and figuring out how much money you can expect to make (and lose) and how much of your capital stake to put into trades is a tedious, complicated, and time-consuming project. You may think you can skip this step. To calculate expectancy and apply it to find out your money gain and number of trades needed is more about money or risk management than about technical analysis itself. Note how many times in this book I say "No indicator works all the time." You should want to know how many times it fails and how much those failures will cost you. I stress again and again that technical analysis is about more than the indicators; it's also about the technical mindset that acknowledges no indicator works all the time, so be prepared. All that fiddly arithmetic may be tiresome to you. But when that tiresome arithmetic starts reducing losses and starts helping you make some real money, you'll dislike it less and less over time until it becomes second nature.

The cost of books on risk management is far higher than the cost of books on indicators or crowd psychology. That price difference shows which topic is more important.

2

Building Indicators from the Ground Up

Start your understanding of indicators by examining their building blocks, bars. A ton of information resides in each bar and each small collection of bars. You can actually trade on bars alone. Don't skip this step!

Review a special set of small patterns containing only a few bars. These small patterns are reliable predictors of upcoming price action.

Make the alternative to standards bars, the candlestick notation version of bars, part of your toolkit. Candlesticks were immediately adopted wholesale within a few years of being introduced in the West from Japan, and for the very good reason that they add to your visual recognition of trendedness.

Chapter **6**

Reading Basic Bars: How to Pounce on Opportunities

The standard bar seems so basic and ordinary — it depicts the open, high, low, and close — but bars contain more information than you might think. Reading price bars is the perfect application of the saying "Actions speak louder than words." Traders may *say* that the price is going up, but the price bar tells you what they really think by showing you what they actually *do*. This chapter gives you the basics on how to read standard bars.

The standard bar I talk about in this chapter isn't the only bar notation method out there. There are also the tick bar, momentum bar, point-and-figure bar, and most importantly, candlestick bars. I describe each of these later in the book. The candlestick bar (see Chapter 8), which came on the scene only 30 years ago, has zoomed to the top of the popularity rankings and is likely used by at least half of the technical analysts working today. That's because it's visually compelling, whereas the standard bar appears boring in contrast (until you tease out all its meanings). A variation on candlestick bars is the *heiken ashi* bar, which rejiggers the bar components. I don't cover heiken ashi in this book, but if you're interested in knowing more about it, you can check out the Investopedia entry.

Building Basic Bars

The price bar is the basic building block of technical analysis. After you have a grip on the price bar, almost nothing in technical analysis can confuse you for long. Honest. Resist the temptation to skim over the bar material to get to more glamorous-sounding stuff.

TIP

The bar is the building block of most indicators, which are nothing more than an arithmetic manipulation of the four price bar components of a series of bars over some period of time. Get the classic bar concept down pat and you can make a giant leap into technical analysis. For example, one of the most popular indicators is named the stochastic oscillator (see Chapter 13). It uses a formula that includes the high, the low, and the close. You should have to a firm grip on the high, the low, and close if you're going to appreciate this indicator.

In addition to being able to grasp indicator construction, you want to figure out how the bar works because every change in a trend *begins* with a bar or small series of bars. Some traders never bother to move on to indicators at all and trade solely on classic bars. In fact, I made more profit in my own trading while I was writing this chapter than at any other time in my trading life. I start off here with a brief overview of the price bar and then detail each component in the sections that follow.

Reality in a nutshell

The *price bar* describes and defines the trading action in a security for a given period, meaning actual deals done with cold, hard cash, not what somebody wished, imagined, or contemplated. For the sake of simplicity, this chapter refers to the *daily* price bar because that's what you'll be working with most of the time. A price bar can be in any increment — a minute, 10 minutes, 240 minutes, or a week. It doesn't matter; all price bars contain an open, high, low, and close. The price dynamics I describe here are valid for all bars of any time frame.

REMEMBER

Check out the standard price bar in Figure 6-1. Like all bars, it consists of four components:

>> **Open:** The little horizontal line on the left is the opening price.

>> **High:** The top of the vertical line defines the high of the day.

>> **Low:** The bottom of the vertical line defines the low of the day.

>> **Close:** The little horizontal line on the right is the closing price.

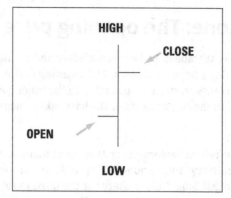

FIGURE 6-1:
The standard
price bar.

© John Wiley & Sons, Inc.

REMEMBER

This Open-High-Low-Close component set of the price bar is often abbreviated OHLC.

The two little horizontal lines on the price bar are called *tick marks*. In trading parlance, a *tick* represents a single trade at a single price, so the tick mark representing the open or the close refers literally to a single transaction or a batch of transactions all at the same price and at the same time. The high and the low don't need a tick mark because the end of the bar conveys that information.

The daily price bar shows the effects of every price factor in the market for that day, including the overall environment, the fundamentals, and market sentiment.

REMEMBER

The price bar tells you the outcome of the battle between the buyers (bulls) and the sellers (bears). Every bar identifies the winning group and the losing group. If the price opened at the low and closed at the high, the winners that day were the buyers. If the price opened at the high and closed at the low, the winners that day were the sellers. Each bar reflects a very real contest whose outcome is measured in dollars. If the bar is very tall, encompassing a $10 range when the normal bar for this security is only $3, the trading was a Titanic battle. If the bar is very short, say $1, it was a pillow fight. On every single trade, one party wins and the other party loses. That is why trading — like war — is called a zero-sum game.

REMEMBER

The relationship between price and volume is important in judging the bar. Everything that you infer from prices about the state of mind of the market needs to be confirmed by volume. For example, if the price bar is three times the usual size, you should verify from volume that a large number of traders were active that day. It's a mistake to see a battle if only one trade was done at the $10 high. That makes the $10 price an anomaly.

Setting the tone: The opening price

The *opening price* is the first trade done between a buyer and a seller on the trading day. It reflects the new day's hopes and fears. The meaning of the open, like all the price bar components, comes from its relationship to the other components of the bar as they develop and to the components of the bars that came before, especially yesterday's close.

REMEMBER

The opening price may reflect factors other than sentiment about the security. Some decisions are arbitrary and random. Maybe Aunt Henrietta got up this morning and decided to sell Blue Widget shares at the open to raise money to buy a racehorse. Also, fund managers may buy or sell at the open to rebalance their portfolios to reflect new money in or out the day before.

WARNING

In U.S. equities, the open often isn't actually the first trade of the day, but a synthetic price (like an average of the first five trades) devised by the exchange or the data collector. This is why the opening price varies from one source to another. Not having accurate data drives some technical analysts nuts because the opening price sets the tone and if somebody made it up, it doesn't matter how reasonable the calculation process — it's not literally the first price of the day. This problem is now compounded by the existence of several exchanges trading the same securities and related options.

Some equity analysts say that they ignore the open because it's not accurate. And although in futures trading the open is the real McCoy, in many instances (such as equity index futures and foreign exchange), trading has been going on in the overnight markets, so every time zone has opens. In other words, the actual open on a U.S. exchange may not be the written-in-stone benchmark you may think it is.

So should you heed the open? Yes. In equities, any particular opening price may not be accurate, but over a series of days, the open adequately represents the sentiment at the beginning of the day and serves as a benchmark for evaluating the upcoming price action over the course of the day. And the placement of the open relative to the close the day before and the close today are two of the criteria for judging whether a security is trending.

REMEMBER

The opening price's most important relationship is the close of the day before.

When the open is up

If the open is higher than the previous close, you deduce that the first trader of the day spotted fresh news favorable to the security, is expecting favorable news, or has some other reason to think his purchase will return a gain. If you, too, see a price rise coming, his action reinforces your analysis. The first trade sets the tone.

When the open is down

If the opening price is below the close of the day before, look out! Maybe bad news came out after the close last night. The bad news may pertain to a political event, a change in interest rates, a bankruptcy in the same industry, or a dozen other factors.

Summarizing sentiment: The closing price

The *closing price* is literally the last price at which a buyer bought and a seller sold before the closing bell. The close is the most important part of the price bar. If you were to draw a chart by using only one of the bar components, you'd pick the close. A series of closes over a small number of days is an indicator in its own right. The close remains the most important price bar component despite after-the-bell trading. When you see a line chart at websites (including Yahoo! Finance or the *Wall Street Journal*), the line is comprised of a series of closes. Every site has a little icon, usually on the upper right, where you can convert the line to standard bars or candlesticks.

REMEMBER

The close is the most important component because it summarizes trader sentiment. Traders have watched this price all day, and by the end of the day they have a sense of how popular it was near the lows (lots of buying going on) or how unpopular near the highs (lots of selling going on). They're also looking at volume to confirm these impressions. As the close approaches, traders have to decide whether to hold the security overnight, something they will do only if they think it's going up further overnight and tomorrow.

Note also that the close is what brokers use to value your portfolio at the end of an accounting period, named *mark-to-market*. Say it's year-end, and you're holding 100 shares of Blue Widget. You want to know what it's worth. You'd apply the close on December 31 to get a mark-to-market value. Mark-to-market is always hypothetical. The closing price on December 31 isn't available for an actual transaction until January 2. Professionals whose job performance (and bonuses) depends on end-of-period accounting care passionately about the close and will sometimes engineer a higher close in the last few minutes of trading to make their mark-to-market positions look as valuable as possible.

WARNING

After-hours trading creates a problem in evaluating the close. How do you treat the close when your security makes a new high or new low in after-hours trading — only 10 minutes after the close? The answer is that you don't adjust the close. In terms of managing your data, the open and close are associated with the trading hours of the primary exchange where the security is listed, like the New York Stock Exchange or the Chicago Mercantile Exchange. No matter how the security trades after the "official" close, the new information is included in the price data for the next day. This can result in some peculiar outcomes, such as the price opening at $5 and closing at $7 on the primary exchange during regular hours, but both the high and the low occurring in after-hours trading — and reaching (say) $4 at the low and $9 at the high. The new high and low gets incorporated in the next day's data.

As with all price bar components, what's important is the relationship of the close to other bar components, especially the open today and the close yesterday. Over time, the cumulative relationship of the close to the close the day before gives you a good impression of directional bias.

When the close is up

If today's close is consistently higher than yesterday's close, day after day, buyers are demanding more and more of the security and are willing to pay an ever-higher price to get it. In other words, the close is up. See Figure 6-2. With the exception of Day 4, every close is higher than on the day before.

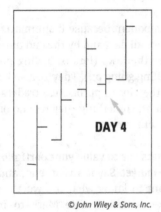

DAY 4

FIGURE 6-2:
A series of up-days.

If you see a trend like the one shown in Figure 6-2, you may want to join the crowd and buy into the trend.

When the close is down

In Figure 6-3, you can see that Day 3 starts a series in which each close is lower than the day before. Here the sellers are willing to take ever-lower prices to get rid of the security. You can assume that those holding an inventory are willing to sell at lower and lower prices to prod buyers to demand it, just like the car dealer puts last year's cars on sale before the new models arrive. When you see a downmove like the one in Figure 6-3, you may want to join the crowd and be a seller.

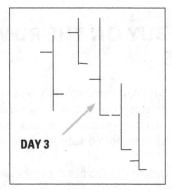

DAY 3

FIGURE 6-3:
A series of
down-days.

Hope, fear, and risk management at the close

On an up-day, you hear that "today the bulls won" or on a down-day, "today the bears won," acknowledging the emotional aspect of trading — bulls hope for a profit (greed) and bears fear a loss. But emotion may have nothing to do with it. Traders also make buy/sell decisions to *manage risk*.

REMEMBER

Just as some traders buy on the open as a standard practice, some traders sell on the close, chiefly to eliminate the risk of loss if something happens overnight to push the price down. Institutions as well as individuals use this simple risk-management tactic. Should you? Yes, if you fear the market could gap over your stop.

Because so many people exit on the close, the close is seldom the high of the day. And when the close *is* at the exact high of the day, that's useful information. It means people who do hold overnight positions are buying right up to the last minute, offsetting the usual end-of-day sales. This is a strongly bullish signal.

Going up: The high

The *high* of the price bar is literally the highest point of the bar. It's the highest price at which a buyer and seller made an exchange of cash for the security. The buyer thinks the price will rise some more. The seller holds the opposite view — that the price will likely fall.

REMEMBER

The high of the day has meaning only in the context of its relationship to other parts of the same bar, especially the close, and to the high the day before.

CURRENT EVENTS: BUY ON THE RUMOR, SELL ON THE NEWS

New highs and lows are often the seed of a new trend and usually arise directly from a specific piece of news. Fresh news that causes a new high or a new low is an *event*. The risk that a new high or low will ensue from the news is an *event risk*. It may seem odd, but most events aren't surprises, but rather scheduled, such as

- News or a rumor about the security, such as a company's earnings announcement
- Market-related events, such as options expiration dates or tax and calendar period dates
- Scheduled releases, such as the Fed's interest rate statement or any of a dozen economic reports

Event risk also refers to unexpected developments:

- Acts of terrorism and war.
- Natural disasters.
- Correlation of a stock to the performance of the major indices. Even if your stock is doing well, for example, it can open down from the close the night before as a side effect of a drop in the index or sector to which it belongs.
- Previous technical levels, such as a round number or a historic high or low (see Chapter 4).

Traders treat forecasts prepared by economists and analysts as though the event had already happened precisely as predicted. In other words, they "build in" the forecast to the price, creating the very high on the price bar that the news is supposed to produce. This practice is named *buy on the rumor*, where "rumor" refers to the forecast.

The rest of the phrase is *sell on the news*. The news is the event itself. You sometimes get the seeming paradox of a price reaching a new high *before* the event and falling lower immediately *after* the event, even when the news matches the forecast. The lower price arises from the early birds taking profit on the upmove that they themselves engineered. The new low is usually short-lived when the forecast of good news was justified.

If the news is much better than forecast, though, traders may not take profit because they know better-than-expected news draws in new players and sends the price higher still. Then the early birds are positioned to make even better profits. Should the news fail to match expectations, traders and investors alike sell, and the dip may turn into a longer-lasting price drop. Either way, to buy on the rumor pays off for the short-term trader who keeps his finger on the trigger. Still, evaluating forecasts and being mentally ready to buy or sell at the moment of impact of the news is a difficult and risky business. More risk-averse traders get out of the market altogether around scheduled event dates. Buy on the rumor, sell on the news is a primary cause of technical price developments, and in many instances, the only "technical analysis" that commentators mention (along with the 200-day moving average — see Chapter 12).

Getting to the bottom of it: The low

The *low* of the day is the cheapest price at which the buyer and seller exchange cash for the security. The buyer thinks the price will rise. The seller believes the price is going to fall or is already falling.

As with the high of the day, the low has meaning in the context of its relationship to other parts of the price bar and the bars that precede it. When the low is lower than the open, it probably means that some fresh news has come out after the opening bell that offsets any buy-on-open orders or initial sentiment. When the close is at the low, it means that bad news or negative sentiment ruled for the day.

TIP

You can judge the power of fresh negative news by checking whether it inspired traders to produce not only a close at or near the low, but also a low that is lower than the low the day before.

Putting It All Together: Using Bars to Identify Trends

The relationship of the bar components to one another contains useful information, and even more information comes from the components across a series of bars. In fact, sometimes you get so much information that you risk information overload. As I discuss in Chapter 2, the law of supply and demand states that for every security, you can find some price that persuades buyers to buy it or owners to part with it. After a price is established through the execution of a real cash trade, traders have a baseline from which to track all ensuing prices. *Any* transaction may occur at a random price, but not *every* transaction can occur randomly, or the market in that security would collapse.

The central observation of technical analysis is that the price bar embodies all the supply-demand dynamics of the day and that a series of bars on a chart shows the evolution of the supply-demand dynamics over time. Some percentage of the time, the evolution is visible in the form of a trend. In this section, I describe how to use combinations of bars to identify a trend.

Identifying an uptrend

The textbook-perfect *uptrend* is a series of up-day bars (close higher than the close the day before) that have higher highs *and* higher lows in a majority of the bars. A series of higher highs implies the fourth factor: close above the open.

>> **Higher high:** When the high today is higher than the high yesterday or higher than the high of the past few days, you have a *higher high.* Higher highs refers to visible peaks, not a higher high every single day. A series of higher highs signals bullish sentiment.

>> **Higher low:** You qualify the higher high by the additional confirming condition of higher lows.

Now you have two pieces of evidence that bulls outnumber bears. A series of higher highs together with higher lows hints that a trend is forming. After two days, you aren't yet sure what is happening, but you're starting to get excited. After all, your goal in identifying a trend is to buy near the beginning of the trend. Your key assumption is that a trend, once formed, will continue. If you have two higher highs with two higher lows, can you assume that Day 3 will also deliver a higher high and a higher low?

Not necessarily. Alas, prices don't move in straight lines. You often see a series of two or three higher highs interrupted by one or two lower highs. This can happen for several reasons:

>> Traders already in the security are taking an early profit.

>> The market is reconsidering whether the new high is really justified.

>> The higher highs were just a random accident.

You seldom see an unbroken series of higher highs on every single day. Go back to Figure 6-2. You see a series of days on which the close is higher than the close the day before. At the same time, the price is making a fresh high nearly every day, but not every day without fail. See the bar marked Day 4. On that day, the close was higher than the open and the low was higher than the day before, but the high of the day wasn't higher than the day before. Oh, oh. What does that mean? Remember, you don't know yet what Day 5 is going to bring at the time you're looking at this chart.

Most analysts tell you not to worry about this particular configuration of bars. It's an uptrend, all right, and you know this because you have an unbroken series of higher *lows*. Day 4 is a disappointment — it doesn't deliver a higher high — but the low is higher than all the previous lows. By considering the additional factor of higher lows, you confirm that the probability is pretty good at getting a higher high, if not also a higher close, on Day 5.

Pinpointing a downtrend

A *downtrend* is a series of down-day bars (a close lower than the day before) characterized by lower lows and lower highs in a preponderance of the bars. Moreover, the lower lows tend to lead to the close coming in below the open (although not in every case). Look at the down-days in Figure 6-3. After the first day, each of these bars has a close lower than the close the day before. Day 3 has the same high as the day before, but a lower low. On Day 3, you start to get the idea that this may be the beginning of a downtrend.

When identifying a downtrend, a series of lower highs is a good confirming indicator to the series of lower lows. The same psychology applies as when an uptrend starts, only in reverse. Sellers see that new lows are occurring — somebody must know something negative about the security. Traders aren't willing to hold a falling asset, and they unload it at ever-lower prices.

Overcoming Murky Bar Waters

Reading bar charts isn't always a clear-cut process. In bar terms, a trend has two identifiers — a series of higher highs (or lower lows) and a series of up-days (or down-days). Technical analysis doesn't offer a hard-and-fast rule on which identifier is more important. Traditional technical analysis emphasizes that you need higher lows to confirm the higher highs in an uptrend, but candlestick analysis, which I cover in Chapter 8, says that the position of the close trumps every other factor, including a new high or low.

Difficult and confusing bar configurations arising from strange placement of highs or lows is usually overcome by the candlestick notation method. The high and low appear on the bar, but only as a barely visible, skinny little line at the top or bottom of the main body of the bar, which features the open and close. In fact, in the candlestick-based ichimoku indicators, the moving averages are calculated using the midpoint of the open and close, not the close alone as in standard bar analysis and most indicators. This makes sense from the viewpoint of trying to identify the main thrust of sentiment by the majority of participants in any security. After all, a high or low may represent an extreme of sentiment or a random event. The midpoint of the bar is much closer to the concept of reversion to the mean or central tendency in trending markets. See Chapter 8 for candlesticks and Chapter 18 for more about ichimoku.

If you usually prefer standard bars but find yourself confused by a particular set of bars, toggle your software to show the bars in candlestick format. You may get a flash of insight.

Paying heed to bar series

Usually a series of higher highs with higher lows or a series of lower lows with lower highs does mean that a trend is emerging, even if the close doesn't yet confirm. Higher highs imply higher closes aren't far behind as the logical outcome, just as lower closes are the eventual logical outcome of a series of lower lows. Market players start wondering why other traders are taking the price to new highs or lows. What do they know that you don't? New highs and lows arouse emotions. A sufficiently large number of new highs triggers greed — better buy now so you don't miss out, even if you don't know why the new high is occurring. Alternatively, new lows scare just enough traders that they sell their positions, even in the absence of any fresh news that would justify it.

Sometimes you get higher closes without getting a preponderance of higher highs. Pay attention anyway because new highs may start to appear. These new highs may happen solely because so many people are aware of the meaning of up-days and down-days. In other words, so many people look at technical indicators — and a series of up-days or down-days is a basic indicator — that they *anticipate* higher highs or lower lows. By acting on that expectation — buying or selling ahead of the actual appearance of a higher high or lower low — they make it happen. You'll observe this type of self-fulfilling prophecy often in technical analysis.

If it's not already provided, turn on the feature in your charting software that graphically differentiates between up-days and down-days (white or green for up and black or red for down). It takes no practice to see where a trend is interrupted by bars that don't qualify.

Knowing when bar reading doesn't work

Some price series are unreadable. You can't figure out what the market is thinking because the market is changing its mind several times a day and from day to day. Figure 6-4 is such a chart. The series of gray up-days is a minor uptrend and the following series of black down-days is a minor downtrend — but then things fall apart. You see higher highs followed by lower lows and no consistency in the placement of the close (up-day or down-day).

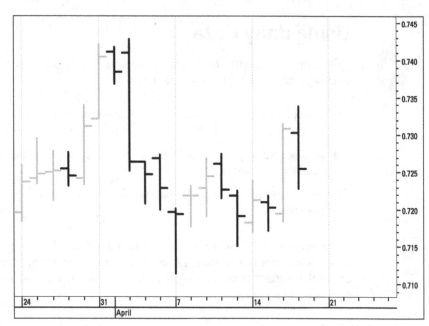

FIGURE 6-4:
Nontrending
bars.

What do you do in a case like this? Nothing — at least not anything based on interpretation of the bars. When bars are messy as in Figure 6-4, the probability of picking the right direction (up or down) is very low. You'd just be guessing. And although you have to accept imperfection and a certain amount of ambiguity in bar-chart analysis, the whole purpose of technical analysis is to obtain a higher probability of making the right decision. Guessing defeats the purpose.

Framing Your Bars

In this chapter, I talk about the price bar as a daily bar. In practice, looking at data in different time frames is useful when you're facing a trading decision. You can zoom out to a higher time frame (such as weekly) or zoom in to a shorter time frame (hourly).

Price bars are *fractal*, meaning you can't tell by looking at a chart what time frame the bars represent. If it's not labeled, a chart of 15-minute price bars can't be distinguished from a chart showing daily bars. The bar components look the same, and traders attribute the same supply-demand assumptions to them. No matter what time frame you select, everything in this book (including the following sections) about the price bar and its components is valid.

Using daily data

TIP

Most traders start with the daily price bar. Daily data is widely available and free or cheap. Daily data is the standard because

>> Most of the commentary in newspapers and on websites and TV refers to daily bars. It's the *base case*.

>> Embracing daily price bars puts you on the same page with the majority of people in the market.

>> Even people who use intraday data (such as hourly bars) also look at the daily price bars.

Technical analysis writers are sensitive to the increased use of intraday data, and today usually speak of *periods* rather than *days*. Changing the vocabulary has the unfortunate effect of making some technical analysis writing sound pompous — but it's more accurate.

Zooming out to a higher time frame

You can display prices in a weekly or monthly format. Mutual fund bars containing all the components are available only weekly. Quarterly and annual charts are seen less often. The universality of standard bar notation isn't hard to understand — after all, a week has an opening price (the first trade on Monday morning) and a closing price (the last trade on Friday afternoon), with a high and a low somewhere in between. The weekly close is a summary of the sentiment of the majority of market participants for the week, just as the daily closing price summarizes sentiment for the day.

TIP

You can often see trends and patterns over longer time frames that are hard to detect on a daily chart. When you look at charts, make the habit of toggling the chart from a daily time frame to the weekly and monthly time frames to see whether anything pops out at you. In addition, you can use, say, a weekly chart to confirm a new trend that you discover on a daily chart.

Zooming in to a shorter time frame

Many traders today track and trade prices on shorter time intervals, like the 60-minute bar. They use a shorter time frame to study price developments and imagine the supply-demand dynamics behind them as news comes out and to make trading decisions as pre-set targets get met. Websites, broker platforms, and TV channels like CNBC and Bloomberg offer rolling hourly prices, for example. If you have a trading rule that says "buy when the price rises above the previous high and also above the 20-period moving average," it's useful to spot that target being met when it's met and not after the trading session has closed and you have to wait for the next session before you can place your trade.

Getting the data

Live, real-time data used to be too expensive for the little guy and only big firms could afford to buy it for their staff. All of that has changed. Now, with a 10- or 15-minute time delay, you can get intraday price bars for free on many websites. All the brokers offer free live data, and most offer free charting capability, some of it very advanced, in return for opening an account.

If you subscribe to a data service, you can organize intraday data in any interval you like — 5-minute bars, 15-minute bars, 60-minute bars, and so on. You could have 7-minute bars or 73-minute bars, if you really wanted to. The notation is the same as in daily bars. The opening price is the price of the first trade during the period, and the closing price is the last trade done during the period, and so on. You can also see tick bars, a somewhat weird way of looking at prices in which a bar is created every 20 or 50 ticks no matter how much time it takes. Because each tick represents a true trade, you're incorporating volume in the representation of the bar. I don't cover tick charts in this book, but if you come to like and excel at bar-reading, you should explore tick charting.

Choosing an interval

If you start using intraday price bars, how do you select the interval? Experts are reluctant to give advice on this point. In equities, many traders look only at the hourly chart. In foreign exchange, traders often use bars covering 240 minutes (4 hours), a tidy way of keeping track in a 24-hour market as it travels around the globe.

The only logical way to select an interval is to treat it like shopping for a new pair of jeans — try them all on your favorite security and see how they look. If an hourly charts looks noisy to you, go up a notch to 2 hours. Selecting the interval to use in displaying bars is subjective. Remember, bar reading is a visual art. Other times you may prefer to look at what everyone else is looking at, on the principle that following the crowd is usually the right way to forecast.

You want an interval that accurately represents activity in the security and suits your needs at the same time. If you're trading an equity that has trading volume of only 10,000 shares during the day and all of that is done in five trades, spacing your bars at 3-minute or 15-minute intervals is silly. Your result would be a chart that is mostly blank, and every trade looks like it gapped from the one before. Don't sabotage your analysis by selecting a time frame that's out of sync with the normal flow of trading in the selected security.

REMEMBER

The key to selecting the right interval is the liquidity of the security you're trading. *Liquidity* refers to existing and potential volume — not only the players on the field but also the bench players waiting around for their chance at bat, meaning a price that pleases them and triggers a trade, with an opposing bench of sellers willing to throw balls until somebody takes a swing. A liquid security has lots of buyers and sellers, with some of them active at all times, including *market-makers* who are required to post a bid-offer at all times. Liquidity results in real trades that are measured as volume. A security with only one or two interested parties isn't liquid, as you may have discovered if you ever tried to sell a thinly traded penny stock. When markets freeze up, as the interbank money market did during the 2008–09 financial crisis, it means no trades are getting executed, and that in turn has a domino effect on many other activities.

Applying Bar Reading in Real Time

Not all bars are created equal. How do you rank bars from those that offer a good profit potential to those that are duds? Keith Fitschen offers methods for "bar scoring" that aims to identify the best bars in his book, *Building Reliable Trading Systems* (John Wiley & Sons, Inc.). Techniques include fancy processes like finding how far the close varies above (or below) the standard deviation of the past x number of bars.

The simplest bar-scoring exercise takes four bar types and checks how these bars would have worked to generate a profit on the next day. Fitschen examined the bars against 3,372 stocks from 2000 to June 2011 that qualified by having liquidity of at least $20 million per day. He also ran the bar-type test against 56 futures contracts going back to 1980 and ending in June 2011. In total, he had 3.5 million equity bars that qualified and 363,000 futures bars. Here's what they look like and how the bars shake out.

>> **Bar-type 1:** Close over the open and the close in the top half of the range.

>> **Bar-type 2:** Close over the open but the close in the lower half of the range.

>> **Bar-type 3:** Close under or near the open and the close in the upper half of the range.

>> **Bar-type 4:** Close under or near the open but the close in the lower half of the range.

Now add the close from the preceding day's bar so the current close is higher or lower. This multiplies the four types of bars to eight. Quick, which bar-type is the winner? See Figure 6-5.

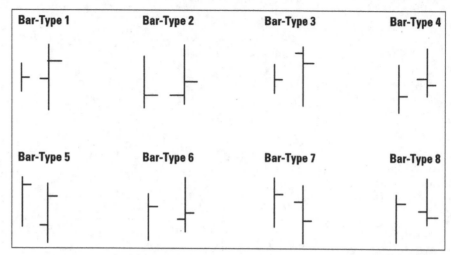

FIGURE 6-5:
Fitschen's simple
bar-scoring.

© John Wiley & Sons, Inc.

You might think that Bar-type 1 would be the winner — the close on the second day is higher than the close on the first day and it's in the top half of the bar. But for both equities and futures, Bar 1 isn't the winner. And to complicate matters, equities have a different winner than futures.

In equities, the winner is bar-type 4, which returned 0.1045 percent or roughly $5.00 on a starting stake of $5,000, by the close the next day. It has a higher high and higher close, but the close is in the lower half of the bar and below the open.

In futures, the winner is bar-type 7, returning $18.63 from tomorrow's open to tomorrow's close. The dollar gain is higher than in equities because contract sizes are bigger than the $5,000 assumed for equities. If you assume an average contract size of $20,000, the return is 0.09 percent, roughly comparable to the return on equities. Fitschen notes that in futures, bar-types 5 through 8 are all profitable even though the close is below the close the day before, implying that futures closes are counter-trend, because a lot of futures traders prefer not to hold positions overnight and they tend to exit near the close. He also says three of the four bar types that close up on the day go down the next day, which means bar reading in futures is trickier than in equities.

Fitschen's bar-scoring demonstrates that you don't need all four bar criteria lined up simultaneously to make profitable trades on bar-reading.

Chapter **7**

Special Bars — An Early Warning System

The price bar is the basic building block of technical analysis. Bar configurations come in endless combinations and permutations, and you can't possibly memorize them all. But knowing about the special bars is useful because they can be powerful predictors — and everyone knows it.

Special bars are a small series of two to five bars — called *combinations* or *configurations* — that stand out on a chart. You can see them immediately, and so can everyone else. Most special bars and configurations are either trend-confirmation or trend-reversal patterns, but even when they're ambiguous, you need to sit up and take notice. This chapter takes a closer look at these special bars and explains what you need to know.

Finding Clues to Trader Sentiment

You use price bar combinations to determine whether your security is starting a trend, staying on a trend, or losing its grip on the trend. The start of a new trend is sometimes the end of an old one, called a *reversal*. Keep reading for more about the clues you may find.

Tick and bar placement

In any set of bars that describes an upmove or downmove, a bar or two may be a little out of line without ruining your interpretation, as I describe in Chapter 6. And then sometimes you see bars that really stand out. It takes almost no practice at all to differentiate ordinary out-of-line bars from special configurations that traders consider to be associated with specific interpretations.

In a series of three bars, each having four components, you can get any one of 2,463 permutations of configuration. When you specify joint conditions, such as higher high together with higher low, the number of combinations reaches into the millions — and that's just with three bars! So, when you see the special cases, you know that you've got a valuable clue to upcoming price behavior.

WARNING

Even so, the interpretation guidelines aren't right all the time. In fact, nobody can tell you even roughly what percentage of the time the standard interpretation is correct because it may be correct all the time in one security but only 30 percent of the time in another or correct 75 percent of the time in one year but only 50 percent in another in the same security. This inconsistency is probably why some technical analysts get very fussy about defining special bar configurations. They'll argue passionately that their definition of a key reversal bar is the only right one, or their idea about gaps is the only way to look at gaps. Don't let such differences of opinion get under your skin. What matters is your ability to spot special bar configurations on your charts and strive to make the deductions about what they mean for your trading purposes.

REMEMBER

A bar component or the placement of the entire bar can be a function of noise (see Chapter 2). After discounting noise, remember that each security has bar configuration habits that reflect the trading habits of the crowd that trades it. Some securities are prone to hysteria (resulting in gaps, such as the Commodity Research Bureau commodities index) and others are beset by indecision (leading to inside days, such as the Japanese yen and Swiss franc). Refer to the following section "Identifying Common Special Bars" for definitions of these special bars.

Trading range

In every instance of special bars in this chapter, the size of the daily high-low range is a key factor. The *daily trading range* is the difference between the high and the low of the day. You can also say that the range defines the emotional extremes of the day:

> » If you have a bar with a small range in a sea of larger bars, the market is indecisive. Indecisiveness isn't the same thing as indifference. Indecisiveness can be dangerous — nobody wanted to buy at a higher high, so perhaps

buyers are getting tired of that security at current prices. A change in sentiment may be brewing, such as deceleration in a price rise that precedes the end of the trend.

» When it's one very large bar in a sea of smaller ones, pay attention. Something happened. Traders are willing to pay a *lot* more for a rising security, or they want to dump a falling one so badly that they'll accept an abnormally low price.

Identifying Common Special Bars

Special bars usually mean the same thing, and therefore you can focus on a few of the special bars with confidence in their reliability. In this section, you can get a feel for the common special bars as shown in Figure 7-1.

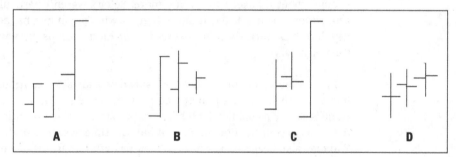

© John Wiley & Sons, Inc.

FIGURE 7-1:
Common
special bars.

A   B   C   D

Closing on a high note

It's bullish when the price closes at the high over several days. A series of *closes at the high* — and its downtrending counterpart, *closes at the low* — indicate that the existing trend is likely to continue. In Figure 7-1, Configuration A illustrates closes at the high for three days running, and the third bar is much longer than the others, which means the high-low range is wider than the previous two days. So, what's up?

The first two bars show the close at the high at about the same level. On the second bar, the low of the day was lower than the low the day before, meaning that sellers came out of the woodwork. But the bulls fought back, buying more and more, so that the close was still at the high, trumping the lower low. Day three delivers a whopping gain — and a third close at the high. By now you may be ready to bet the ranch on this configuration.

Your instincts are right, with one word of caution: A big gain is often followed by *profit-taking* by active traders. Three days isn't enough to call this configuration a *trend*, so traders call it a *move*. It doesn't matter whether the closes-at-high occur at the start of a trend or while the trend is in progress — a fat gain always inspires some traders to take profit. Profit-taking doesn't change a trend, but it can dent performance the next day. You can use your imagination (or turn the book upside down) to envision the parallel configuration on Configuration A of Figure 7-1 — closes at the low. As you may expect, a series of closes at the low imply that a downtrend is forming or worsening.

Spending the day inside

Configuration B in Figure 7-1 shows the inside day. An *inside day* refers to a price bar in which the high is lower than the previous day's high and the low is higher than the previous day's low. In other words, today's high-low range is inside the previous day's high-low range. It reflects indecision. Buyers didn't feel strongly enough about this security to buy more. Sellers weren't particularly inspired to sell, either. The inside day doesn't suggest what's going to happen the following day, but does warn that the market is starting to reconsider what it feels about this security.

Some commentators opine that an inside day is always a continuation bar. If you had an uptrend and it's punctuated by an inside day, don't worry about it. Your trend is safe. This opinion isn't borne out by statistical work, which finds an inside day leads to continuation only about half the time over tens of thousands of tests. You may also hear that it's not the next day after an inside day to watch, it's the second day after the inside day. Bottom line: You may not know immediately what an inside day means when you spot one, but you do know to keep an eye peeled.

Getting outside for the day

Configuration C in Figure 7-1 is the outside day, meaning the high-low range of the bar is outside the range of the preceding bar. The open and close ticks can appear anywhere on the outside day bar, but two variations stand out:

>> **The open is at the low, and the close is at the high.** This configuration suggests that something new has happened to inspire bullish buying right up to the end of the day.

>> **The open is at the high, and close is at the low.** You can deduce the opposite supply-demand setup here. Sentiment turned bearish and sellers overwhelmed buyers, right to the end of the day.

TIP

The sheer size of an outside day bar gets your attention, but it doesn't mean much on its own — you also need to consider the placement of the open and close and the configuration of the preceding bar. If the price series is untrended, the outside day alerts you to a possible trend beginning. If a trend is in place, the placement of the close relative to the open may be a hint of an upmove or downmove — but not always.

Finding the close at the open

Configuration D in Figure 7-1 shows a series of bars where the close is at or near the open. As you can guess, a close at or near the open reflects indecision among market participants. Trader opinion is divided as to whether this bar generally signifies a continuation or reversal pattern. Consider it a clue to look at what else is going on, such as trading volume. In candlestick charting, the open at or near the close is named a *doji*, a term I promise you'll come to use with ease (see Chapter 8).

Decoding Spikes

While the inside day and the outside day in Figure 7-1 have high-low ranges noticeably different from the preceding bars, they don't make your hair stand on end. Sometimes, though, the market delivers an exceptionally big bar with a wildly out-of-whack high or low. Figure 7-2 shows two of these uncommon price bars, called spikes.

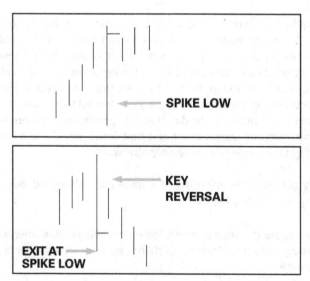

FIGURE 7-2: Uncommon special bars.

© John Wiley & Sons, Inc.

A *spike* is a bar that encompasses a much wider high-low range than the bars immediately preceding it. Do spikes matter? Yes, a spike is often the harbinger of an important price reversal and that's why traders keep an eye peeled for spikes.

But sometimes a spike is just randomly generated by rumors and market silliness. The spike turns out to be an anomaly. The top example in Figure 7-2 shows such a case. The spike low suggests that some people panicked and were selling so much and at such a frantic pace that buyers got a bargain at abnormally low prices. But panic was misplaced. The next day, the price resumed its uptrend and its same "normal" high-low range. The spike was just noise. Maybe the panicked sellers believed a rumor that the buyers didn't hear or knew was false. Or perhaps the sellers were deliberately trying to break a support line, as I describe in Chapter 10. Jack Schwager in his book *Technical Analysis* (John Wiley & Sons, Inc.) writes that the return of prices to a previous spike extreme means a failed signal.

The bottom spike example in Figure 7-2 is, in contrast, an important bar named a *key reversal* because over the next few days, the price proceeds to make lower highs and lower lows, signaling a trend reversal. Commentators today make a big deal out of the key reversal bar and say that after a spike low, the next bar opens over the spike bar close and makes a new higher high, but then closes below the previous day's close. In practice, you don't need a new higher high; you just need the series of lower highs and lower lows. And it can take more than one bar after the spike low to confirm the reversal because the confirmation point is the close surpassing the spike low. In fact, a key reversal bar can be an ordinary bar and isn't always a spike, but when you see a spike, always ask yourself whether it might be a setup for a pending reversal.

As the spike is occurring, you don't know where the low is going to come until after the bar is completed, and obviously you can't exit the trade until then (in other words, in the next trading session). You still don't know what bars will ensue, but you can make note of the spike low after it forms and keep it in mind as a benchmark for a stop, even if the bars that follow the spike retrace some of the downmove, as they do in Figure 7-2. You seldom know whether a spike is random or meaningful on the day that it happens, unless there is a specific news event that everyone knows about and that dominates the headlines. All too often you find out the cause of a spike only afterward.

You may not know the meaning of a spike until afterward, but you can still use spikes right after they appear:

>> **Investigate the environment.** Sometimes you *do* know when a spike is a harbinger of a major directional change because you know what shock caused it.

>> **Trust the close.** As a general rule, you're safe assuming that the close is the most important part of the bar because it sums up the sentiment for the day. To see the usefulness of the close, take a look at the two examples in Figure 7-2:

- **Continuation spike:** In the top chart showing a spike low, the close is near the high. The wider high-low range and the lower low are a worry, to be sure, but the position of the close near the high trumps those worries.

- **Key reversal day:** The bottom chart in Figure 7-2 shows three components to worry about — not only the wide high-low range but also the lower low and close near the low.

TIP

A conservative trading tactic is to order your broker to sell the security if the price falls below the low of the spike day over the next two or three days. This method is plain old crowd-following. Everybody can see the same spike low and many will have sell orders at that level, and you should, too. The bar following a spike is often an inside day. Other times the following bar has a new higher high only a few pennies above the spike high and a close lower than the spike bar close. Neither bar is helpful. They're simply inconclusive, and you have to wait for additional evidence to get guidance on how to trade.

Getting Gaps

A gap is one of the most important special bar configurations. A *gap* is a major, visible discontinuity between two price bars on a chart. Because every bar encompasses all the transactions made during a specific period, a gap marks the absence of any transactions at the prices covered by the gap. In this section, I give you pointers to identify gaps and how to use them.

Pinpointing a gap

The gap is a void — no supply is offered at the prices the gap encompasses. Check out the gap in Figure 7-3. Prices had to shift upward in order for supply and demand to meet again and for both buyers and sellers to be satisfied. On daily charts, you can often see an opening gap when the opening price today diverges dramatically from yesterday's high or low, although you can also see gaps between bars on intraday charts.

REMEMBER

You can *identify* a gap at the open of the bar, but you can't *measure* a gap until the day's trading is over. Then you measure it from yesterday's high to today's low (for an upside gap) or from yesterday's low to today's high (for a downside gap). The gap is between the bars' highs and lows, not between the opens and closes.

If the security opens on a gap but then the gap is filled during the day, the gap doesn't show up on a daily chart. The same thing happens when a security gaps during the day on an hourly chart — the daily bar doesn't show it.

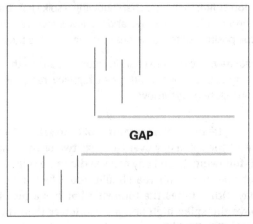

GAP

© John Wiley & Sons, Inc.

FIGURE 7-3:
Price gap.

Gaps are usually triggered by news, like earnings or some other event, whether true or invented. That's why gaps are such a valuable pattern — you know instantly how the market is interpreting the news.

The reason to read bars is to get an accurate assessment of whether news is big or merely ordinary — noise. Some news is easy to interpret. News will start a new uptrend if it's wildly favorable or halt an uptrend dead in its tracks if it's wildly unfavorable. But much of the time, you don't know how to interpret news — and everyone is overloaded with too much news! — until you see how the market treats it in the form of the bar on the chart. Traders often get the bit between their teeth on news and this is especially clear with gaps.

Consider how a gap develops. Say that Blue Widget stock closes on Monday at $15 per share. After the closing bell, it announces bad news — the bookkeeper embezzled $20 million and ran off to Rio. The market is unforgiving and the next day, Blue Widget opens gap down at $10. Most people deduce that the opening gap down implies further price drops, and they proceed to sell — in droves.

The total gap for the day may not be $5, though. During the course of the day, Blue Widget may trade as high as $12, making the net gap a $3 gap. If the price of Blue Widget normally trades in a $2 high–low range, $3 is still a significant number — 50 percent higher than normal. Gaps are significant when they're proportionally large compared to the trading range (see the "Kicking things off: Breakaway gaps" section in this chapter).

Gaps occur with good news, too. If Blue Widget announces a fabulous new discovery, the opening price on the following day may be a gap up, like the one in Figure 7-3. You may deduce from this gap that some traders (including well-paid professional analysts) had a whole night to evaluate the news, and *they* bought the stock at the open, so you should buy it, too. The gap implies buyers anticipate the stock rising throughout the day from the opening price, and you want to jump (if not leap) on this bandwagon. In equities, you can pretty much count on an opening gap on the day after an initial public offering.

Using gaps to your advantage

Gaps are, indeed, a wonderful trading opportunity if you can differentiate between a common gap and uncommon gaps. In the following sections, I describe the main types of gaps and how to use them.

Lacking opportunity: Common gaps

A *common gap* is one that appears out of nowhere for no particular reason and should be considered noise. Common gaps can occur in trending and nontrending prices. If the price is trending, it fails to change the trend. If the price isn't trending, it fails to initiate a trend. Common gaps are generally insignificant.

What causes a common gap? Usually it's a simple error. A trader heard or thought he heard a market-moving bit of news and made an offer above (or below) the market. Or the trader was trying to break a trendline or had some other hidden agenda.

Common gaps often occur when liquidity is low, meaning only a few players are in the market. A security that normally has low volume tends to have more gaps than heavily traded securities. A low-volume security is described as *thinly traded*, meaning few market participants. Don't try to interpret gaps in thinly traded securities. These gaps are usually just common gaps and mean nothing at all. At the same time, a heavily traded security can also have gaps as traders flail around trying to validate the new gap direction because it favors their existing position or fight against the new gap direction because if the price keeps going, their existing position will suffer a loss. Another cause of gaps in heavily traded securities is the fist-fight between bulls and bears changing their interpretation of a new event. This is fairly common in the foreign exchange and commodity markets.

TIP

To judge an opening gap, consult volume. If volume is low or normal, traders aren't jumping on the bandwagon, and it's probably a common gap. If volume is abnormally high, traders are jumping on the bandwagon, and the gap will probably lead to a big rise or fall in the coming days.

Kicking things off: Breakaway gaps

A *breakaway gap* (refer to Figure 7-4) is an important event because it almost always marks the start of a new trend. Not only do you get the gap and a new trend, but you also get a major change in the appearance of the chart, such as a widening of the normal high-low daily trading range, an increase in day-to-day volatility, and much higher volume. A breakaway gap is often confirmed as significant when the price breaks support or resistance, or a channel or band. All these changes occur because the breakaway gaps draw in new traders. A breakaway gap is event driven, usually on some news about the security itself.

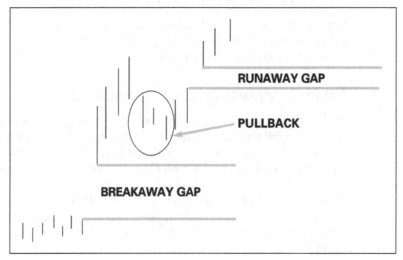

RUNAWAY GAP

PULLBACK

BREAKAWAY GAP

FIGURE 7-4:
A breakaway gap and a runaway gap.

© *John Wiley & Sons, Inc.*

To qualify as a breakaway gap, the gap has to

>> **Be proportionately big to the usual trading range:** If the security normally trades in a $3 range between the daily high and low, and the gap is $15 between the preceding day's high and the gap-day open, you can instantly recognize that something big happened.

>> **Occur when a price is only slightly trending or moving sideways:** Nothing much is going on in the chart, and then bam! Fresh news creates new supply-and-demand conditions and ignites a trend.

You interpret a breakaway gap depending on whether it's upward or downward, according to supply and demand.

>> **Upside breakaway gap:** Good news creates demand. New buyers want to own the security and are willing to pay ever-higher prices to get it. Volume is noticeably higher than usual.

>> **Downside breakaway gap:** Traders can't wait to get rid of their holdings and accept ever-lower prices to achieve that goal. Volume is usually (but not always) abnormally high.

Continuing the push: Runaway gaps

A *runaway gap* occurs after a security is already moving in a trended way and fresh news comes out that promotes the existing trend. See the second gap in Figure 7-4. What's the difference between a breakaway gap and a runaway gap? A breakaway gap *starts* a trend. A runaway gap *continues* a trend. In both cases, buyers become exuberant and offer higher and higher prices. Sometimes fresh good news bursts forth, sometimes traders make up fresh good news, and sometimes the buying frenzy is just feeding on itself in the absence of any news at all.

TIP

Notice in Figure 7-4 that after making new highs following the runaway gap, the price fell a little. A falling price after a dramatic move up is called a *pullback.* The security stops making new higher highs and may make some lower lows, but it doesn't go as far as the low on the breakaway day. A pullback after a dramatic price move represents profit-taking by the early birds and is very common. In fact, professionals count on the pullback to "buy on the dip." If they get really enthusiastic, reentering professional traders often supply the energy for a runaway gap that follows a breakaway gap.

Calling it quits: Exhaustion gaps

Exhaustion gaps occur at the end of a trend, signaling that the party's over. Volume is usually low. What's exhausted is the news that propelled the security up in the first place and the energy of the early buyers. An exhaustion gap is usually followed by a reversal.

Here's how it works. This example is an exhaustion gap at the end of an uptrend, but the mechanics are similar for a downtrend exhaustion gap as well. When you see a gap up in an existing uptrend *and* volume is low on that day, you have to wonder why the gap appeared. Volume tells you that buyers aren't pounding on the sellers' doors to get the security.

Presumably some greedy seller is out there, along with one last fool who's willing to pay a gap-worth more than the last trade. The buying frenzy is over, but the buyer doesn't realize it. He fails to see that there are a lot of offers and few bids. In short, everybody who wanted to buy has already done so. But somebody has to be the last buyer, and this particular one got taken to the cleaners — in the form of the gap. When he turns around and tries to unload his recent purchase, he finds no buyers, at least no buyers at a profit to him, and has to dump the security at a loss.

TIP

You can distinguish an exhaustion gap from a runaway gap by looking at volume, which is usually low at an exhaustion gap. Anytime you see wild new highs (or lows) that aren't accompanied by wild new high volume, be suspicious of the staying power of the move. You can exit altogether or move up your stop-loss order.

Scoring big: Island reversals

Sometimes an exhaustion gap is followed immediately by a breakaway gap going in the other direction (see previous sections for details on exhaustion and breakaway gaps). This occurrence is how an island reversal forms. An *island reversal* is a single, isolated price bar with a gap up on one side and a gap down on the other. It looks like an island in a sea of price bars and is almost always an unusually long bar — a wide high-low range.

Take a look at Figure 7-5. You see a series of higher highs, including a minor gap up, but then the last buyers realize that they're all alone on top of the mountain. They start to sell in a panic and are willing to accept a much lower price. Now the price takes off in the opposite direction on a breakaway gap. Remember, a breakaway gap tends to have high volume.

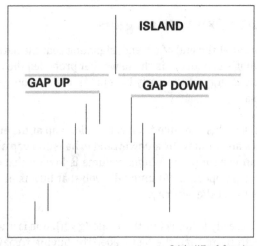

FIGURE 7-5:
Island reversal.

© John Wiley & Sons, Inc.

This figure shows a single bar sandwiched between two gaps as defining the island reversal, but it's also possible to get two or three bars forming the island. As in the case of the key reversal bar, some analysts insist an island reversal is a single bar, whereas others insist it can be or should be a set of bars. The important point is two gaps, not how many bars form the island. What is being defined is a change in sentiment so powerful that it signals a reversal.

Watching volume can get a little tricky. The island reversal bar has a higher high but is accompanied by low volume. This combination is the warning. The next day, as the breakaway gap develops, it has unusually high volume. High volume in combination with the downward gap is an indication that early selling is strong; later prices aren't going to go back and fill that gap.

Now consider this case in reverse order. Everyone and his brother has been dumping the security, and it's been gapping downward as it trends downward. This time the frenzy is a selling frenzy. At some point, traders realize that the selling has gone on long enough and maybe the price is now too low — a bargain. Another trader agrees and buys it from him, and offers it on in the market at a gapping price — and wins. Turn Figure 7-5 upside down and you can see how an island reversal at the bottom looks.

TIP

Examine enough charts and you'll see a lot of gaps. Seldom, though, do you see an island reversal. But when you do see it, here's how to respond:

>> An island reversal at the bottom: Buy.

>> An island reversal at the top: Sell.

Despite its rarity, chances are good that a large number of other people will identify the makings of an island, too, and cause the expected reaction — the self-fulfilling prophecy aspect of technical analysis.

WARNING

Although you can't know for a day or two after the second gap that you have an island reversal, many commentators speculate that an island is forming when they see the *first* gap. Close your ears when you hear market chatter like this. Form your own judgment. "Is an island reversal forming?" is one of the most-asked questions that market technicians hear and one that can't be answered on a technical basis until a day or two *after* the second gap.

Filling the Gap

You may hear that a gap *must* be filled. This emphasis on filling the gap is usually nonsense uttered by people who are trying to sound worldly and wise, but really don't know what type of gap they're dealing with. *Filling the gap* (see Figure 7-6) means that prices return to the level they occupied before the gap.

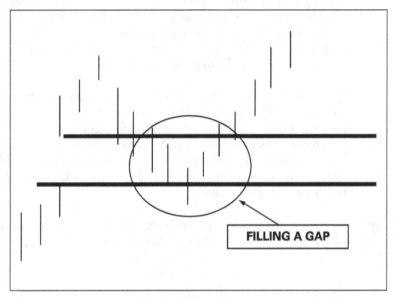

FIGURE 7-6: Filling a gap.

If a security takes off on a breakaway gap, sometimes the price doesn't return to fill the gap for many months or even years — if ever. Stop and think about it: When the fundamentals of a security change dramatically, why would market participants sell it back down to the level it was before the big event? Conditions have changed permanently and so has the price of the security. If a company has invented some new must-have product, the new higher stock prices may not be the right price, but the old prices based on the old conditions aren't right either.

A runaway gap or common gap is another matter. Demand for the security is normal and not under the influence of news or changing conditions, so the gap may be filled by bargain hunters. Sometimes a gap gets filled because the chatter about filling the gap makes it a self-fulfilling prophecy.

TIP

How do you know whether a gap will be filled? If it's a breakaway gap, it probably won't be filled, at least not in the near future. If it's a common or runaway gap, it might get filled or it might not. You need to look at other indicators (such as momentum in Chapter 13) to confirm whether a price move is at risk of going back to fill a gap.

Using the Trading Range as a Tool

The length of the price bar, the *trading range*, plays a role in the special bar configurations such as spikes. But the trading range also has meaning in its own right. As I define in the "Trading range" section earlier in this chapter, the trading range is the difference between the high and the low. If you see a security that has been averaging a $3 high-low range and suddenly it starts trading consistently in a $5 range, something happened — no matter where the opens and closes are. The following sections discuss how you can utilize the trading range.

Paying attention to a changing range

When market conditions change, the average trading range is sometimes the first aspect of price behavior to change.

REMEMBER

A change in the high-low range, which you can see in Figure 7-7, usually precedes or accompanies a change in the direction or slope of a trend. Take note — it's often a leading indicator.

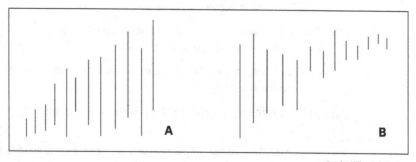

FIGURE 7-7:
Range expansion and contraction.

© John Wiley & Sons, Inc.

>> *Range expansion* is a lengthening of the price bars over time — the high-low range is getting wider (visible in Chart A of Figure 7-7) — and usually suggests a continuation pattern.

>> *Range contraction* is a shortening of the price bars — the high-low range is getting narrower (check out Chart B in Figure 7-7) — and suggests that a trend reversal may be coming soon.

WARNING

A change in the size of the bars — range expansion or contraction — doesn't tell you anything about the *existing* direction of the price move. The range can expand or contract in both uptrends or downtrends.

Determining the meaning of a range change

As a general rule, an expanding range is a continuation pattern and a contracting range suggests that a trend reversal is impending. Sometimes your only clue to a shift in market sentiment about your security is a change in the high–low range, but check for these confirming conditions as well:

>> **Volume:** Look to see whether the volume is rising or shrinking.

- **Rising volume:** More people are trading the security, or existing traders are taking bigger positions. This rising volume usually accompanies range expansion and is an excellent indication of an accelerating trend. The acceleration can be in either direction, up or down. If you see an expansion of the range and it fails to have an accompanying rise in volume, you have a mystery and need to look at some other indicators, like momentum (see Chapter 13).

- **Shrinking volume:** Fewer people are in the market for this security, or existing traders are reducing their allocations to this security. Falling volume often accompanies range contraction.

>> **Open-close position:** Here's an outline of the four possible open-close combinations and what they likely mean:

- **Expanding range, higher closes:** Buyers are excited about the prospect of the price going higher still.

- **Expanding range, lower closes:** Sellers are ever more anxious to unload the security.

- **Contracting range, higher closes:** In all range contractions, traders start to feel uneasy about the direction that the security has been trending. But a higher close can offset some of the negative sentiment inherent in a contracting range.

- **Contracting range, lower closes:** This combination is doubly negative. Traders may not be causing lower lows, but they're unloading at or near the close, forcing it lower. Range contraction usually means that activity is drying up and volume is low — so if you see high volume and a lower close in a contracting range, you probably want to get out of Dodge.

Looking at the average trading range

The trading range is a valuable analytical tool. But you want to capture a change in the range in some more-efficient way than eyeballing a bunch of bars and trying to figure out whether they're getting bigger or smaller. What you want is an average.

You know what an average is — you measure ten of something, add up the measurements, and divide by ten. If you have ten days' worth of high-low ranges that add up to $32, you know that the average daily trading range for the ten-day period was $3.20.

REMEMBER

The average trading range is one of the best tools around for keeping your sanity and perspective. If you know that the average daily trading range is $3.20, the most you can expect to make on this security in a single day is $3.20, and that's assuming that you could buy at the exact low and sell at the exact high — and assuming that it's an average day.

When your broker, your brother-in-law, or an email solicitation says you can make $500 in the next month in a specific security, you can use the average range to judge whether it's even remotely possible. If the security moves up by its full average $3.20 range every day with no pullbacks for the entire 22 days in a trading month, your gain would be $70.40. Unless your informant has certain knowledge of some news or event that is going to change things, his forecast is silly. Under normal, average conditions, you can expect the normal, average trading range to persist.

Checking out the gaps

But how do you measure average range when your prices series has gaps? Say that you're merrily averaging your daily high-low ranges and suddenly you have a gap. You need to account for that gap or you will be literally missing something. Figure 7-8 displays the problem. On Day 1, the high-low range is $2. The next day, the price opens gap up, but the daily range is the same $2. Therefore, the average range for the two days is also $2. Looking at the average range alone, without inspecting the chart itself, you wouldn't know that the gap occurred. Well, so what? Maybe the gap is just a common old gap that doesn't mean anything. If it's an important gap, like a breakaway gap, the range would automatically expand.

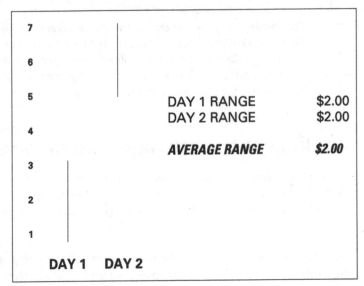

DAY 1 RANGE $2.00

DAY 2 RANGE $2.00

AVERAGE RANGE   *$2.00*

DAY 1   DAY 2

FIGURE 7-8:
The averaging gaps problem.

© *John Wiley & Sons, Inc.*

So what's the issue? The reason you need to account for the gap is that it often precedes a longer-term change in the range, which is what you're looking for. If you measure each day separately and average those numbers, the range looks the same from day to day. For the first two days in Figure 7-8, though, the range is actually from the low on Day 1 at $1 to the high on Day 2 at $7 — or a $6 range. In short, the range doubled but the averaging process doesn't capture this change. In fact, if the range on Day 2 had been smaller, say $1.50, the average would be less than $2. Just looking at the average range on a numerical basis, you would think that the range had contracted — exactly the opposite of what really happened.

Discovering the average true range

If you want to make a trading decision based on a change in the average trading range, you need to adjust the averaging process to account for possible gaps. You do this by starting at the most important component of the price bar: the close. As a rule, to calculate the true range today after a gap, you start from the close on the day before and end at today's high. You're substituting the first day's close for the second day's *open* in order to incorporate the gap.

In Figure 7-8, Day 1's range was ordinary. The gap happened afterward. Why not use Day 1's high rather than the close? Aren't you double-counting by including the space between the high and the close from Day 1? No, because in range work you don't really care about the gap itself — you care about the total range of prices *today*. The close was the end of trading yesterday, and you're now considering it the start of trading today. Because the close is the most important part of the bar, traders are hypersensitive to an opening gap away from yesterday's close.

Figure 7-9 shows this new measurement. Pretend that the close on Day 1 was $3, or $2 over the open at $1. Subtracting that close from the high on Day 2 at $7, you get a true range of $4. Averaging that with the original Day 1 range of $2, you get $3, the average true range. If Day 2's price bar gaps downward, you incorporate the gap by measuring from the close on Day 1 to the low on Day 2.

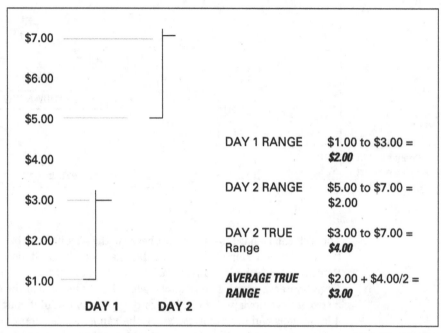

DAY 1 RANGE	$1.00 to $3.00 = *$2.00*
DAY 2 RANGE	$5.00 to $7.00 = $2.00
DAY 2 TRUE Range	$3.00 to $7.00 = *$4.00*
AVERAGE TRUE RANGE	$2.00 + $4.00/2 = *$3.00*

DAY 1   **DAY 2**

© John Wiley & Sons, Inc.

FIGURE 7-9: The average true range.

Why the word *true?* Because the inventor of the idea, J. Welles Wilder, Jr., selected this word. The average true range is sometimes called *Wilder's average true range,* or simply ATR. ATR is generally shown as a 14-day moving average, although you're welcome to fiddle with the number of periods.

TIP

The bigger the shift in the size of the range, the bigger the trading opportunity (or warning to exit). You judge a shift in average true range the same way as in a regular high-low range but with greater confidence that you're measuring and not just eyeballing. If your security normally trades in a daily range of $10 and then it starts trading at $6, $4, and $2, something is happening. Go find out what — or get out.

In Figure 7-10, for example, you see a price in the bottom window on an uptrend, but the average true range in the top window is falling. It reaches a low level just as the trend is ending (note the circle). Notice that after the trend reversal, you get a big-bar down day and corresponding rise in ATR.

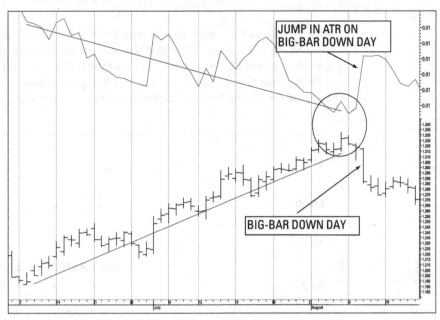

JUMP IN ATR ON
BIG-BAR DOWN DAY

BIG-BAR DOWN DAY

FIGURE 7-10:
Change in ATR
as a warning
indicator.

© John Wiley & Sons, Inc.

The ATR can be hard to use, in part because the ATR line can be choppy, it doesn't track the trend slope, and it can diverge from it, as it does in Figure 7-10. Remember, ATR isn't a directional indicator, but rather a measure of volatility (see Chapter 14). In this chapter on special bars, the value of the ATR is to confirm a strong new move prefigured by a gap, especially useful if your security displays a lot of gaps and even more so when the gap is near a support or resistance line (or breaking the line). A rise in the ATR confirms the move is likely significant, whereas a steady or shrinking ATR means nothing much is really happening.

In Figure 7-10, by the time you get the big-bar down day, you already know this trend is ending. But don't neglect ATR as a warning indicator — sometimes it's the only warning you get. If you're going to use several indicators as confirming indicators for your primary "ruling" indicator (see Chapter 16), ATR is a good supplemental confirmer.

Chapter 8

Redrawing the Price Bar: Japanese Candlesticks

C andlestick charting displays the price bar in a graphically different way from the standard bars described in Chapters 6 and 7. Candlestick charting was developed in Japan at least 250 years ago in the 18th century, where traders applied it to prices in the rice market.

A trader named Steve Nison brought candlesticks to the attention of western traders in 1990. Candlestick patterns became instantly popular because they embody the principle of imputing trader sentiment to the bars, as in "shaven top," where the close is at the high. As I say in Chapter 6, the close at the high means strong bullish sentiment. Today every software program offers to display bars in the conventional way or in candlestick format. Trading guides abound on how to use candlesticks. Steve Bigalow has several books on candlestick trading (and software add-ons), including *Profitable Candlestick Trading* and *High Profit Candlestick Patterns* (both published by John Wiley & Sons, Inc.).

In this chapter, I break down the components of a candlestick and explain why candlesticks are so useful. Note that in some instances, a stand-alone candlestick is a pattern in its own right, and such candlesticks always have a name. (For more on patterns, check out Chapter 9.) Named candlesticks and small series of candlestick patterns number in the dozens, and I can't cover all of them in this chapter. Here I select a few that stand out.

Appreciating the Candlestick Advantage

Candlesticks are visually compelling. You can quickly and easily figure out how to identify a handful of the top candlestick patterns. The following are some of the advantages you can get from candlesticks:

» Many candlesticks are simple to use and interpret, making them a splendid place for a beginner to start figuring out bar analysis — as well as for old hands to achieve new insights. Your eye adapts almost immediately to the information in the bar notation.

» Candlesticks and candlestick patterns have delightfully descriptive and memorable names — charming and sometimes alarming — that contain the seeds of interpretation. The names help you remember what the pattern means. Among the colorful names are "abandoned baby," "dark cloud cover," and "spinning top."

» Candlestick bar patterns and their interpretation are widely known so you can expect other participants in the market to respond in a specific way to specific patterns.

» You can use candlesticks on any chart, with any other indicators, just like standard bars.

» Candlestick shapes can be dramatic, so they can often bring your attention to a trend change earlier than standard bars do. As I describe in Chapter 7, some exceptional bar patterns embody a forecast that's usually correct, such as the breakaway gap and the island reversal. Standard bar analysis offers very few such patterns, but candlestick analysis offers dozens.

» Candlestick patterns excel in identifying strategic market turning points — reversals from an uptrend to a downtrend or a downtrend to an uptrend.

Dissecting the Anatomy of a Candlestick

Candlestick notation emphasizes the open and the close. Figure 8-1 shows the open and the close mark at the top and bottom of the box, named the *real body*. A thin vertical line at the top and bottom of the real body, named the *shadow*, shows the high and the low. (See Chapter 6 for a discussion of the basic bar components — open, close, high, and low.)

I present some more details on the candlestick bar components in the following sections.

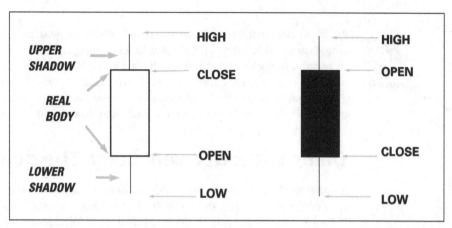

FIGURE 8-1: Candlestick bar notation.

Drawing the real body

The *real body* encompasses the range between the open and the close. The color of the real body tells you how the daily struggle between the bulls and the bears played out. Note that in candlesticks, the real body emphasizes the open-close range, whereas in traditional bar charting, you look at the high-low range, as discussed in Chapter 7.

The colors mean the following:

>> **White real body:** The close is higher than the open. A real body is bullish, and the longer the body, the more bullish it is. A long candlestick indicates that the close was far above the open, implying aggressive buying. In the daily battle of bulls and bears, the bulls won.

>> **Black real body:** The close is lower than the open. A black real body is bearish, and the longer the body, the more bearish it is. A long black candlestick indicates a preponderance of sellers throughout the session. In the daily battle of bulls and bears, the bears won.

The two candlestick bars in Figure 8-1 show the identical open and close, but coloring one of them black creates the optical illusion that it's bigger. That black bar demands your attention, which is one reason candlestick charting is appealing and effective. (For more appealing aspects, see the section "Appreciating the Candlestick Advantage" earlier in this chapter.)

As in all bar analyses, *context* is crucial. Although you may sometimes use a single candlestick bar as an indicator in its own right, most of the time you use it in relation to the bars that precede it. One small white-body bar in a sea of black bars, for example, may mean the bulls won that day, but it was a minor event. The one white bar may signal that the bears are losing power, but you wouldn't use it all by itself to call the end of a black-bar downtrend.

Doing without a real body: The doji

A candlestick that has no real body or only a very small one is named a *doji*. In a doji, the open and the close are at the same or nearly the same level. See Figure 8-2 for three types of dojis. On its own, a doji doesn't tell you much about market sentiment except that traders are indecisive and sentiment is in a transitional phase. It's a neutral bar, neither bullish nor bearish, that gains meaning from its placement compared to the preceding bars.

FIGURE 8-2:
Doji candlestick patterns.

PLAIN DOJI   DRAGONFLY DOJI   GRAVESTONE DOJI

When you see a doji after a prolonged uptrend, the doji may mean that the buyers are coming to the end of their bullish enthusiasm. A doji immediately after a very long white bar in an uptrend shows that the market is tired. This particular doji is named a bearish doji star. A bullish doji star is a mirror image — it comes after a big black bar in a downtrend. In most cases, it signals an impending reversal.

The doji form contains important information, regardless of the shadows, although shadows have their own additional meaning and are covered in a later section. Always take notice of a doji or series of dojis after a trend has been in place for a while. It's a transitional bar, and you should always be on the lookout for any transition that can affect your trade.

Catching the shadow

The high and the low prices are shown in the *shadows*, which you can think of as a wick (on the top) or a tail (on the bottom). Although the shadow is secondary to the real body in importance, shadows contribute useful information about market psychology, too, and modify your interpretation of the body. Shadows offer special interpretive clues in three instances:

» The real body is a doji.

» The shadow is missing.

» The shadow is extremely long.

Shadows in the doji bar

In many instances, the doji is just a plain one with ordinary, same-size shadows, as shown in Figure 8-2. However, the two most useful types of doji bars, also shown in Figure 8-2, are the following:

» **Dragonfly doji:** Look for the long lower shadow that means the open, high, and close were the same or nearly the same. Sellers were trying to push the price down and succeeded in making a low — but they didn't succeed in getting it to close there. Because the close was back up at or near the open, buyers must have emerged before the end of trading and bought enough to move the close to or near the high.

How you interpret the dragonfly depends on what bar patterns precede it. Your options include the following:

- If the price move is a downtrend, the dragonfly may mean that buyers are emerging and the downtrend may be ending.

- If the dragonfly appears after a series of uptrending bars, buyers failed to push the price over the open to a new high while sellers succeeded in getting a low, so the uptrend may be in trouble.

» **Gravestone doji:** Take a look at that long upper shadow in Figure 8-2. This bar, the exact opposite of the dragonfly, is formed when the open, low, and close are the same or nearly the same, but a high creates a long upper shadow. Although buyers succeeded in pushing the price to a high over the open, by the end of the day the bears were fighting back and pushed the price back to close near the open and the low. This push is a failed effort at a rally, but you can interpret the bar best in the context of the other bars that precede it:

- If the gravestone bar appears after a series of uptrending bars, buyers failed to get the close at the high. Sellers dominated and the uptrend is at risk of ending.

- If the price move is a downtrend, the gravestone doji may mean that buyers are emerging and the downtrend may be ending.

Missing shadows

The absence of a shadow at one end is called a *shaven top* or a *shaven bottom*. To get a shaven top or bottom, the open or close must be exactly at the high or the low, as you can see in Figure 8-3. These candlestick bar notations are called *marubozu candles*, and you can classify the types of candles by using the following descriptions:

>> **Shaven top:** No upper shadow exists when the open or close is at the high. A shaven top can be black or white, and come about in two ways:

- If the open is at the high, the day's trading was all downhill. Not only is it a black candlestick, bearish to begin with, but it's also doubly bearish that no net new buying occurred after the open.

- If the close is at the high, the net of the day's trading was at higher prices, which is bullish. The candlestick is also (by definition) white — a bullish sign.

>> **Shaven bottom:** No lower shadow exists when the open or the close is at the low of the day. A shaven bottom can come in two ways:

- If the open is at the low, bulls dominated all the day's trading.

- If the close is at the low, all the day's trading points to bearish sentiment.

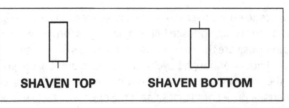

FIGURE 8-3:
Missing shadows.

SHAVEN TOP   SHAVEN BOTTOM

© *John Wiley & Sons, Inc.*

Really long shadows

When the shadow is as long as the real body, or longer (see Figure 8-4), traders are expressing a sentiment extreme. They may or may not follow through the next day by pushing the *close* to the high or low breaking point, though. Evaluating a long shadow is therefore tricky.

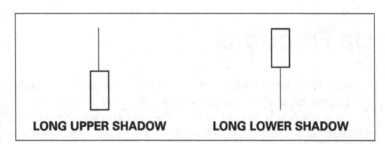

© John Wiley & Sons, Inc.

FIGURE 8-4: Very long shadows.

REMEMBER

As a general rule, judge a long shadow by its placement on the chart (relative to preceding bars), such as the following:

>> **Long upper shadow:** The high of the day came well above both the open and the close, whether the real body is black or white. Here's how you can interpret a really long upper shadow:

• If the price series is in an uptrend, the long upper shadow is a failure to close near the high. If the uptrend is nearing a resistance level (see Chapter 10 for a discussion of resistance), the long upper shadow may signal a weakening of the uptrend. If a long upper shadow follows a doji bar indicating indecisiveness, you should worry that the uptrend may be over.

• If the price series is on a downtrend, the long upper shadow suggests that some market participants are buying at higher levels. Especially if a long upper shadow follows a doji bar, you should wonder if the downtrend might be ending.

>> **Long lower shadow:** A long lower shadow means that the low of the day came well under both the open and the close, whether the real body is black or white. Here's what that probably means:

• If the price series is trending down, the long lower shadow is a failure to close near the low. If the downtrend is nearing a support level (see Chapter 10), the long lower shadow may signal a weakening or an end of the downtrend.

- If the price series is trending up, the long lower shadow suggests that traders weren't willing to keep buying at the high levels right up to the close. They were exiting under the high, and therefore think that new highs aren't warranted. This signal can be a warning sign of the trend decelerating or ending.

Sizing Up Emotions

Identifying when traders are reaching the end of their emotional tether is one of the primary goals of candlestick charting. And a change in the size of the bar is one of the best indicators of this. The candlestick technique sensitizes you to spot extremes of emotion, which is why it's a valuable tool for marking possible support and resistance at overbought or oversold levels (which I discuss in Chapter 2). You can also easily spot range expansion or contraction (see Chapter 7).

For example, at the beginning of the "Dissecting the Anatomy of a Candlestick" section, I discuss the idea that the longer the bar, the more bullish or bearish it is. If you're looking at a series of medium-sized bars and suddenly see one relatively long bar (as you can see in Figure 8-5), it may be telling you that support or resistance has been reached. Support marks an extreme level where buyers perceive that the price is relatively cheap, and resistance marks an extreme level where sellers perceive that the price is relatively high, inspiring profit-taking or least an end to accumulation. (See Chapter 10 for support and resistance.)

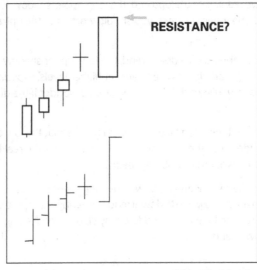

RESISTANCE?

FIGURE 8-5:
Bar placement.

© John Wiley & Sons, Inc.

In the top illustration in Figure 8-5, you see a series of three white bars making higher opens and higher closes, followed by a doji and an exceptionally long white bar. If you look at this chart in standard bar notation, as shown in the bottom illustration of Figure 8-5, you might say to yourself, "Higher high, higher lows, higher closes, trend okay." But the unusually tall bar stands out more prominently in candlestick mode — especially following the transitional doji — and alerts you to the possibility that all the buyers who were going to buy have just done so in one last burst, and the price may have formed a resistance level at the top of the bar (the close, in this case).

If the long bar were a black bar, denoting that the close was lower than the open, you would find it easy to deduce that the upmove might be ending. A long black bar implies panic selling. But to interpret the white bar as an ending burst in an uptrend is more subtle. In fact, an expert in reading standard bars would see the same thing. Candlesticks just make it easier, especially for traders just starting out.

Identifying Special Emotional Extreme Candlestick Patterns

Dozens of possible bar placement combinations and permutations are possible. In this section, I cover several of the most popular patterns and how you can tell the difference between them. These special emotional extreme candlestick patterns are unique to candlestick analysis and don't appear in the standard pattern analysis I discuss in Chapter 9.

Interpreting candlestick patterns

Two similar candlesticks or candlestick patterns often have the exact opposite interpretation, depending on where they fall in a series. You have to memorize the exact patterns to avoid getting confused. I select just two of the many candlestick patterns to illustrate how tricky some candlestick interpretation can get.

Hammer and hanging man

Both of these candlestick types have a small real body and only one shadow — a long lower shadow. While similar, noticing their differences is crucial to your interpretation. The long shadow of the hammer extends to the downside off a white body, while the long shadow of the hanging man extends to the downside off a black body. See Figure 8-6 for an example. How can it be a hanging man if the body is white? You can tell from the placement among the rising and then falling bars on either side. This is a subtlety that may be easy to miss.

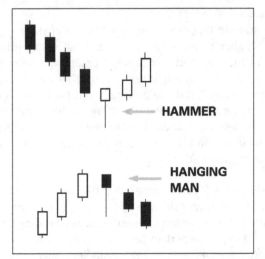

© John Wiley & Sons, Inc.

FIGURE 8-6:
Hammer and
hanging man
patterns.

You'd think that the white-body version would automatically be a bullish indicator and the black-body version a bearish one, but interpreting this candlestick depends on its placement on the chart, regardless of the real-body color. If the candlestick appears in a downtrend, for example, it marks the likely end of the trend even if the real body is white.

You may see a hammer in many other contexts, but when it has a white body and comes after a series of black downtrending bars, it implies a reversal. Note that the close is higher than the previous close, too. In this context, the long lower shadow means the sellers were able to achieve a new low, but buyers emerged at some point during the day and the close was higher than the open, indicating last-minute buying.

The hanging man looks the same except it appears after a series of white uptrending bars. The long lower shadow marks the bulls' failure to prevent the bears making a new low and also from keeping the close below the open. You may see this bar in other places within a series of bars, but when you see it at the top of an uptrending series, consider that the trend is probably over. The wise course is to take your profit and run.

Harami

A small real-body candlestick that comes after a bigger one is called a *harami*, which means "pregnant" in Japanese. A harami (see Figure 8-7) implies that a change in sentiment is impending. Technically, the harami pattern requires two bars, so it doesn't stand alone. On this chart, I show the shadows of the harami bar as inside the range of the first big bar, although this isn't essential to identifying the pattern.

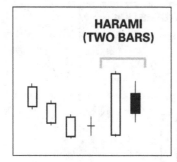

FIGURE 8-7:
Harami.

© John Wiley & Sons, Inc.

A harami can be a white session followed by black (bearish) session or a black session followed by white (bullish). If the second session is a doji, the pattern is called a *harami cross*. The smaller the real body, the more powerful the implication that a reversal is impending. In Figure 8-7, the white bar in the first session signals a likely downward reversal.

As I discuss in the section "Sizing Up Emotions" in this chapter, the size of the bar is important. Both the exceptionally small harami and the exceptionally big bar preceding it express extreme emotion. Seeing just the big white bar after a series of smaller ones that are downtrending, you may think that the bulls finally got the upper hand, and this movement is the start of an uptrend — especially because you have an indecision doji just ahead of it. But then the small black harami following the big white bar should disillusion you. If an uptrend was forming, the harami just put the kibosh on it.

Turning to reversal patterns

Reversal patterns number at least 40, and identifying reversals is the one of two applications of candlesticks (the other being continuation). The following are some of the most popular and easily identified candlestick reversal patterns.

Bearish engulfing candlestick

An *engulfing pattern* signals the reversal of a trend. The word *engulfing* refers to the open and close of the bar encompassing a wider range than the open and close of the day before. In Figure 8-8, the engulfing nature is the dominant characteristic so that the lower close pops out at you even though the bar also has a higher open. When a bar starts out at a higher open but then closes at a lower level, the bears won that day. Not shown in Figure 8-8 is a *bullish engulfing candlestick*, which is white. The higher close is visually compelling because the real body is so big. Like the harami, the engulfing candlesticks require two bars.

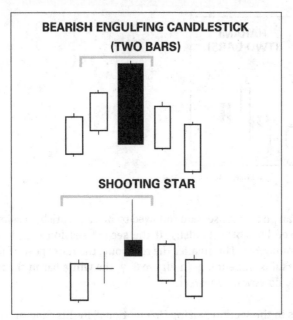

FIGURE 8-8:
Reversal patterns.

BEARISH ENGULFING CANDLESTICK
(TWO BARS)

SHOOTING STAR

© John Wiley & Sons, Inc.

Shooting star

You can characterize the *shooting star* pattern by a small real body and a long upper shadow, as you can see in Figure 8-8. As I discuss in the section "Really long shadows" in this chapter, the long upper shadow in an uptrend implies a failure of the trend — a failure to close near the high. The addition of the doji bar indicates traders were already becoming indecisive the day before.

Continuation patterns

Candlestick patterns are most often used to identify reversals, but continuation patterns do exist. As the name suggests, a continuation pattern gives you confirmation that the trend in place will likely continue. This section covers three continuation patterns you may see.

Rising window

Rising window is the term for a gap, in this case, an upward gap. (A downward gap is a *falling window.*) You can get more on gaps in Chapter 7.

In Figure 8-9, the gap separates two white candlesticks, which are themselves bullish. The next bar doesn't "fill the gap" (called *closing the window*). The gap between the two price bars is confirmation of the existing trend, and the market's refusal the following day to go back and fill the gap is further confirmation that the trend is okay.

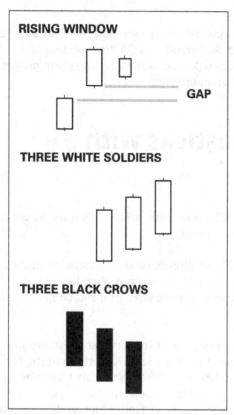

FIGURE 8-9:
Continuation
patterns.

© John Wiley & Sons, Inc.

Three white soldiers

The second exhibit in Figure 8-9 shows three white soldiers. In this pattern, note the three large white candlesticks in a row. Seeing the close consistently over the open for three days confirms that the price series is in an uptrend, and the size of the bars indicates its robustness. Three white soldiers is a pattern that has to come after a series of bullish (white) candles to be considered a continuation pattern. It goes by the boring name *advance block.*

In contrast, when three white soldiers comes at the end of a downmove, it's a reversal pattern. In both instances, the pattern is even better if the top wick is small or not there at all, meaning the close was at or near the high — bulls won all the way to the end.

Three black crows

Three black crows is the upside-down mirror image of three white soldiers, only with black real bodies. In this pattern (refer to Figure 8-9), you have three periods of the close under the open and lower each time, with the bars fairly sizeable. The price series is now in a downtrend. As with three white soldiers, three black crows is a continuation pattern when a downmove is already in play and a reversal pattern when it comes after an upmove.

Combining Candlesticks with Other Indicators

You can combine candlesticks with other indicators to get a more-powerful description of trader sentiment.

TIP

Many traders who don't act directly on the information contained in the candlestick patterns still use the notation on every chart because of its visual appeal and because a candlestick bar or pattern often confirms some other indicator to which they give priority.

Figure 8-10 shows a set of parallel support and resistance lines called a *channel* (which I cover in Chapter 11). You use a channel to outline the probable limit of future prices moves, either up or down. Note that I describe each of the candlesticks on this chart in preceding sections in this chapter. The harami is followed by a rising window (upward gap) and a tall, white candle. These three candlesticks together are bullish and alert you to go back and start the channel at the lowest low, the bar before the harami.

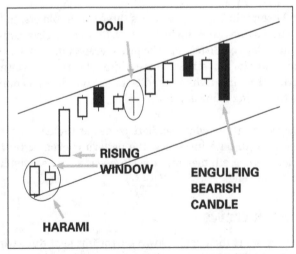

FIGURE 8-10:
Candlesticks as confirmation.

© John Wiley & Sons, Inc.

The real bodies in Figure 8-10 proceed to push against the top of the channel resistance line, but the doji, which suggests that traders are having second thoughts, is followed by two higher white candles. The two white candles indicate that the reconsideration of the move on the doji day culminated in traders' decisions to keep taking the price up. In this occasion, the doji wasn't a reversal indicator, at least not for the next day. After the two white candles comes a bearish engulfing candle, a reversal warning that this upmove may be ending. The engulfing candle alerts you to watch the next day's activity, especially the open, with an eagle eye.

You can also use candlesticks to confirm relative strength, momentum, and many other indicators. Check out Chapter 13 for details on relative strength and momentum. Note that in Japan, a favorite indicator to use with candlesticks is the moving average, which I cover in Chapter 12.

Some traders use specific candlesticks to identify *setups*, or a pattern configuration that is believed to have a high probability of delivering a specific outcome. Say that after a long series of falling bars, you see a doji (indicating indecisiveness) or a harami that closes near the upper end of the previous candle — and then a bullish engulfing candlestick. At the same time, another indicator like the stochastic oscillator or relative strength index shows the security to be deeply oversold. This scenario is a high-probability trade setup, which means to get out the big guns because you want to buy! You can find many resources out there, including in print and online, for great ways to combine candlesticks with other indicators.

Trading on Candlesticks Alone

Reading candlesticks is like reading standard bars — endlessly fascinating, even addictive. But be aware that all bar reading takes practice. Some specific bars and patterns of bars are well known — and thus likely to get the expected response from market participants. But to do a good job interpreting candlesticks, you need to understand the dynamic and complex relationships of many patterns all at once, like juggling six oranges rather than three.

REMEMBER

As with standard bar interpretation, the predictive power of a particular bar or pattern of bars may be limited to the next day or next few days. Like all technical indicators, candlesticks work only some of the time to deliver the expected outcome. Evaluating candlesticks alone, without confirmation from other indicators, is a daunting task. First, you have to define carefully what each candlestick looks like. As noted in the section "Harami" in this chapter, a harami (for example) can be bullish or bearish, depending on the other bars around it.

Tom Bulkowski took on the task of measuring the predictive value of candlesticks in his book *Encyclopedia of Candlestick Charts* (John Wiley & Sons, Inc.). Carefully defining each candlestick and set of candlestick patterns for a total of 103, Bulkowski ran them through a gigantic database of 500 U.S. equities over ten years and found that 69 percent of the candles delivered the outcome expected, such as continuing higher closes following three white soldiers. Bulkowski tested 412 combinations of the 103 candlestick patterns and found that only 100 candles or patterns got the expected outcome, or 24 percent.

Wait — it gets worse. In statistics, you need a bare minimum of 30 to 40 instances of a pattern occurring to see whether it delivers the expected outcome. But Bulkowski found that patterns meeting his definitions didn't occur all that often. In fact, only 10 percent were found a sufficient number of times to qualify for workability testing. In short, you find only 10 percent of the candles in sufficient number, and these candles work as expected only 60 percent of the time. Refining the criteria further to a 66 percent success rate, meaning that the candle works as advertised in two out of three trades, only 6 percent of candles (or 13 candles total) are what Bulkowski calls "investment grade." These candles include some that I describe in this chapter, including the bearish doji star, bearish engulfing candle, and rising and falling windows.

Bulkowski's findings don't mean that you cannot find a specific candlestick that works most of the time in your security. A higher incidence of success in candle-reading may be due to other traders in the same security seeing the same candlestick pattern and believing it will work — and so it does. In foreign exchange trading, for example, the hammer, shooting star, and engulfing bull or engulfing bear candles work nearly all the time.

A qualification of the Bulkowski study is that it was applied to U.S. equities, not commodities or other securities, and over a specific ten-year period. Still, the study confirms what you already knew — no technical indicator works all the time. That doesn't mean specific candlesticks won't work for you, especially if you add confirming indicators like the MACD. This only emphasizes once again that chart-reading is an art.

Finding Patterns

Build familiarity with classic chart patterns that you probably see quite often, like double top and double bottom, plus some fun-sounding patterns like dead-cat bounce.

Focus on the true purpose of technical analysis, identifying a trend, with basic support and resistance lines. These are the first lines you'll draw and S&R will become second nature to you — you'll likely draw thousands of them in your trading lifetime.

Expand the support and resistance concept to a wider perspective with channels that contain embedded forecasts. Examine how useful and reliable channels can be.

Chapter **9**

Seeing Patterns

A pattern is a type of indicator traditionally drawn on the chart by hand but placed on charts sometimes by software. You still need to understand pattern recognition, though — don't count on software to do interpretation for you. You may think that you'd rather have an objective indicator on the chart instead of a subjective pattern, but consider that many traders use nothing but patterns and make a good living from it. In addition, because common patterns are so widely known and even mentioned in the press and on TV, they can become self-fulfilling prophecies.

Technical traders have been developing patterns from the earliest days of technical analysis. Until personal computers came along, *Technical Analysis of Stock Market Trends* by Edwards and McGee was a Bible for chart readers starting at its publication date in 1949. This was the first book that took ideas partly or mostly devised by Charles Dow but written up only in newspapers and magazines. The central idea is recognizing that after a trend moves up substantially (a primary trend), it pulls back on profit-taking or second thoughts (a secondary trend), and then resumes the upmove. You'll see this pattern many, many times. Edwards and Magee identified support and resistance, gaps, triangles, head-and-shoulders, and many other patterns still in wide use today.

I cover some classic patterns in other chapters, such as the inside day (Chapter 7) and support and resistance lines (Chapter 10). Other bar patterns are also covered in Chapter 7 (island reversal), and all the candlestick formations are considered patterns, too (see Chapter 8), as well as the Fibonacci retracement (see Chapter 17). In this chapter, I describe a few of the most common patterns. Traders have devised and named literally hundreds of patterns, and you can't expect to memorize them all. But master a handful.

Introducing Patterns

Chart patterns are indicators consisting of geometric shapes drawn on the chart, such as a triangle. As with most indicators, a price forecast is embedded in the pattern identification. Here's a quick pattern primer:

» Most patterns employ straight lines (such as triangles), although a few use semicircles (such as head-and-shoulders).

» Pattern lines generally follow either the highs or the lows.

» Pattern types are organized according to whether they forecast a continuation or a reversal of the current price move, although you can apply many patterns (like triangles) either way.

The lingo of pattern analysis — double bottom and dead-cat bounce, for example — can be amusing. You also see cup-and-handle, belt-hold, scoop, fry-pan, cradle, and jay-hook. Some of the names do seem a little silly, but they describe the price action efficiently. Nowadays you can have an analyst walk you through specific patterns on websites like www.candlestickforum.com and You-Tube, which is especially useful for patterns. For a comprehensive review, go to www.ThePatternSite.com. And keep going back. The author, Tom Bulkowski, wrote the definitive book on patterns and often updates material on the site. In the following sections, I cite performance data from Tom Bulkowski's path-breaking *Encyclopedia of Chart Patterns*, Second Edition (John Wiley & Sons, Inc.) and www.ThePatternSite.com.

REMEMBER

A pattern is always a work in progress. You may see a pattern developing only to have the price action change course and fail to complete the expected formation. This makes pattern identification frustrating and time consuming. Resign yourself to mistakes and to indicator failure. The reason to tolerate the pattern recognition process is that when you get it right, you have a powerful forecasting tool that can deliver high returns.

Using imagination

Humans are awfully good at pattern recognition — are you? Just about every chart containing at least a month of data offers a pattern or two. At the beginning, you won't see any patterns at all. After a little practice, you'll see patterns everywhere, including some that aren't there (which is why you need to apply the rules for identifying patterns).

For example, consider Figure 9-1. Do you see the pattern?

FIGURE 9-1:
Find the pattern.

The pattern in Figure 9-1 is a symmetrical triangle, as you can see in Figure 9-2. This pattern is sometimes referred to as a *coil*. The triangle is characterized by a series of lower highs along which you can draw one trendline and a series of higher lows along which you can draw another trendline. The two lines eventually come together at an apex. Before that point is reached, the price must pierce one of the trendlines simply in the course of trading in its normal range. Which one? Because most of the bars are trending downward, you imagine the odds favor a break to the downside.

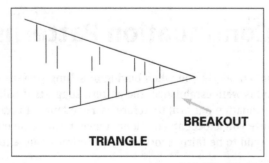

BREAKOUT

TRIANGLE

FIGURE 9-2:
Pattern revealed.

And you're right. In the Bulkowski study of triangles, the outcome is a downside breakout well over 50 percent of the time, making this triangle a continuation pattern. But sometimes the breakout is to the upside. In the same study, the price delivered an upside breakout only 43 percent of the time. In this instance, the pattern forecasts a reversal, not a continuation. Most patterns don't deliver a gift-wrapped buy/sell signal until near the end of the formation. As the symmetrical triangle pattern develops, the forecast is only that a breakout will occur, not the direction of the breakout.

TIP

You usually see a burst of higher volume when a pattern reaches completion, implying other chartists in the crowd see the same pattern. For triangles, low volume often *precedes* the breakout and serves as a bonus warning of an impending move.

Coloring inside the lines

WARNING

Pattern identification doesn't require that each single price in a series line up perfectly. Not every price high hits an overhead resistance line, for example. It suffices that several hit the line. All triangles — symmetrical, ascending, and descending — incorporate support (top) and resistance (bottom) lines, as do flags and pennants, and other patterns. Some analysts say it's okay for a bar or two to break one of the lines by a tiny amount. But Victor Sperandeo in *Trader Vic: Methods of a Wall Street Master* (John Wiley & Sons, Inc.) — another must-have book in every technical analyst's library — says that ignoring a break of the trendline is *always* wrong.

TIP

You don't have to trust your pattern recognition ability alone. Curtis Arnold, author of *Timing the Market* (Probus Publishing) and *Curtis Arnold's PPS Trading System* (McGraw Hill), recommends using patterns (like triangles) together with moving averages to confirm. PPS stands for *pattern profitability strategy*.

Cozying Up to Continuation Patterns

A *continuation pattern* alerts you when buying or selling pressure is pausing. If a big-picture trend is well-established, the pattern suggests it will accelerate after the pause. A continuation pattern, therefore, is a good place to add more money to a position, because you expect an additional move in the same direction. Continuation patterns tend to be fairly short term, sometimes only a few days, and can be easily missed.

TIP

Continuation patterns serve as reassurance that you've identified the trend correctly. They also often point you to the ideal level at which to place a stop-loss order, such as the ascending line in the ascending triangle that I describe in the following sections.

Ascending and descending triangles

To draw ascending and descending triangles, you draw a line along the highs of a price series and another one along the lows (see Figure 9-3) — just like you do with symmetrical triangles.

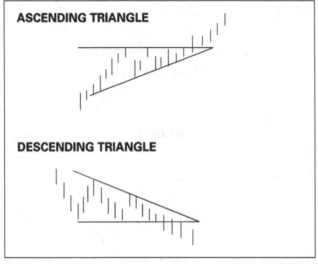

© John Wiley & Sons, Inc.

FIGURE 9-3:
Ascending and descending triangles.

In the ascending triangle, the price isn't making new highs, and the topmost (resistance) line is horizontal. You may worry that the failure to make new highs means that the upmove is over. But the price isn't making new lows, either. You can often expect a breakout of the top line to the upside.

TIP

When you can draw a horizontal line along a series of highs, remember to look for a rising line along the lows at the same time. Not only does the ascending line of lows confirm the trend continuation, but it also provides you with a ready-made stop-loss level at this ascending support line. The ascending triangle pattern delivers the expected rise about two-thirds of the time (and obviously fails about one-third of the time). If you wait for prices to *close* above the top trendline, then the failure rate drops to a mere 2 percent. The *expected rise,* by the way, is equal to the height of the triangle pattern. See the section later in this chapter on "Evaluating the Measured Move."

A descending triangle is the mirror image of the ascending triangle. In this case the important point is the price is failing to make new lows in the prevailing downtrend. You wonder if the trend is failing. But if you can still draw a line along the series of lower highs, it would be a mistake to buy at this point — the probability is high that the downtrend is going to continue.

Dead-cat bounce

A *dead-cat bounce* (refer to Figure 9-4) is a peculiar continuation pattern that looks like a reversal at the beginning, with a sizeable upward retracement of a downmove, but then fades back to the same downward direction. Note that a dead-cat bounce occurs mostly in downmoves, although there is a less-seen inverted dead-cat bounce (see www.thepatternsite.com/idcb.html).

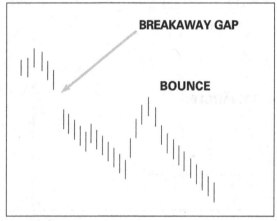

FIGURE 9-4:
Dead-cat bounce.

© John Wiley & Sons, Inc.

The dead-cat pattern starts off with a negative fundamental event that triggers a massive downmove. The average size of the downmove is 25 percent — but the price can shoot down by 70 percent or more in only a few days. The *bounce* is an upward retracement that may fool you into thinking the drop is over. The pattern includes a breakaway downside gap about 80 percent of the time, and sometimes the bounce upward fills part of the gap. Many traders mistakenly think that if a gap is filled, even partly, the preceding move has ended. The dead-cat bounce is one of the patterns that disproves that idea — by the end of six months after the gap, only a little more than half of price moves close the gap, according to Bulkowski's studies.

The dead-cat bounce is one of the most successful patterns of all, delivering a success rate nearing 90 percent and steady over three decades.

Recognizing Classic Reversal Patterns

Patterns come into their own when you use them to identify a trend reversal. No matter how a trend comes to an end, chances are good that a pattern exists to identify it. The reversal patterns I mention in the following sections are definitely ones you want to be able to recognize.

Double bottom

A *double bottom* (refer to Figure 9-5) looks like a W. The double bottom is essentially a retest of a low and predicts a price breakout to the upside, but only under certain conditions.

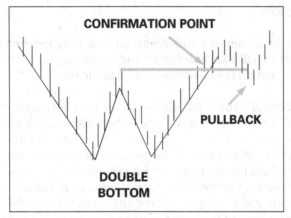

FIGURE 9-5:
Double bottom.

REMEMBER

The identification guide for a valid double bottom includes these factors:

>> A minimum of ten days between the two lows and sometimes as long as two or three months.

>> Variation between the two lows shouldn't be more than 4 percent.

>> A center upmove of at least 10 percent from the lower of the two bottoms.

>> The price must rise above the confirmation line to confirm that the pattern is indeed a double bottom and the forecast of a continued rise is correct. The *confirmation line* is a horizontal line drawn from the highest high in the middle of the W. The point where the price rises above the line is called the *confirmation point.*

REMEMBER

Reaching the confirmation line drawn horizontally from the confirmation point, shown on Figure 9-5, is the most important identification key of the double bottom. This is where you buy.

Some of the price bars break the lines that form the double bottom pattern. Breaking some of the bars is allowed in a formation where the line isn't a support or resistance line. Note the pullback, too. A *pullback* is a retracement to the downside right after the price breaks the confirmation line. A pullback occurs 68 percent of the time in confirmed double bottoms, making it hard to trust your pattern identification.

TECHNICAL STUFF

Bulkowski prefers the term *throwback* for the retracement after an upside break-out, as in the double bottom, and *pullback* for the retracement after a downward breakout, as in a double top, but these words aren't engraved in stone. You can use the words *retracement*, *correction*, *throwback*, and *pullback* (more or less) interchangeably.

WARNING

Not every twin bottom is a true double bottom. Only about one-third of all the patterns that look like a double bottom end up meeting the confirmation criterion. In short, the pattern fails about two-thirds of the time.

These odds sound terrible, but wait — on the occasions when you do get confirmation, the double bottom is tremendously reliable. If you wait for the price to break above the confirmation line, the pattern delivers a profit more than 90 percent of the time. The version of the double bottom that Figure 9-5 illustrates is clear and obvious, but not every pattern is so easy to detect. For example, one or both of the two lows of the double bottom could be rounded rather than pointed. When the first bottom is pointed and the second is rounded, Tom Bulkowski names it the *Adam and Eve* double bottom. You can imagine the other combinations, including two pointy bottoms (*Adam and Adam*) and the first one rounded with the second one pointed (*Eve and Adam*). This is, by the way, as racy as technical analysis ever gets.

REMEMBER

Often the two lows of a double bottom are separated by several months and you can easily miss the pattern altogether. Also, minor retracements and other patterns within the W can obscure the pattern. Some analysts note that big patterns lasting months are easier to see on weekly charts that skim off the aberrations in daily data. Some analysts believe they can see double bottoms and other classic patterns on charts using hourly bars or other time frames (such as 240-minutes or 4-hours). This is probably true, and the interpretation remains the same whatever the time frame, assuming other traders are using that time frame and see the pattern, too.

Double tops

A double top is the mirror image of the double bottom — it looks like the letter M. In a *double top,* the price makes a high, pulls back on profit-taking (as usual), and then bullish traders try but fail to surpass the first high. The failure to rally a second time through the first high means that the bulls were beaten and the bears are now in charge. A true double top is usually accompanied by falling volume as the second top is being formed.

As with the double bottom described earlier, you need to see the price surpass the confirmation level (the lowest point in the center bar of the M) for the pattern to be valid. When that condition is *not* met, twin tops fail to deliver a sustained downmove more than half the time. When the condition is met, however, the pattern delivers a downmove more than half the time.

REMEMBER

Topping reversal patterns like the double top are usually more short term than bottoming reversal patterns like double bottoms. Tops take less time to form than bottoms because traders are more fearful of taking losses after a big gain than they are trusting of early signs of a bottom. Topping reversals are often more volatile, too, although they occur with equal frequency. According to Bulkowski, nearly all bottom chart patterns — of any type — perform better than tops. These statistics confirm market lore that bull markets are easier to trade than bear markets. Bull markets are more orderly and may suggest that greed is stronger than fear. Bull markets also tend to have wider and deeper participation because there are more traders who can go long than there are traders who can go both long and short, at least in equities. In equities (but not in securities like foreign exchange), buy-side gains are theoretically unlimited while gains on the short side are always limited — a stock can't sell for less than zero.

The ultimate triple top: Head-and-shoulders

A triple top or bottom is somewhat rarer than the double version, but the meaning is the same — the price fails to surpass the previous low or high, signaling a trend reversal.

The *head-and-shoulders* pattern is a triple top that's easy to see: One bump forms the left shoulder, a higher bump forms a head, and a third bump forms the right shoulder. (See Figure 9-6 for two examples.) The head-and-shoulders pattern is the most widely recognized of all the patterns and deserves its popularity because when the price surpasses the pattern's confirmation line, it delivers the expected downmove a whopping 90-plus percent of the time.

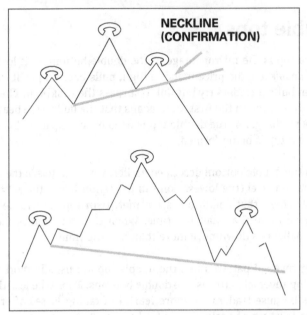

NECKLINE (CONFIRMATION)

© John Wiley & Sons, Inc.

FIGURE 9-6:
Head-and-shoulders patterns.

The confirmation line connects the low point of each shoulder and is named the *neckline*. The price breaking the neckline predicts a price decline, whether the neckline is sloping upward or downward. Seldom do you see the neckline perfectly horizontal. A downward-sloping neckline tends to deliver the biggest price move.

If you stop and think about it, a head-and-shoulders pattern is a logical development of crowd behavior. A head-and-shoulders usually forms after a long uptrend. The dip from the first shoulder represents the normal retracement after a new high. The head then represents the triumph of bullish sentiment and sets a new higher high. The dip after the higher-high head represents more profit-taking, whereupon the bulls buy again. When the bulls are making their third try at a rally, their price target is the last highest high, which is the top of the head. The failure of the second shoulder to surpass the head is the end of the rally. Buying demand diminishes and selling pressure takes hold, forcing prices down, completing the pattern. Note that if you get three tops at about the same level, it's not a head-and-shoulders but a triple top. The bullish version occurs to the bottom of the chart and is called an *inverse head-and-shoulders*. It's bullish because after the three bottoms, the price is expected to move to the upside.

WARNING

As with double tops and bottoms, however, some traders refuse to accept the pattern, and they cause a pullback to the confirmation line on many occasions. Pullbacks are short-lived, only a week or two, before the security resumes its decline. This is your last chance to jump off before the price hits the wall. Don't listen to that little voice that says, "See, it's coming back." That little voice is wishful thinking. The pullback is the only free lunch in technical analysis.

As with every trend that is losing steam, volume falls after the head, although about half the time the highest volume is at the left shoulder and about half the time at the head. Volume is low at the second shoulder. Volume on the breakout day and the next few days after the breakout day, however, tends to be very high. This isn't surprising, because by now a great number of chart-oriented traders have identified the pattern and its neckline. Some traders may see only the break of support without having seen the head-and-shoulders pattern, adding to the number of traders who now want to sell.

The head-and-shoulders patterns shown in Figure 9-6 are easy enough to see, but many head-and-shoulders patterns are more complex and contain other patterns within them. The second head-and-shoulders pattern in Figure 9-6, for example, contains a little double top and a gap.

Evaluating the Measured Move

The term *measured move* is used in a number of contexts in technical analysis, so it can become confusing. In essence, a *measured move* is a forecast of the upcoming price move after a chart event, including completion of a pattern. Unfortunately, these forecasts are seldom correct, or rather, they vary by too much from actual outcomes to serve as reliable trading guides. Here, I outline three types of measured moves. (Point-and-figure charting also features its own version of the measured move — see Chapter 15.)

Taking dictation from the pattern

One definition of *measured move* is the price change expected to result from a particular pattern. For example, in the ascending triangle pictured at the top of Figure 9-7, the gray lines denote the height of the pattern. Imagine that the distance between the high and low within the pattern is $5. After the price breaks out above the top of the triangle, you expect the subsequent rise to be about the same amount, $5. This is most likely an overestimation.

Instead of an equal measured move, the size of a move after a pattern is *proportional* to the size of the pattern.

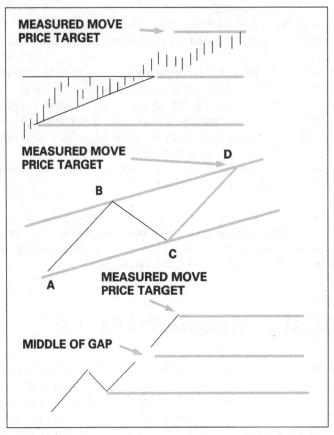

MEASURED MOVE PRICE TARGET

MEASURED MOVE PRICE TARGET

D

B

A

C

MEASURED MOVE PRICE TARGET

MIDDLE OF GAP

FIGURE 9-7:
Measured
moves.

© *John Wiley & Sons, Inc.*

Bulkowski provides measurement guidelines for the range, average, and *mode* (most often seen) price change upon the completion of a pattern. Seldom are they exactly 100 percent of the height of a pattern. Every pattern is measured in its own way. The expected move after a head-and-shoulders pattern described earlier in this chapter, for example, is measured from the top of the head to the neckline. You then subtract that number from the neckline at the breakout point to derive the expected stopping point of the downmove. This target will get met more than 50 percent of the time, but not every time.

Resuming the trend after retracement

Another type of *measured move* is when a price repeats the extent of a first move after a retracement. The retracement takes back 30 percent of the gain from the low to the high, or some other percentage. The point is that after the retracement, you often see the price resume the trend at the same slope and to the same extent as in the first move.

This type of measured move is illustrated in the second chart in Figure 9-7. Here you see an already established channel consisting of support and resistance lines. (The price is oscillating between the two channel lines. After you see the price stop at Price C, you simply copy and paste the A-to-B move to C to arrive at price target D.)

In the updated performance stats for the measured move up (as of mid-2018) Bulkowski found that a measured upmove hit the price target 67 percent of the time. The measured move down met the price target 55 percent of the time.

Measuring from the gap

A third type of *measured move* is when you have a gap. A *gap* is a price bar whose high or low is separated from the preceding bar by open space, meaning that no trades took place at those intervening prices. A gap is important because it shows graphically that something happened to alter perception of the security. In Figure 9-7, you measure the distance from the lowest low in the upmove to the middle of the gap, and then project that height from the middle of the gap to the upside (in an uptrend). You do the opposite in a downtrend.

In my experience, measured moves in gaps are unreliable, probably because the gap itself shows the market for this security has the collywobbles; traders are fearful and uncertain and do unexpected things.

Chapter **10**

Drawing Trendlines

The human brain instinctively seeks order and creates meaning from patterns. When looking at a chart of a security, you may think you see a pattern of directionality — *trendedness* — but is it really there? Or are you seeing a pattern when randomness is all there is?

To be sure, you need to connect the dots by drawing a visible line along what you think is the trend. A *trendline* is a straight line that starts at the beginning of the trend and stops at the end of the trend. Today everyone uses software to draw trendlines, but note that you have to do the drawing; websites and charting software won't do it for you.

In this chapter, I cover support and resistance, two of the most important concepts in technical analysis, and also the linear regression, which depicts pure, true trend.

Looking Closely at a Price Chart

When you take your pencil (or cursor) to draw a line, sometimes you get it right the first time out. But take another look — is there a better, more representative line? Don't give up. You want to master the rules for drawing lines for two reasons:

>> You have more confidence that your trade is going to be profitable when prices are following your trendline, especially when they follow it tightly.

>> A break of a trendline is a high-probability indication that the trend has ended and you need to take action.

WARNING

You never know in advance when a trendline will start or stop. You know only after the fact. So a trendline is a work in progress that needs constant reevaluation. This means persistent price-checking to see where the latest prices are placed relative to the trendline. You probably know people who check their prices every day. It's a mystery why they do that if they don't have an analytical framework in which to judge the day's outcome, even just a rough hand-drawn trendline.

Following the Rules with Rule-Based Trendlines

You're welcome to draw any old line that your eye dictates, but rule-based lines have a long history of actually working to improve trading results, in part because everyone knows the rules and draws the same or similar lines. This gives some practical meaning to the phrase "reading the mind of the market."

Rule-based trendline is therefore better than an impressionistic line for three reasons:

>> It doesn't let you impose your personal view of what the trend should be.

>> It improves your ability (and self-confidence) to buy a security when its price is rising or sell it when the price is falling.

>> It helps prevent loss by showing you the exit at the right place.

Understanding the seductive zigzag

How about a line that tracks a price move until the moves reverses by (say) 5 percent? Then you start a new line going in the other direction. This is named a zigzag and forms the basis of a trading system designed by Arthur Merrill in the 1977 book *Filtered Waves* (Analysis Press). The *zigzag pattern* is available online and in most charting software packages, and you get to experiment with different percentages. Obviously if you choose 2 percent, you'll get many zigs; if you chose 8 percent, you will get fewer zags. Some analyst match up zigzags with Elliott Waves and other cycle ideas (see Chapter 17). As cycle ideas have come back into fashion, so has the zigzag.

The problem with zigzag is it looks splendid on the chart, until it doesn't. That happens when your security undergoes a change in variability. For a long period, a 5 percent trigger for a reversal is effective. Now the security is jumpier with higher volatility and changes directions after every 2 percent move. Or it may be trending heavily and doesn't reverse until it reaches 10 percent. In each case, you'd need a different percentage number to capture the moves. You never know in advance whether your percentage trigger is truly representative of upcoming ranges. Securities can go through periods of relative calm when the average range shrinks down to practically nothing and then a period of excitement or agitation, usually based on fresh news, in which the range expands dramatically. In Figure 10-1, notice how you get whipsawed in the middle of the chart. Then the 5 percent trigger rule works well for a long time, only to give a false signal near the far right-hand side of the move.

FIGURE 10-1:
A 5 percent
zigzag.

© John Wiley & Sons, Inc.

Zigzags are a great idea, especially if the crowd that trades the security is reliably consistent (and perhaps using zigzags, too). Although many use zigzags, *everyone* uses another technique, based on market sentiment — support and resistance.

Drawing support and resistance lines

A *support* line is interpreted as defining where latent demand lies waiting, and *resistance* means latent supply. In other words, a support line is the price level where a downtrend pauses or stops and represents the lowest price for trading in the current range; resistance is the highest price in the current trading range.

The appropriate trendline for an uptrend is the support line. Here's how you draw it.

1. **Start at the lowest low and connect the line to the next low that precedes a new high.**

2. **As long as new highs are being made, redraw the line to connect to the lowest low before the last high.**

3. **When prices stop making new highs, stop drawing.**

   Extend the line out into the future at the same slope.

The appropriate trendline for a downtrend is a resistance line. Here's how you draw it.

1. **Start at the highest high and connect the line to the next high that precedes a new low.**

2. **As long as new lows are being made, redraw the line to connect to the highest high before the last low.**

3. **When prices stop making new lows, stop drawing.**

   Extend the line out into the future at the same slope.

Notice that this is a dynamic process. You often have to erase one line and draw another one as conditions change.

Using the support line to enter and exit

The trendline illustrates a *support line* in Figure 10-2. It's named *support* because you expect the line to support the price — traders who like this security will step in and buy at support, preventing the price from falling below the line. You start at the lowest low and draw a line to the next low. This generates a line that can be extended at the same slope, but it becomes a trendline only when another daily price low touches the line and bounces off it back to the upside. This touch-bounce is confirmation that the line isn't just any old line but rather a true trendline. When you use the support trendline as a trading guide, you initiate a new position on the confirmation, right after the third touch.

FIGURE 10-2:
Drawing a
support line.

SELL ON BREAK
OF SUPPORT LINE

BUY ON THIRD
TOUCH OF SUPPORT

© John Wiley & Sons, Inc.

Some technical traders say that to require a third touch is to be overly cautious and to miss out on some perfectly good trends that fail to meet the third-touch qualification. This is true — many valid trends do have only two touches before they end. If you're waiting for the third touch, you may miss the entire move. You may even say that two touches is better than three or more because that means this security doesn't have a crew of wiseguys always testing support. It's up to you to gain the experience from drawing support lines on *your* securities to determine whether two touches are enough.

REMEMBER

You use the support line to identify an uptrend. The *support line entry rule* says: Buy on the second or third touch of the support line. On the flip side, the support line exit rule says: Sell as soon as possible after the low of the price bar falls below the support line. Notice that the buy/sell rules are asymmetrical. You buy only after a tough entry test, but you sell fast at the first sign of trouble. In some securities, including foreign exchange (FX), traders like to play games and push the price to break the support line but then buy it back so that the *close* remains over the support line. This is a trick to weed out weak hands and let the pros buy at a lower price. You need to examine the behavior of the crowd that trades your security to see whether it's the low or the close breaking the line that matters.

TIP

The more times that a low-of-the-day touches the support line without crossing it, the more confidence you should have that it's a valid description of the trend. This is called a *test of support* and encourages buyers of the security to buy more after the price passes the test. Fresh buying constitutes demand for the security.

Those who already own the security are reluctant to sell after support has passed the test because they now expect a flood of new buyers who also saw support hold.

Noting breakouts and false breakouts

A break of the support line doesn't automatically mean the trend is over. In Figure 10-2, the upmove resumes after the support line was broken, but experience teaches that the trendline is no longer reliable. The loss of reliability is due to all the other traders in this security seeing the break.

A minor trendline break (by the low but not the close) has more to do with your risk management practices than to identifying trendedness. If you didn't have a stop near the support line, you need to get one. If you did have such a stop but it escaped being hit, you may want at least to reduce your exposure by selling half of your position (or some other percentage).

REMEMBER

A *breakout* is any part of the price bar penetrating a line that you drew on the chart. Some traders insist that it has to be the close breaking the line to qualify for the term "breakout." The word *breakout* is used in a dozen contexts in technical analysis, but it always refers to a significant violation of the trend. Sometimes the offending breakout is quickly roped back into the herd, but even if the trend doesn't change direction, its nature has changed. For example, a downside breakout of support that is *immediately* followed by a series of higher highs indicates that bulls got a second wind and are violently repudiating the breakout. But will they be there the next time?

Sometimes the low breaks the support line for just one day, and then prices obediently fall back into line. Subsequent prices respect the support function of the line. A one-day (or two-day) break of the line is called a *false breakout*. The word *false* is misleading because the price really does break the line; what's false is the conclusion you draw from it.

To estimate whether a breakout might be false, master trader Larry Williams (author of *How I Made $1,000,000 Trading Commodities* [Windsor Books] and many other books) recommends that you consider the position of the close on the day before the breakout. In an uptrend, if the close is at or near the high, chances are good that it's a false breakout. The breakout was due to profit-taking that got carried away, it was triggered by a false rumor, or it was noise. If the close on the day before is at or near the low, though, chances are the breakout is real.

TIP

Discard the support line as a trading tool after it has been broken. However, you may want to leave it on the chart for a while. Sometimes old support becomes new resistance, and vice versa. This market lore — of old support becoming new resistance — goes in and out of favor. During one recent decade, it wasn't in evidence in the FX market. But it came back starting around 2010; considering that the decade before starting around 2000 brought a surge in the availability of software-based indicators, not to mention new techniques like ichimoku (check out Chapter 18), it's more a little strange that old-fashioned lore became active and relevant again, although perhaps it makes the point that technical analysis never throws out any ideas.

Using resistance to enter and exit

Resistance is the mirror image of support: A line drawn along a series of highs marks where buyers resist buying more — the price is too high for them, and they expect profit-taking sellers to emerge at the resistance line. You should care about identifying a downtrend using the resistance line for two reasons:

>> **When a downtrend ends, the next move may be an uptrend.** You want to get in on the action as early as possible, so you care when a downtrend is broken to the upside. The breakout is an important clue that an uptrend may be starting and you should start paying attention.

>> **You may someday do the unimaginable — sell short.** If you have been trading exclusively in the U.S. stock market, chances are you're not familiar with taking *a short position,* or selling a security first and buying it back later after its price has fallen. Commodity traders, on the other hand, are familiar with the practice. After all, traders are striving to be emotionally neutral about whether prices are rising or falling. Why not profit symmetrically? To make a profit only when a price is rising is to lose 50 percent of the opportunity presented by trend-following.

Figure 10-3 shows two resistance lines drawn according to the rule. The uppermost line correctly advised shorting this security at the third touch of the line. The price falls off the cliff. But the price never returns to this first resistance line. Instead you get the opportunity to draw a new resistance line a few months later.

An experienced trader would probably see the new line as an opportunity to increase his short position. A long-only trader would be watching this second resistance line for the opportunity to buy the security — with a holding period that lasts only until the price nears the topmost resistance line, where it will face (you guessed it) resistance. Note that selling this security on the third touch of resistance and covering the short position when the price breaks the second resistance line would have given you a return of 20 percent.

The logic for trading using resistance lines is the same as for the support line, but in reverse. The more times the high-of-the-day touches the resistance line and doesn't cross it, the more confidence you have that it's a valid description of the trend. This is called a *test of resistance* and encourages sellers of the security to sell more after the price fails the test of resistance.

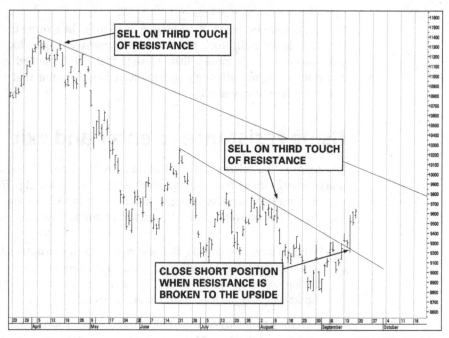

FIGURE 10-3:
Drawing
resistance lines.

© John Wiley & Sons, Inc.

But remember, you can get a false breakout in a resistance line just as in a support line. This occurs when some bullish traders decide the price has gone low enough and the security is now a bargain. They push the price upward to a test of resistance and succeed in getting the high of the day to break the resistance line. But unless others chip in with buying of their own, the breakout can fizzle.

REMEMBER

To trade using support and resistance exemplifies the ruling principle of trend-following trading: You never enter at the absolute high and never exit at the absolute low. The goal is to capture a portion of the trend. Famous trader Bernard Baruch said he was willing to let others have the first third of a move and the last third of a move — he just wanted the middle third.

Being aware of the 1-2-3 Rule

You need patience and persistence to work with trendlines because you need to adjust the lines often, sometimes daily. You'll hardly ever be lucky enough to get a clear uptrend along a support line and then a breakout of the support line that turns into a downtrend with a tidy resistance line, the classic inverted V. Instead the price will wander around and perhaps test the last high, which can be very annoying if you sold at the break of support.

TIP

This chart (see Figure 10-4) is an adaptation of one shown by Victor Sperandeo in *Trader Vic: Methods of a Wall Street* Master (John Wiley & Sons, Inc.). It's probably the most important chart in his book. First is the break of the support line. But instead of an inverted V-shaped downmove coming right afterward, the price tests both the highest high and a significant low along the upmove. It's only when it crosses under this previous significant low that you're 100 percent certain that the move is over. Sperandeo calls it the *1-2-3 method* for identifying a change in trend. Not every break of support looks like this, of course, but it's an excellent model, not least because it reminds you that trends hardly ever end and reverse in one fell swoop.

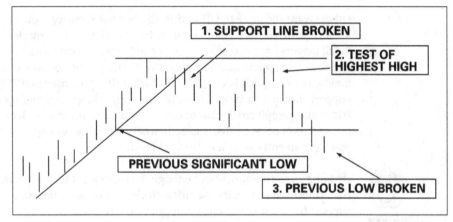

© John Wiley & Sons, Inc.

FIGURE 10-4:
Classic break
of support.

If you grasp the 1-2-3 concept, congratulations! You have just met the most irksome, vexatious phenomenon in technical analysis — the pullback. The *pullback* is usually characterized by minor countertrend or roughly sideways movement that occurs after a trendline breakout. The pullback is a symptom of *congestion,* aptly describing the market participants milling around like people on a crowded sidewalk trying to dodge one another and impeding progress in both directions as a result. Another term for a sideways price movement is *consolidation,* referring to market participants consolidating their ideas about the security being traded.

TIP

Congestion and consolidation describe the same thing — trendless prices trading in a range. Often the range is defined by a previous high or low. Consolidations often precede *and* follow a breakout. If you see a period of sideways price movement and can't find the trend, widen your chart to include more data and switch to a longer time frame (such as weekly). Chances are you are about to get a breakout. *Remember:* Nearly every technique in technical analysis pertains to taking advantage of trends to make a money gain. A congestive/consolidative/nontrending market offers no trend-following opportunities. Stop trading until you see the next trend. A true trend-follower is never in the market all the time.

Playing games with support and resistance lines

Support and resistance lines occur so often on charts (and so many people are aware of them), that to some extent they become self-fulfilling prophecies. A large number of people draw and respect the same lines. If they're holders of the security, they may defend the price by buying more at support, hoping to ward off a break of support that would force them to sell. They don't want to sell, for whatever reason, so they take action to prevent the chart event — breaking support — that would force them to sell.

Others want the price to fall so they can buy the security more cheaply, or to cover a short position. In some instances, the big players in a market know where the small players have placed their buy or sell orders, because as amateurs, they select the obvious support or resistance levels. The professionals can then pick off the amateurs for a quick buck. As I note earlier, the pros may punch the price under a support line just to spook the amateurs into selling. You end up going through a tricky and complicated train of thought whereby you don't place your order at an obvious level because that's exactly where the big guys expect you to — and then you miss an entry or exit at the best level.

REMEMBER

Drawing good trendlines isn't enough. You also want to study how often the crowd that trades your specific security chickens out at a resistance level or breaks support by a hair only to take the price up afterward.

Drawing Internal Trendlines

Wouldn't it be nice to know the true trendline? This line would reveal the hidden trendedness of the prices without at the same time alerting everybody and his brother to attack or defend specific levels.

Such a line does exist. It's a line that goes through the center of the price series rather than along its edges, like the support and resistance lines I describe earlier in this chapter. How do you draw a straight line through the center of each price bar? You can't, at least not by eye, because prices jump around and the centers of the bars never line up properly.

But scientists have a solution to jumpiness. They calculate a line that minimizes the distance from itself to each price close along the line. This is called *fitting*. The best-fit line is named the *linear regression line*, *linear* referring to *line* and *regression* referring to the mathematical calculation.

TIP

Drawing a linear regression line requires a complex statistical calculation, but relax — all charting software and websites come with the linear regression already built in. Look up the mathematical formula if you must, but spending time observing how it works on your charts is a more productive use of your time. You don't need to know how the line is calculated to be able to use it. You probably can't explain an auto transmission, either, but you can still drive your car.

Rules for drawing a linear regression

You get to choose your own rules. The obvious place to start the line is at a significant high or low in the recent past, usually the starting point of the current move. Ah, but what's the "recent past" and how am I defining "current move"? For most traders, the recent lowest low or highest high entails looking back a few weeks or months. I prefer to include two or more successively lower lows or higher highs as long as the slope of the line still contains a directional bias. I also generally start a linear regression line at the next bar after an abnormally big bar. I do this by eye, but "abnormally big" is a high-low range at least 35 to 50 percent bigger than the rest of the current bars. I'm looking for "standard," and therefore exclude what is nonstandard at the starting point.

The history check can be trickier than it sounds. Starting at the previous lowest low, a chart of orderly prices yields a nice linear regression line with prices clustered tightly around the line. The clustering tendency gives you comfort that the trend is a solid one and upcoming prices won't stray far from the line.

But as you go further back in price history and add more price data, the tight clusters start to spread out. The more time you add, the more comfort flies out the window.

And some securities have widely dispersed prices to begin with. You see a lot of outlier bars that seem to bear no relationship to the line. The line is still mathematically correct and the slope of the line may be identical to the orderly price chart, but the dispersion is telling you that you can't count on upcoming prices to be anywhere close to the line, let alone cling to it. So, if you're averse to risk, pick short time frames on which to draw linear regressions, or pick orderly price series, or both.

Where do you end a linear regression? Normally you end it at the current period's bar, or maybe one period before if today's bar is exceptional in some way. After all, you're trying to gauge where the current price is relative to a standard.

TIP

The linear regression doesn't contain embedded buy/sell trading rules but can be used in other ways. You may choose to trade only securities that have tight price clusters around a linear regression line or to reduce or close your position when tight clusters give way to scattered outliers.

You may see charts by self-appointed gurus that show a linear regression and advice that prices are *mean reverting* and exhibit a *central tendency,* meaning that a big variation away from the linear regression line will automatically correct back to the linear regression. This is nonsense. No reputable trading system features the linear regression alone as a trading tool.

Identifying trendedness

In Figure 10-5, the linear regression line doesn't actually go through the center of each price bar. In fact, some price bars are outliers fairly far away from the line. But if you look more closely, you can see that no other line gets you as close to Point A *and* to Point B at the same time. Only one linear regression exists for any set of prices on the chart. Despite its somewhat intimidating name, the linear regression should have you breathing a sigh of relief right now because nothing is subjective or judgmental about it. It's a scientific measure. Everybody gets the identical line if they're given the same chart and the same starting and ending points.

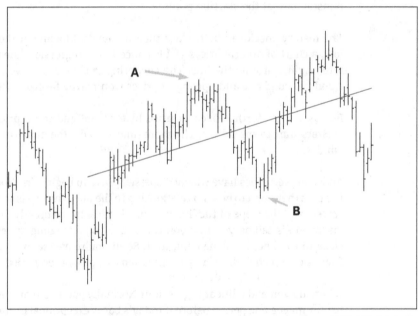

FIGURE 10-5:
Simple linear
regression.

© John Wiley & Sons, Inc.

REMEMBER

A linear regression is the true, pure trendline. This is wonderful news. If you accept the core concept of technical analysis, that a trend will continue in the same direction, at least for a while, then you can extend the true trendline and obtain a *forecast.* In some software packages, a linear regression extension is called exactly that — *a time-series forecast.* This tool is tremendously useful. You have created a high-probability forecast for the upcoming period that delivers perspective on what to expect.

In fact, you could dress up the linear regression to get a mathematically respectable forecast that is better than just extending the line. It goes by the intimidating name *autogressive integrated moving average,* or ARIMA, and fortunately for me, is beyond the scope of this chapter. But if you really, really like math, see Perry Kaufman's *Trading Systems and Methods* (John Wiley & Sons, Inc.).

Assuming you're using a simple extension of the linear regression line, if some self-appointed guru says that the price of Blue Widget stock is going from $5 to $10 in one month, you can test the claim by extending the line out one month at the same slope. Is the forecast even probable or is it hype? Unless the guru claims to have inside information or is predicting a big, fat news Event, it's hype. That's the good news.

The bad news is that the linear regression line can slope this way or that way or no way (horizontal), depending on where you start and stop drawing. If you take a V-shaped price series like the one in Figure 10-6 and draw a single linear regression line, you get . . . garbage. This chart shows two trends, and you need two linear regression lines to reflect that. It's common sense to observe that the less daylight between the line and the price points on the chart, the better the fit and the more likely it is that extending the line is a valid technique.

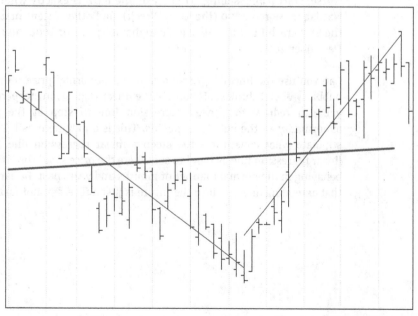

FIGURE 10-6:
Invalid linear
regression.

In other words, you can draw linear regression lines that are totally useless. They'll still be scientifically accurate in that they depict the best fit possible to the data, and everyone else will get the same result. However, they won't advance the cause of making a profit in the market or preventing a loss.

Using the linear regression

The linear regression doesn't take the place of support and resistance lines. It should be viewed as a supplementary, confirming indicator to identify the trend. If you select a good starting point, the linear regression delivers pure trend. The linear regression line may not contain embedded trading rules, but visually, the linear regression line is the most informative. You can see both trendedness and orderliness, and thus have a modicum of confidence that your trading plan isn't going to be turned upside down by mere noise.

Sometimes you can draw a linear regression line and it lands smack on top of a support or resistance line, or is parallel to it. Start cheering! It implies that the market players in this security are attuned to the true trend.

However, if you draw a support or resistance line whose slope varies dramatically from your linear regression line, one of them is wrong. In a similar vein, if the line has a very steep slope and this security never before had such a steep slope, you can deduce that the price movement is statistically abnormal. It's probably unsustainable and likely to come to a sad end when traders start taking profit, or worse, start panic-selling. This crash and burn is exactly what happened in the Nasdaq in March 2000 (the Tech Wreck), and other recent market collapses like the S&P crash in 2007–09, the Shanghai Surprise in 2008, and the S&P crash in December 2018.

Can you use the linear regression to detect abnormal price moves that are likely bubbles? Well, I think so. If you see the linear regression steepening dramatically, you can redraw the linear regression line to stop at the point where the abnormality — the bubble — begins. This is a judgment call. There is no rule to stipulate what constitutes too steep a linear regression line. Then extend the linear regression line by hand to see where the price *should* be if the price were still behaving in the normal manner of months and years past. Be careful to remember that extending any line into the future is just a forecast, not fact.

Chapter **11**

Transforming Channels into Forecasts

A straight-line trendline that extends into the future suggests where the price may go, but only in the general neighborhood. You expect future prices to cluster around a linear regression line, for example, but you don't always know how to think about the outliers. It's not realistic to try for a pinpoint forecast, but you can aim to draw a range of probable futures prices. *Range* refers to the high-low scope of prices over a number of periods, generally weeks and months.

In this chapter, I describe the straight-line channel and its forecasting capabilities. I show you how to build a straight-line channel forecast and outline how to interpret the information you see on the chart. I also talk about using pivot point analysis to draw horizontal support and resistance.

Diving into Channel-Drawing Basics

A *channel* is a pair of straight-line trendlines encasing a price series. It consists of one line drawn along the top of a price series and another line, parallel to the first, along the bottom of the price series.

The purpose of the channel is to train your eye to accept prices within its borders as *on the trend* and to detect prices outside its borders as *off-trend* or statistically abnormal. The channel is a wider measure of trending behavior than a single line. You deduce the trend is in place as long as prices remain within the channel. I describe several types of channels in the following sections.

The swing bar problem

How do you know when a high or low is obvious and the right place to start a trendline and thus a channel? You're looking for the significant high or low that's a turning point in price movement, often named a *swing bar*. In practice, the trend may continue for a few more bars after the highest high or lowest low — you don't always get a sharp, clear-cut reversal exactly at a single bar. But a few periods after the highest high or lowest low, you deduce from bar placement, tick placement, a pattern, or simply the absence of new highs or lows, that the move is over. This can be done only in hindsight, of course. Can you mistakenly identify a swing point? You bet.

If you look online for "swing bar," you'll find many methodologies for identifying a swing bar. You may begin to wonder if the swing bar isn't a unicorn — it doesn't exist. Net-net, you can't possibly hope to memorize every set of bars that could potentially constitute a swing low or swing high. The combinations and permutations that could qualify are almost without limit.

Channels organize your vision. You expect the resistance line to cap price rises (a *ceiling*) and the support line to provide a *floor* that prevents further price lows. The parallel lines tell you the maximum probable future price range. Note that word *probable*. Channels are visually compelling and can seduce you into thinking that the forecast range *must* occur. It's all too easy to start drawing channels and forget that they're only a forecast and terribly vulnerable to noise and events.

Drawing channels by hand

You may be astonished at how often you can draw a support-resistance channel on a real security. Here's how:

1. **Start by connecting the two lows at the lower left.**

   This is the support line. Notice that they're the two relative lows because a bar with a higher low comes in between.

2. **Extend that line with your cursor or the "extend line" command in your software into the future.**

3. **To form the top of the channel, you have to wait for the next relative high.**

   A relative high can be seen only after you get an intervening lower high (got that?). On the chart, the highest high is the last of three higher highs. You go back to the highest high and start a line parallel to the support line from it. This is the resistance line.

4. **Extend the resistance line into the future.**

Note that sometimes you later get a higher high and have to shift the entire resistance line up, keeping it parallel. Oddly, a high proportion of new highs stop at the old resistance line, even though some stop at the new resistance line, too. It's like having two equally valid resistance lines. To be on the safe side, consider the farther-away channel line as the more-important one. The same thing is true of a second, farther-away support line.

On the chart in Figure 11-1, the extension lines are gray. At the time they're first drawn, the extended lines are hypothetical support and hypothetical resistance. *Hypothetical* means, among other things, not proven.

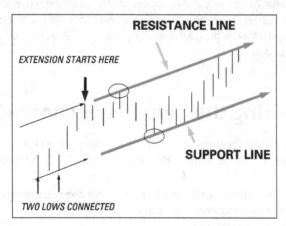

FIGURE 11-1:
A model channel.

© John Wiley & Sons, Inc.

REMEMBER

The lines stop being hypothetical and become *actual* support and resistance when the next high or low touches the extended line but doesn't break it, validating the extension process. The circles in Figure 11-1 mark where the next high and low occur in this price series — and they do occur at the hypothetical support and resistance lines. As with all support and resistance lines, the third touch is a confirmation point.

WHY ARE THE LINES PARALLEL?

When you draw a support line connecting a series of lows, you often see a parallel resistance line that mysteriously connects the highest highs. This is so common that most charting software programs have a standard command — "create parallel line" or "duplicate." No one knows why support and resistance lines are so often parallel. Here are a few possible explanations:

- Channel orderliness arises from an orderly trading crowd. Market participants know where the price is relatively high — at the top of the channel. They expect no more gains at this point. Die-hard buyers, in turn, see when the price is relatively cheap — down around the support line. They buy more, propelling the price upward.

- Many technical analysts perceive a cyclical quality to the ebb and flow of prices within a channel. Their trading plan relies on the security alternating between support and resistance. This often works as long as you don't project the price bouncing off support and resistance indefinitely. In other words, don't get cocky.

- Humans have an innate need to impose order and patterns. Parallel lines don't always appear, of course, but they appear often enough that observers speak of channels with a certain air of authority. This kind of parallel support and resistance channel is usually what the commentator has in mind. Beware — channels aren't inevitable or divinely inspired.

Considering the benefits of channels

When you use straight lines to represent a range, you get a chart that's easy to read. Your eye fills in the blanks. The benefits include the following:

>> Straight-line channels imply absolute limits that give you comfort and the sense that you know where you stand.

>> When a new price touches the channel top or bottom, but then retreats, named a *retracement*, you believe that the channel limits are correctly drawn and valid — and will likely work next time, too. As I explain in Chapter 10, the more often a price touches a support or resistance line but doesn't cross it, the more reliable you can consider the line to be.

>> If a channel line is broken, you feel certain that something significant has happened to the perception of the security by its market participants. Violation of the channel alerts you to changing conditions and the need to consider making a trading decision.

Delving into the drawbacks of channels

REMEMBER

On an orderly price series, the straight-line channel is fairly narrow. But if your chart contains a disorderly price move where prices jump around all over the place, the channel is so wide that you can't judge what is usual or normal.

When you draw a channel so wide or so narrow that only you can see it, you can't expect other traders to respond to it. To forecast a price range is really to forecast the probable collective behavior of the people who trade the security. The validity of a channel depends on other traders in the same security seeing the same thing. When everyone can see the same lines, a consensus builds as to what constitutes breaking the lines.

Channeling to make gains and avoid losses

REMEMBER

With confidence that the channel broadly describes the trend, you can

>> Buy near the channel bottom and sell near the channel top — over and over again, as long as the channel lasts.

>> Estimate your future gain. If the width of the channel is $5 and you bought near a support line, your maximum probable gain over the next few days is about $5 — as long as the channel remains in place and you're able to sell near the resistance line. This is more useful than you may think at first, because

- It's a sanity check. You can't reasonably expect a gain that would call for a price far outside the channel.

- It's a reality check. You can use the channel to evaluate a forecast made by someone else. If the forecaster is calling for a price far outside the channel, you have grounds to question the forecast.

>> Calculate your maximum loss. Regardless of where you bought the security, you know that when a price bar breaks the bottom support line of the channel, the channel is no longer valid. The trend is likely over. This is the point at which you want to sell. And you don't have to wait for the actual breakout. You can place a stop-loss order with your broker at the breakout level.

Riding the Regression Range

You can construct a more scientific set of parallel lines by drawing channel lines around the linear regression line. As I describe in Chapter 10, the *linear regression* is the line that minimizes the distance from itself and every close on the chart. It's the true, pure trendline, and thus the channel built on it, named the *standard error channel* (also called the *linear regression channel*) is the true trend channel. You can calculate the standard error by hand, but it's laborious. Software is less prone to error and a lot faster.

You use a channel based on the linear regression line the same way that you use a hand-drawn support and resistance channel, as I discuss in the following sections. By projecting the lines out into the future, you get a forecast of the future price range, and you deem a significant breakout of a channel line as ending the trend.

REMEMBER

Hand-drawn support and resistance channels are formed from lows and highs and thus don't have a center line. In the linear regression channel, you start with the center linear regression line and build the channel from the inside out, so to speak.

Introducing the standard error

The *standard error,* sometimes called the *line of best fit,* measures how closely the prices cluster around your linear regression line. Most chartists use two standard errors, which results in a channel top and channel bottom that enclose a high percentage (95 percent) of the highs and lows. An extreme high or low constitutes a bigger error away from the trendline than 95 percent of the other highs and lows. A variation of the standard error channel was devised by Gilbert Raff, author of *Trading the Regression Channel: Defining and Predicting Stock Price Trends* (Equis International), adding an additional "error" away from the linear regression and thus widening the channel.

Drawing a linear regression channel

How true the linear regression and its channel turn out to be depends on where you start drawing. You start a linear regression channel at an obvious low or high, draw a channel line from there to a second relative low or high, and then extend it out. The parallel lines come along for the ride.

REMEMBER

As with the hand-drawn support and resistance channel lines, you know that you've drawn your channel line correctly when a third relative high or low makes a touch of the line but doesn't cross it. Sometimes the obvious turning point high or low occurs within a previous channel that has been broken and discarded: Go back to the turning point bar and use it as the starting point for the new channel.

Figure 11-2 shows a nicely uptrending security with two channels. Look at the shorter one first. I start it at the lowest low and let the software do the drawing to the bar after the next relative low. Then I stop drawing and extend the lines by hand, using dotted lines to mark them as hypothetical.

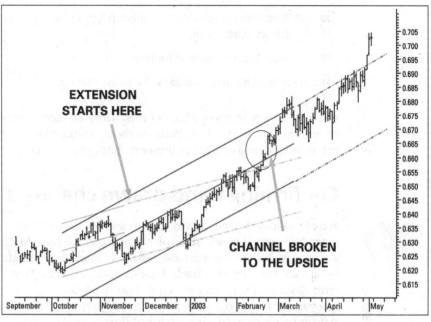

EXTENSION
STARTS HERE

CHANNEL BROKEN
TO THE UPSIDE

September   October   November   December   2003   February   March   April   May

FIGURE 11-2:
Two standard
error channels.

© John Wiley & Sons, Inc.

It isn't until three months later that prices break out of the channel — to the upside. Oh, oh. A breakout always means something. When it's a breakout in the same direction as the trend, you start worrying that it may be a blowout breakout, as I describe later in this chapter in the section "Driving faster is always risky." Whatever it turns out to be, you still need to discard the old channel for analysis purposes. In this case, I left it on the chart.

Now I draw a new linear regression and its channel (the darker lines on the chart) from the same lowest-low starting point and keep drawing until just after a new relative high appears. I know it's a relative high because it's breaking the top of the channel and followed by a lower high. I stop drawing at that relative high and extend the channel lines out, as before. Notice that the price does it again! It breaks out of the top of the channel a second time.

REMEMBER

As a practical matter, every time a price breaks a channel line, you face a higher risk. In this instance, if you already own the security, the risk is in your favor — but it's still considered risk solely because uncertainty is now higher. The channel defines what is normal, and any foray outside the channel isn't normal. What does this breakout in Figure 11-2 mean?

>> The latest high prices can mark a third shift to a new, more steeply sloping channel yet to be drawn.

>> A blowout breakout may be forming.

>> The price series may subside back into the channel.

You have no way to know which of these three outcomes is the most likely from the information on the chart. You may choose to exit on every channel line break-out, or you can add another indicator to guide your decision.

Confirming hand-drawn channels

TIP

You can validate a hand-drawn support and resistance channel by superimposing a standard error channel on top of it. Starting at the same low (or high) point that you used to draw the support and resistance lines, draw the standard error chan-nel and see how closely it tracks your hand-drawn lines. Sometimes the standard error channel falls exactly on top of your hand-drawn lines, which is validation that you drew them right and they accurately represent the trend. More often, the standard error channel has a slightly different slope.

Trading a security that moves neatly within its channel, especially a validated double channel (hand-drawn *and* standard error), reduces the stress of trading.

Sizing up the special features of the linear regression channel

You use the linear regression channel the same way you use a hand-drawn channel — to estimate the future range and to determine when a trend has ended with a breakout of one of the channel lines.

The linear regression has a few special characteristics, though. For instance, you want to know the following:

>> The linear regression doesn't encompass every price extreme in a series, but rather a very high percentage of them. Therefore, some price bars will always break the channel lines without invalidating the channel, unlike the situation in a hand-drawn channel.

>> You can adjust the width of the channel lines by applying the Raff version previously described or by instructing your software to use three errors rather than the usual two. A three-error channel encloses 99 percent of the prices. This usually makes the channel too wide though and blurs your vision of the trend.

>> The linear regression is self-adjusting. Every time you update the channel, your software includes the new day's data and modifies both the linear regression line and the slope and width of the channel accordingly. It's therefore a bit of an odd duck — a set of straight lines that isn't fixed, at least until you fix it by halting the updating process.

>> In order to see a breakout to confirm a trend change, you have to stop drawing at some point. Otherwise, the channel simply adjusts to the new data and you never get a breakout. Don't forget; it automatically incorporates all the price data you put into it. Garbage in, garbage out.

TIP

To determine if your channel is stable, you can draw new channels on top of your existing forecast channel. You begin at the same starting point but continue the true channel to the current day. If the width and the slope of the fresh true channel are about the same as your forecast channel, it's stable and thus reliable. A stable channel implies that the forecast embedded in the farther-out lines is probably pretty good.

Discovering the drawbacks of linear regression channels

Linear regression channels are more difficult to work with than hand-drawn support and resistance; you have to exercise more judgment, and it's more of an art. Some of the complications are

>> **Not a majority process:** A large number of people draw support and resistance lines and channels, but not everyone draws linear regression channels, although analysts have seen them gaining in popularity over the last 20 years. A big part of why technical analysis works is that many people are observing the same thing and acting on it, like breakouts.

>> **May not stand alone:** You can draw a very large number of channels on the same chart, and each of them is right, mathematically speaking. Often you draw one channel from an obvious starting point but after fixing it and extending it out into the future, you find that you can draw another channel from a nearby starting point that points to a different outcome. I call this *dueling channels*, and it always occurs at trend turning points.

>> **Not really scientific:** The linear regression channel is scientific in the sense that the software calculates it to enclose a preponderance of prices, but that doesn't mean that you started it or stopped it at the ideal spot, or that extending the channel delivers a good forecast. The mathematical principle isn't subjective, but your application is always subjective. Consider that your car works on scientific principles of internal combustion, but that doesn't necessarily make you a good driver.

Dealing with Breakouts

REMEMBER

The *breakout* is one of the most important concepts in technical analysis. It's a direct, graphic representation that something happened to change the market's sentiment toward the security. In the simplest terms, a breakout implies that a trend is over, at least in its present form. After a breakout, the price can go up, down, or sideways, but it seldom resumes at exactly the same level and rate of change you had before the breakout.

A breakout must always be respected, but you want to be sure it's authentic, which is what the following sections are all about. As I mention in Chapter 10 and elsewhere, because so many traders draw support and resistance lines, there's always some wiseguy in the market who tries to push the price through the lines. In an uptrend that's retracing downward, he tries to break the support line and panic holders into selling. He may believe in the uptrend; he's just trying to get a lower price for himself. In a downtrend, he's the joker who buys so much that the price puts in a new high and a close higher than on previous days, which scares the pants off sellers, who then cover their shorts and propel the price higher. In addition, a breakout can be error or noise.

Distinguishing between false breakouts and the real thing

You often see a tiny breakout and don't know how to evaluate it. Say your support line is at precisely $10 and the low of the price bar is $9.50. Is that a legitimate breakout or just an accident? Sometimes you have to accept imperfection and live with ambiguity. The channel lines are an estimate, not a certainty.

Or sometimes you get a minor break of a channel line that lasts one or two days but then the price returns back inside its channel and performs just as before. The breakout was a *false breakout*, which is a breach of a trendline that then fails to deliver the expected additional moves in the same direction (see Figure 11-3).

To call it false is misleading, because the price bar unmistakably breaks the trend-line. What's false is the conclusion you draw from it — that the trend is over.

In Figure 11-3, the channel does define the high-low trading range, after all. Sometimes you have to accept one or two violations of your lines. The challenge, of course, is that you don't know right away whether a breakout is meaningful or just a random outcome. How do you know which it is?

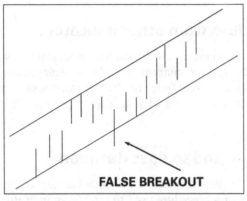

© John Wiley & Sons, Inc.

FIGURE 11-3:
False breakout.

The first line of defense

Your first line of defense is the configuration of the breakout bar. A simple judgment is to see whether the breakout is a violation of the channel line by the *close*, and not just the high or low. As I explain in Chapter 6, the close is the bar component that best summarizes sentiment. A high or a low can be a random aberration, or noise. The close is less likely to be random.

Verifying with volume

Breakouts are often accompanied by a change in volume, usually an easily noticed higher level. Consulting volume for confirmation is in keeping with interpreting events on the chart in terms of supply and demand. You can verify that the breakout isn't random by seeing an equivalent change in volume:

>> **Increase in volume:** Extraordinarily high volume on one or two days is named a *volume spike* and often accompanies the end of a strong trend, either a rally or a crash. Buying and selling interest is frenzied.

>> **Decrease in volume:** If volume declines steeply after holding steady at about the same level over the life of your trend, demand is falling off but so is selling interest. You don't necessarily know what falling volume means, but it may foreshadow a breakout. All the people who wanted to sell have done so, and the people still holding an inventory aren't willing to sell at the current price. It's like a logjam. It will be broken up when either the bullish camp or the bearish camp takes the initiative and causes a new high or new low, with accompanying higher volume.

Looking for clues from other indicators

While the breakout is a powerful technical indicator, you still want as much confirmation as you can get. Momentum and relative strength are useful to confirm or deny that a breakout is real (refer to Chapter 13). A loss of momentum and/or relative strength in an uptrend almost always precedes a downside channel breakout.

Size matters — and so does duration

You can use a filter to estimate whether a breakout is meaningful or can be ignored. A *filter* is a formula or a procedure used to modify an indicator. In this instance, the indicator is the break of the channel line. A filter can modify the amount or duration of the breakout. Here's how you do it:

>> You add some percentage of the total range to the channel line. You stipulate that to constitute a real break of the channel line, the new high or low must surpass this extra amount.

If the channel is $5 wide, you can specify that a price high or low has to violate the line by more than 5 percent (or 25 cents). Anything less wouldn't be a real breakout. Where does 5 percent come from? Why not 10 percent or 20 percent? Either one may be effective, or neither. You need to experiment with each security to see whether it has a habit of breaking its lines by this amount or that amount. You can also specify that the *close* has to break the line by *x* percent to qualify as a real breakout. In either case, the result is a new channel line that is a little farther out, effectively widening the channel.

>> To modify the duration, you can specify that you're willing to accept one price bar violating the channel line, but not two. Or perhaps two violations, but not three. Again, you have to experiment with each security to determine its habits. Also, you can combine the duration rule with the close rule and specify that the close plus *x* percent beyond the line for *y* number of days is the sign of a true breakout. I happen to like 20 percent and two or three days, but those may be totally wrong for your security and your risk profile.

WARNING

Experienced technical analysts warn against making size and duration filters too complex and fancy, for a number of reasons:

>> **Rules count.** The breakout principle is a powerful and well-known concept. A lot of other traders in your security are likely to heed a breakout in a black-and-white way. They *always* exit on a downside breakout of a support line by the low, for example. They feel that a breakout is a breakout, and traders shouldn't try to second-guess it.

>> **One size doesn't fit all.** You can only know that 10 percent is the right amount to put into your filter if 10 percent was the amount that worked in the past on this security. Each security has its own habits, or rather, the people who trade it have their collective habits. In one security, the best filter may consistently be 10 percent, and in another it may consistently be 40 percent. (In the 1930s and 1940s, a filter of 3 percent was standard.) No single correct filter exists for every security under all circumstances. You only know whether a filter is usable by testing different filters on the price history of each security, one by one.

>> **Blending works only with coffee.** The orderliness of your security can change without warning. During some periods, a 5 percent filter may be the most effective, but later, volatility can increase and you'd need a 10 percent filter to capture all the price highs and lows that really do belong inside the same channel. Looking back over historical data to find the best filter has an enormous flaw: Chances are that you'll come up with a blended percentage filter that's too small for an orderly move and too big for a volatile one. And if today is breakout day, you don't know how volatile the upcoming move is going to be.

Putting breakouts into context

A genuine breakout means that your trend channel is now defunct. You need to discard it. To verify that the breakout truly ended the trend, you need to evaluate it in the *context* of the general volatility characteristics of the security itself.

Neatness counts

REMEMBER

As a general rule, a breakout that occurs in the course of an *orderly* trend is more meaningful than a breakout that occurs in a *disorderly* trend (see Chapter 14 for more on orderliness). Orderliness isn't a word you see very often. Instead, the word *volatility* is used, referring to the extent of variation away from a central reference point (like an average). You should see low volatility as orderliness and high volatility as disorderliness.

The more orderly your price bars, the more reliable your channels are. A breakout of an orderly channel is more likely to be the real thing than a breakout of a high-volatility (disorderly) channel. If you choose to trade a disorderly security, you must be able to tolerate a high number of false breakouts — and modify your filters accordingly.

Figure 11-4 illustrates this point. In the first chart, the security is orderly — prices line up neatly within the channel. The breakout is obvious. In the second channel, the security isn't so tidy — prices jump around a lot. The breakout bar is exactly the same size as the orderly channel breakout bar, but in the disorderly price series, you can't be sure that it's authentic. The people who trade this security are accustomed to big bars and big jumps. You can see that it broke the support line, but perhaps others won't find it meaningful.

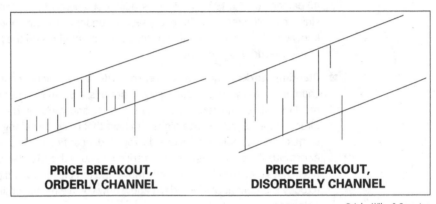

FIGURE 11-4:
Orderly security versus disorderly security.

PRICE BREAKOUT, ORDERLY CHANNEL

PRICE BREAKOUT, DISORDERLY CHANNEL

© John Wiley & Sons, Inc.

If your security generates a lot of false breakouts and they make you nervous, find another security. Seek out software and sites that scan a collection of securities for the low volatility candidates.

TIP

Transition from orderly to disorderly (and back)

When a price series morphs from an orderly to a disorderly mode, the transformation is almost always accompanied by a breakout and a change in volume. Weirdly, a shift the other way (from disorderly to orderly) also foreshadows a breakout. When prices shift from disorderly to orderly, the sharp decrease in volatility warns you that a breakout is impending; buyers and sellers alike don't know what to do, so they do nothing. On the day of the breakout and in the day or two following, you see a big increase in volume.

Driving faster is always risky

You also want to know the context of the breakout in terms of where the prices were located within the channel just before the breakout. The usual breakout is in the opposite direction of the prevailing trend.

But sometimes you see prices pressing against the top or bottom of the channel line, which can lead to a breakout in the *same direction* as the trend. In other words, higher volatility can mean an acceleration of an existing trend. You often see a breakout can be to the upside in an uptrend as well as to the downside in a downtrend.

Figure 11-5 illustrates an upside breakout in an uptrend. It's still a breakout, and you should expect that it still marks a change in the trend even though it is in the same direction. The acceleration of an existing trend may simply signal a steepening of the trend as the crowd develops enthusiasm for the security — but it can also occur near the end of a trend. It's sometimes called a *blowout* (or *blowoff*) *top* or a blowout bottom. In other words, an upside breakout in an uptrend is often a warning of a *downside* breakout to come later, counterintuitive as that seems at first.

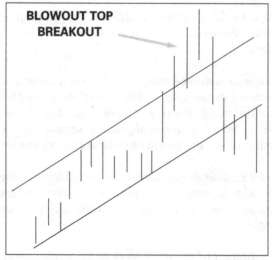

FIGURE 11-5:
Upside breakout in an uptrend.

© John Wiley & Sons, Inc.

How can such a pattern come about? Easy. The crowd becomes overheated with greed to buy a security that is rising with tremendous force or overwhelmed by fear to dump a security that is declining with great momentum. At some point, everyone who was going to buy has bought. Because these are traders who bought only to get a fast profit, when the rise slows down and a lower high or a lower low appears, these buyers exit in a horde. (For a discussion of a lower high together with a lower low in an uptrend, see Chapter 6.) By selling a lot of the security in a very short period of time, the market has an oversupply, and just like the price of tomatoes falling to ten cents in late August, buyers can command a low price.

The same thing happens when a downmove exhausts itself. Everybody who was going to sell has sold. Supply is now limited. Anyone who wants to buy has to start bidding the price up until he induces a longer-term holder of the security to part with it.

TIP

An upside breakout in an uptrend is a buy signal but with a short shelf life. More than likely you know the phrase "buy low and sell high," but trading guru Larry Williams advises you can also "buy high and sell higher."

Examining Pivot Point Support and Resistance Channel

What do you do when you stop getting higher highs (in an uptrend) or lower lows (in a downtrend)? In other words, the price is still within its channel but now it's moving sideways.

REMEMBER

The pause in movement may be temporary, but the sideways action can also be a warning that forward momentum is gone. From this you may deduce that if you're going to take profit, now is the time. The sideways action may also imply that a breakout in the opposite direction is impending, so now you need a benchmark to figure out which it is *before* it gets to directional support and resistance lines.

One technique for dealing with sideways moves within a channel is to draw horizontal support and resistance lines off pivot points. Technical traders use the term *pivot point* in many different ways, and like swing bar, *pivot point* can have many different definitions.

One standard definition of the pivot point is the *median price*, or the numerical average of the high, low, and close. This is probably the most universally applied definition. But some analysts define the pivot points as the center bar of three bars (or more) where the center bar contains the highest high or lowest low. Other traders cook up yet more definitions.

Calculating the first zone of support and resistance

The logic of the pivot point is that when a trend pauses, you need a breakout that's a significant distance from the median price to decide whether the old trend will resume or will reverse. Starting with the median price, you add a factor to get upside resistance and subtract a factor to get downside support.

To calculate the first (inner) line of resistance, multiply the pivot point value by two and, from that number, subtract the low of the pivot day. This is named R1. To calculate the first (inner) line of support, or S1, multiply the pivot value by two and, from that number, subtract the high of the pivot day. This procedure sounds like a lot of arithmetic, but don't sweat it. It's easy enough to do in a spreadsheet or by hand, and many trading platforms and websites offer it as a standard option. A particularly good one for FX is at www.earnforex.com. Plus, the procedure itself is quite sensible — you use a multiple of the median price to estimate a range going forward that subtracts the high and the low to yield a norm. Any price higher or lower would be an extreme. If the upcoming price breaks the horizontal support and resistance lines calculated this way, the direction of the breakout is your clue that the trend is truly over.

You can create a series of pivot support and resistance lines according to these formulas or some variation of them:

Pivot Point = (High *plus* Close *plus* Low) *divided by* 3

Resistance Level 1 (R1) = (2 *times* Pivot Point) *minus* Previous Low
Resistance Level 2 (R2) = (Pivot Point *minus* S1) *plus* R1
Resistance Level 3 (R3) = (Pivot Point *minus* S2) *plus* R2

Support Level 1 (S1) = (2 *times* Pivot Point) *minus* Previous High
Support Level 2 (S2) = Pivot Point *minus* (R1 *minus* S1)
Support Level 3 (S3) = Pivot Point *minus* (R2 *minus* S2)

In Figure 11-6, R3 is very close to the highest high, and S3, while higher than the recent lowest low, meets the hand-drawn support line connecting two lows. Pivot point analysis became popular because, advocates say, by projecting out a reasonable range to the next few days, you can easily see a breakout, and pivot points are therefore predictive instead of lagging, like every other indicator. This is not, strictly speaking, accurate. For one thing, there is no such thing as a leading indicator. All indicators are based on past price performance, and they all lag. Moreover, any band or channel has predictive value in the sense that upcoming prices, if they are normal, will remain within the band or channel and a violation of the channel top or bottom constitutes a breakout. What is valuable about pivot points is when many market participants are looking at the same lines, you can expect price movement at exactly those lines.

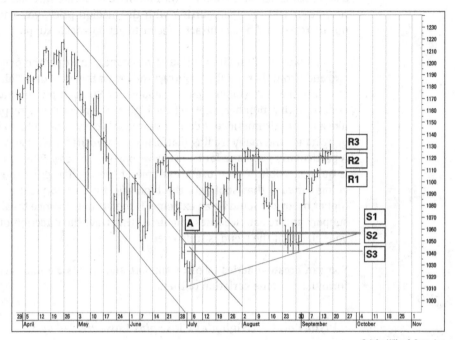

© John Wiley & Sons, Inc.

FIGURE 11-6:
Pivot point support and resistance.

Using pivot support and resistance

You can use pivot support and resistance all by itself, and many day traders do. You can also add other indicators like the two moving average crossover (see Chapter 12). In the case I present in Figure 11-7, if you had bought at Point A, you would set your target at R1 if you're averse to risk, R2 if you're an optimist, and R3 if you're swinging at every ball. Note that a test of a previous high is commonplace in a bounce off a low. If you're able to go short, you may sell at R3 and target a gain to S3, which conveniently meets the hand-drawn support line.

What's important about the pivot-based support and resistance lines is that they effectively outline a period of activity where traders don't know the trend. Bulls try to make a new high and get only a few pennies' worth. Bears try to make a new low but fail to get a significant lower low.

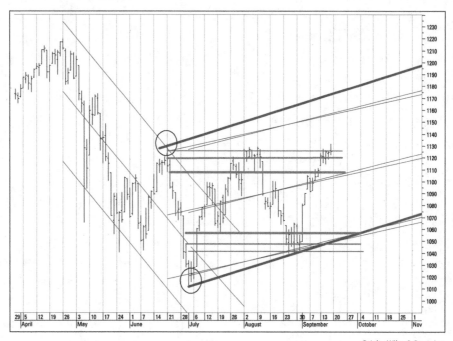

FIGURE 11-7:
Pivot point levels overlaid with a standard error channel.

In Figure 11-7, you can see two standard error channels overlaid on the same pivot point chart as in Figure 11-6. The first channel is drawn from the intermediate high in the topmost oval, and the second channel is drawn from the lowest low in the bottommost oval. Both channels slope upward, suggesting they're a credible identification of the direction, and both are near the hand-drawn support line. This evidence certainly suggests that an uptrend has formed, and yet the moves are choppy and failing to make new highs or new lows. It's a range-trading market, and the up-sloping standard error channel could be just wishful thinking. In contrast, the pivot-based support and resistance channel offers hands-on, specific places to buy and sell whether the trend uptrend is the real deal or not.

Like all technical indicators, the popularity of pivot points waxes and wanes. Not every software package contains pivots as a standard indicator, although you may be able to create them by yourself. In a nontrending (sideways) market, pivot lines may do the trick to identify a significant breakout. The downside is that your chart is cluttered with a bunch of horizontal lines.

4
Dynamic Analysis

Use dynamic moving averages that smooth out price moves and reveal trendedness.

Apply acceleration and deceleration in the rate of price change — momentum — to get confirmation of trendedness and advance notice of trend endings.

Incorporate volatility in your thinking in the form of the Bollinger Band, another dynamic way to judge and predict trendedness.

Strip away time from your vision of the chart to get a picture of underlying structures in price moves with point-and-figure charting and other methods that show pure trendedness.

Examine how to combine techniques to become a systematic trader operating on hard evidence.

Step into the universe of cycle theories that have the power to deliver perspective and a bird's-eye view of the big picture beyond the immediacy of indicators.

Take a close look at the newest popular technical methodology, ichimoku, combining moving averages, a dollop of momentum, a new way to measure volatility, and a forecast of the futures price range projected into the future.

Chapter **12**

Using Dynamic Lines

Prices don't move in straight lines. To make a more dynamic (and realistic) indicator, you want lines that move along with the price move. Enter the moving average.

The moving average is the workhorse of technical analysis. Most traders start out in technical analysis with moving averages, and some never see a need to look at any other technique. The charts accompanying most commentary usually contain moving averages, despite some whippersnappers dismissing averages as "old school" because moving averages lag. Well, all indicators lag to some extent. Indicators are constructed from past prices and can hardly do anything but lag.

A *moving average* is an arithmetic method of smoothing price numbers so that you can see and measure a trend. A straight line is a good visual organizing device, but a dynamic line — the moving average — more accurately describes what's really going on. In addition, you don't need to choose starting and ending points, removing that aspect of subjectivity, although choosing how many periods to put in your moving averages is subjective. In this chapter, I discuss several different ways you can calculate and use moving averages to get buy/sell trading signals.

 WARNING

Moving averages are *trend-following,* and so are all indicators that use them. Be careful not to attribute a forecasting capability to the moving average. The moving average is a lagging indicator — it can still rise after a giant fall.

Introducing the Simple Moving Average

More than likely you know what an *average* is — you measure ten of something, add up the measurements, and divide by ten. To make the average move, you drop the first day's data from 10 days back and add today's to keep the day-count constant at ten. You can assume that all moving averages use the close unless specified otherwise. For example, the moving averages in ichimoku charts use the midpoint price, not the close (refer to Chapter 18 for more discussion about ichimoku charts).

All technical analysis software offers moving average choices. Before PCs, recalculating the moving average every day was a chore. In fact, a preference for the 10-day average started in the 1930s, because it's easy to calculate by hand (plus it measures two weeks), and it remains popular today. Figure 12-1 displays a 10-day simple moving average.

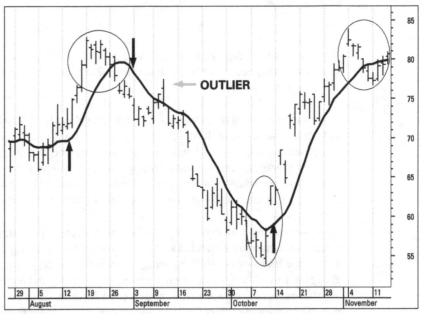

FIGURE 12-1:
Simple moving average.

© John Wiley & Sons, Inc.

Right off the bat, you can see that the moving average clings to the prices and represents their movements better than a straight line and, at the same time, smooths away the occasional erratic price. You almost stop seeing outliers after you draw the moving average on a chart.

A moving average is a visual aid to help you identify a trend. Because the average contains data that is x number of days old, like the tenth day in the past in a 10-day moving average, the average is dragging price history along with it. As the number rises, you know the newer prices must be higher than the prices were nine and ten days ago.

Starting with the crossover rule

When the price is moving upward or downward, so is the moving average line. Because the moving average lags, the price crosses the average after a turning point. At the V-shaped bottom in Figure 12-1, for example, prices are below the line until the gap (ellipse), and then prices cross above the line.

The *crossover trading rule* states that you buy at the point where the price crosses above the moving average line and sell at the point where it falls below the moving average line. In practice, you execute the trades the next day at the open.

You can see that the moving average on Figure 12-1 succeeded in capturing the trends. The crossovers captured the trend reversals, too. The result is buying at lows and selling at highs. The moving average crossover rule generates a profit. What could be better? Right about now, you may be tempted to shout "Eureka! I have discovered a systematic, objective trading system."

Not so fast. For one thing, the price doesn't always obediently stay above the moving average after an upside crossover (or below the moving average after a downside crossover). Refer to the price bars on Figure 12-1 marked Outlier. First is a close over the moving average and then the next bar is almost entirely above the moving average. An *outlier* is just what it sounds like — a data point that lies far off the trendline represented by the moving average. This particular chart is tidy — it has only a pair of outliers. Usually you see a lot more.

If you use the crossover rule to buy and sell a security every time the close crosses the moving average, you get a lot of buy/sell signals that reverse in fairly short order, as this one does. In this figure, you don't know at the time that the outliers are abnormal. For all you know, the crossover above the moving average is a genuine indication of a reversal. You know only after the price resumes the down-move that they were outliers.

Table 12-1 shows the gains and losses following the moving average crossover trading rule. Notice that I include the short side, which is selling something you don't own in the expectation that you'll be able to buy it later at a lower price. To sell short is only to reverse the normal order of the buy/sell equation. Usually it's commodity traders who can easily sell short, but even if you trade buy-only in equities and never sell short, calculating total profitability accurately is important when you evaluate a trading rule like the moving average crossover rule. For one thing, a rule that applies equally well to downmoves as to upmoves is more likely to be correct in all cases. For another, the end of a short sale may be the start of a purchase trade.

TABLE 12-1   Hypothetical Profit from the Simple Moving Average Crossover Rule

No. of Days	Action	Price	Crossover Profit	Buy-and-Hold
19 days	Buy	$70.61	$5.39	$70.61
	Sell	$76.00		
14 days	Sell	$76.00	($.40)	
	Buy	$76.40		
2 days	Buy	$76.40	($4.90)	
	Sell	$71.50		
28 days	Sell	$71.50	$9.50	
	Buy	$62.00		
38 days	Buy	$62.00	$16.50	$78.50
	Sell	$78.50		
Total			$26.09 (37%)	$7.89 (11%)

To evaluate a trading technique, including moving averages, you judge its effectiveness on the basis of its profitability from identifying trends going in both directions.

If you traded every crossover signal as shown in Table 12-1, the return is $26.09 on starting capital of $70.61, or 37 percent in less than one year. This gain is more than three times higher than simply buying at the beginning of the period and holding to the end. But in the process of trading the crossovers, you take two losses caused by the outliers.

This profitability exercise assumes a policy of *stop-and-reverse*, which means you close out one trade and put on another in the opposite direction at the same time and at the same price. This method is the conventional way to calculate the profitability of a trading rule, at least the first time around. Later you may adjust your entry and exit rules, as I discuss in the section "Filtering out whipsaws" section later in this chapter.

Dealing with the dreaded whipsaw

A buy/sell signal that's wrong (in hindsight) is called a *false signal* instead of a false breakout, although in principle it's the same as a false breakout of straight line trendlines. In moving average work, the false signal is a crossover that reverses within a few days, like the outliers in Figure 12-1. False signals usually reverse fairly quickly, putting you back in the trade in the right direction, but in the meanwhile, you take a loss, called a *whipsaw loss. Whipsaw* refers to the whipping action of the price quickly moving through the moving average in both directions, resulting in a series of back-and-forth trades. Whipsaws occur in even the best-behaved trend and are common in a sideways market.

REMEMBER

Whipsaws have a pernicious effect on your profit and loss statement in two ways:

>> When trading a trend-following technique like the moving average crossover, you make most of your gains by riding big trends, and you accept that gains are going to be reduced by the occasional whipsaw at reversal points, sideways periods, and any spiky outlier. But if your big trends also contain whipsaws, you end up *overtrading,* which is to make a lot of trades for only a small net gain or loss.

>> Overtrading almost always results in net losses because on every trade you have to pay brokerage commissions and fees. In all the cases in this chapter, I'm conveniently not subtracting commissions and fees, but remember that they reduce profits and raise losses in real life.

Filtering out whipsaws

Instead of using the crossover of price and moving average alone to generate a buy/sell signal, you can set up additional tests, called *filters.* If the crossover passes the filter tests, chances are it's a valid buy/sell signal and not a flash in the pan. Filters come in several varieties, and you can apply any or all of them to reduce the number of trades. Note that filters may delay entry and exit to an already-lagging indicator and thus reduce total gains. Increasing the lag is a fairly high price to reduce whipsaw losses, but if you're seriously averse to loss, a filter may be just the ticket.

Consider the following filters:

>> **Time:** The close has to remain above (or below) the moving average for an additional *x* number of periods after the crossover date.

>> **Extent:** The price has to surpass the moving average numerical value by *x* percent of the price or *x* percent of some other measure, such as the trading range of the past *y* days. A fancy version specifies the price has to surpass the

moving average by a factor based on the standard deviation of the recent range (yikes).

>> **Volume:** The crossover has to be accompanied by a significant rise in volume. Note that volume is tricky in this context, because an initial big move, including a gap move, can take place on low volume, and the big volume comes later.

>> **Extreme sentiment:** In an uptrend crossover, the low has to surpass the moving average and not just the close; in a downtrend, the high has to be under the moving average, and not just the close.

Using the moving average level rule

Instead of looking at the crossover, you can call the end of an uptrend when the moving average *level* today is less than the moving average yesterday, and you call the end of a downtrend when the moving average today is higher than yesterday's. The moving average level rule usually calls the end of a trend earlier than the crossover, although not always.

REMEMBER

Here's proof the moving average always lags the price action. In Figure 12-1, look at the prices and moving average in the left-hand ellipse. From the peak close, it takes the price six days to cross below the moving average — and *ten* days for the value of the moving average to be lower than the day before. By the time the moving average puts in a lower value than the day before, the price has fallen from $82.49 to $75.38, or by 8.6 percent.

But despite giving up 8.6 percent from the highest close while you wait for the moving average to catch up with prices, to trade *this* stock by using *this* indicator during *this* period would have been profitable. (See the "Fixing lag" section in this chapter for more information.)

The black arrows on the chart in Figure 12-1 mark the buy/sell entry and exit points using the moving average level rule. You buy and sell at the open the day after the moving average meets the rule. Table 12-2 shows the profit you make by applying the rule. Your gain is $43.07 on an initial capital stake of $71.05, or 61 percent, compared to 14 percent if you buy on the first date and account for the gain on the last date.

Accounting for the gain is what *mark-to-market* means in Table 12-2. Cash in the bank from closed positions, named *realized gain*, is the main way to keep score in trading, but mark-to-market is the way to keep score on positions that are still open. It means to apply today's closing price to your position to see how much it's worth in cash terms, even though you didn't actually exit the position today. Mark-to-market gains are named *unrealized*, and it's a good phrase, meaning that the gain is only an accounting convention. Needless to say, a mark-to-market valuation is valid only until the next market price becomes available.

TABLE 12-2   Hypothetical Profit from the Moving Average Level Rule

No. of Days	Action	Price	Level Rule Profit	Buy-and-Hold
22 days	Purchase	$71.05	$7.19	$71.05
	Sale	$78.24		
42 days	Sale	$78.24	$16.70	
	Purchase	$61.54		
29 days	Purchase	$61.54	$19.18	$80.72
	Mark-to-market	$80.72		
Total			$43.07 (61%)	$9.67 (14%)

TIP

Be on the lookout for trading system vendor performance track records that rely on mark-to-market gains for wonderful end-of-period gains. Mark-to-market gains are only paper gains and can vanish in a puff of smoke. To evaluate a technique, look at its performance on closed trades.

Dealing with limitations

REMEMBER

Table 12-2 is pretty exciting — a 60 percent plus return in four months. But before you dive off the deep end, consider that I rigged the case by finding an ideal chart like Figure 12-1. It wasn't hard to find, but for every ideal situation like this, thousands more can be found where applying a 10-day simple moving average crossover or the moving average level rule results in heartache and losses.

The security in Figure 12-1 is trending, and in a tidy fashion. Aside from one outlier, prices don't vary much away from the moving average. But not shown are the periods when it's neither trending nor tidy. Moving averages lose their power to help you make money when the price move is nontrending (sideways). A sideways movement defeats trend-following by definition. Some traders consider a sideways move a trend in its own right, because sideways is, technically, a direction. The value of identifying a sideways move is to prepare for a breakout that delivers an up or down direction.

The other drawback arises from a disorderly (noisy) chart with lots of outliers far away from the moving average. The second chart in Figure 12-2 shows a tidy trend with few outliers. The third chart is the same moving average, but it arises from a price move with many outliers.

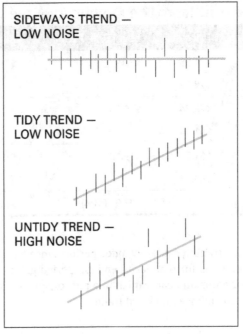

SIDEWAYS TREND —
LOW NOISE

TIDY TREND —
LOW NOISE

UNTIDY TREND —
HIGH NOISE

FIGURE 12-2:
Trend tidiness
and the moving
average.

© John Wiley & Sons, Inc.

The trader using moving averages faces a perpetual task of reducing noise while also reducing lag, and these two goals are hard to achieve simultaneously. You can fix noise by using a higher number of periods in the moving average, while fixing lag entails using a shorter number — as you can see in the following sections. Alas, you can't have it both ways.

Fixing noise

You can't do anything about a sideways move, but you can do something about noise. Just apply a moving average with more days in it. You want to minimize losses, and a noisy price series makes you vulnerable to false buy/sell signals. When you use a higher number of days in the moving average, say 50 days, noisy outliers get put in their place, arithmetically speaking. An abnormally high or low price relative to the existing average is less important in a 50-day moving average than in a 10-day moving average, because it literally carries less weight in the calculation.

But if you're using a 50-day moving average, your buy/sell signals are even later than the 10 days that cost 8.6 percent in the previous case. Besides, in some periods, the security is tidy, and in other periods, it's noisy, and you don't know in advance which it's going to be. Fixing noise by altering the number of periods in the moving average is an endless challenge that has launched a gazillion hours of research. Because new data comes along all the time, a lot of this noise-targeting research is wasted.

Another idea is to normalize the price data. This is an arithmetic process in which you reduce the effect of outliers. You create a new moving average line that uses this formula:

$$\text{Current Price} - \text{Lowest Price} \div \text{Highest Price} - \text{Lowest Price}$$
$$\left(\text{High} - \text{Low Range}\right) \times 100$$

If you notice that a 20-day moving average is a darn good period for an uptrend to last before it falls apart, you'll use 20 days for the high-low range. Charting software tends not to include a default normalization option, but it's easy enough to give the formula to the software and see what happens. You can also instruct your software to discard any price spikes that are $x\%$ away from the average in order to calculate a more representative average. The drawback of this procedure is that you're changing the number of periods in the moving average — after you discovered the optimum moving average for your specific security. It's generally better to apply one of the other modifications to the moving average I describe in the section "Adjusting the Moving Average."

Fixing lag

Often you can see a dramatic price move, but you know it's going to take days for the moving average to catch up. You're disciplined and committed to following the crossover rule, but potential profits are going up the chimney while you twiddle your thumbs. Why not simply reduce the number of days in the moving average? It will be more sensitive to current prices.

As a general rule, you want to use as few days in the moving average as possible without running into a high level of wrong signals. When you use a very short moving average, like three days, you not only lose the descriptive visual power of the line on the chart, but you also get a lot of whipsaws. In fact, using a three-day moving average on the same data in Figure 12-1 cuts the profitability to under 5 percent — worse than if you used the buy-and-hold approach.

No single number of days is best for a moving average. The best number is the one that fits how noisy the prices are. If your prices are so noisy that you would have to use a high number of days in the moving average, resign yourself to getting late exits long after the price peak. Or you can find a different, more orderly security to trade.

Comparing moving average rules with Donchian rules

The Donchian entry rule (named for Richard Donchian, one of the pioneers of technical analysis and a founder of the managed futures industry) calls for an entry when the price hits an x-day high, usually 14 days, and an exit when it hits the x-day low, also usually 14 days. If you connect successive 14-day highs and lows, you get a form of channel.

I bring up the Donchian rule here because I want you to think about the difference between an entry at the crossover of price above a moving average compared to buying at the x-day high. The chief benefit of the Donchian rules is keeping you out of a range-trading market, which the moving average can't do. However, you can get misled by spiky highs or lows, and the problem of selecting the best number of days is the same for Donchian rules as for moving averages.

Magic moving average numbers

Some technical traders think that securities prices move in cycles that are relatively fixed, such as three-to-four weeks, three-to-four months (and its double, six-to-eight months), and so on. They imagine that you should gear the number of days in your moving average to these cycles. Although cycles do exist, too many of them exist at the same time. They overlap, and nobody can say which one is ruling the market at any one time. Whether fixed-length cycles are true doesn't matter. If a sufficient number of traders believe they're true, sometimes traders cause the predicted cycle to occur. Popular moving averages are 28 days and half of 28 days (14 days), and the combination 5-10-20 days, or a variation, 4-18-40. The 28-day number was devised as a monthly number in apparent disregard of the trading month having 20 to 22 days compared to the lunar or calendar month.

Systems designers joke that the four-day moving average was devised to ace out the people using the 5-day and the 9-day to get in front of the traders using the 10-day moving average. The ichimoku moving averages use 26 days because in Japan at the time the technique was invented, trading took place on Saturdays, making 26 days an accurate count for a month. Weirdly, nobody adjusts the ichimoku moving average to match the Western week, presumably because it works well the way it is. This should give you a clue that the exact number of days in a moving average isn't terribly important when the moving average is a building block in a more complex indicator. You see the same thing in the moving average convergence-divergence indicator that I discuss later in this chapter.

WARNING

The bottom line: Be skeptical of buying into a magic number. The spirit of technical analysis is empirical: *What does the data say?* If you find that 17 days works on your security today, then you should use the 17-day moving average. Just don't get married to it. At some later point down the road, a better one might be 13 days, or 23.

REMEMBER

One moving average really does stand out — the 20-day. When a security is trending, the 20-day moving average often works the same way a support line works — sellers stop selling when it's reached. Less often, the 20-day moving average constitutes resistance. The virtue of a moving average that works as support or resistance is that you don't have to choose a starting and ending point — the moving average is nonjudgmental and everyone gets the same line. Many traders plot the 20-day moving average on every chart to get a feel for what other traders in the market may see as a benchmark level.

FOLKLORE VERSUS TRADING TOOLS

You see reports that Blue Widget stock just surpassed its 50-day moving average, or its 200-day moving average, or that its 50-day moving average crossed its 200-day moving average, a so-called *golden cross*. This type of information may or may not be interesting and useful. Maybe the price had been within a few pennies of the 200-day moving average for months on end and just managed to inch over it. Why is this news?

Without a context, a price crossing a moving average of a fixed number of days is just another statistic. Because of research by technical trader Richard Donchian, the 5-day and 20-day moving averages became popular, and that makes sense — 5 days is a week and 20 days is (roughly) a month. But 50 days and 200 days are just round numbers unrelated to the calendar (the number of business days in a year is about 240). And as I note in this chapter, the best number of days to put in a moving average is the *smallest* number that still generates as few whipsaws as possible. By choosing a number as high as 50 or 200 days, you're condemning yourself to an inefficient parameter practically by definition.

But that would be to mistake a *barometer of the environment* for a *trading tool*. If you're looking for an indicator to describe the general tone of a security or market index, the 200-day moving average is pretty good — mostly because it has been in vogue for decades. To use a fixed number like 50 or 200 makes sense only if everyone else is looking at the same number, and increasingly, they are. Even people who profess to dislike and distrust technical analysis give credence to the 200-day moving average.

But what *exactly* does it mean? Well, the 200-day moving average doesn't have a proven meaning. A security whose price falls below the 200-day moving average has fallen out of favor with traders, and one whose price is in the process of crossing above the 200-day moving average is in favor. The financial press sometimes reports a death cross, or the 50-day moving average crossing below the 200-day. *Death cross* is a semantically loaded term that has no statistical basis for reliably predicting outcomes. This technical jargon example is an instance where language influences the outcome far more than the event the language is purportedly describing.

You may also see the 20-day moving average tracking the linear regression. When you see this confluence, you get a sense that maybe the market has some underlying order after all. Beware of superstition! The sense of orderliness may not be an illusion in any particular case, but remember that no trend lasts forever. At a turning point, the 20-day moving average is dead wrong, so enjoy it while you have it.

Adjusting the Moving Average

You can adjust the moving average to make it track current prices more closely without sacrificing all the benefits of the averaging process.

Moving averages are often abbreviated. You may see SMA and wonder what *that* is. SMA stands for the *simple moving average* (and you feel like an idiot after you figure it out). Likewise, the moving averages I cover in the following sections are also often abbreviated: WMA refers to *weighted moving average*, EMA refers to *exponential moving average*, and AMA refers to *adaptive moving average*.

Here I describe some of the fancy adjustments you can make to a moving average, but it's by no means an exhaustive list. Don't let the arithmetic put you off your feed. Modifying moving averages is a proven method of raising their effectiveness (that is, profitability). And it's not as though you have to do the math yourself — your software will do it for you.

Weighted and exponential moving averages

Instead of reducing the number of days in the moving average, a different way to make the moving average more responsive to the latest prices is to weight the latest prices more heavily. You get the *weighted moving average* by multiplying each price in your series according to how fresh it is. In a five-day moving average, for example, the price on Day 5 (today) would be multiplied by 5, Day 4 by 4, Day 3 by 3, and so on. Remember to divide the total by the sum of the *weights*, not the sum of the *days* (5 + 4 + 3 + 2 + 1 = 15).

More popular than the weighted moving average is the *exponential moving average.* This moving average is hard to calculate, and fortunately, all the charting software and websites do it for you. The principle is to create a factor that minimizes the change between the existing moving average and the latest price, creating a smaller bridge than the simple moving average, which has to bridge the entire distance between today's price and yesterday's.

This factor gives the moving average a numerical value closer to the last price and thus makes it more representative of recent prices. The fewer the number of days in the moving average, the bigger the factor.

Adaptive moving averages

The *adaptive moving average* works like a long-term moving average in that it diminishes the effect of outliers, but without sacrificing sensitivity to trendedness. You always want a moving average to be as short as possible to identify the beginning of a trend quickly, but as long as necessary to avoid whipsaw losses.

In other words, sometimes you want the moving average to contain a small number of days, and other times you want it to contain a higher number of days. You don't want to be forced to select the number yourself because you have no way of knowing in advance which is right. You want some automatic mechanical adjustment to kick in when variability changes, to adapt the moving average to the new condition. You can't change the number of days according to conditions, but you can get the same effect by making the moving average *adaptive*.

Software today contains many versions of adaptive moving averages, generally some form of detrending. *Detrending* the series makes the current price more important; you simply subtract the current price from the moving average. This smooths the line right away. Other adjustments can get horribly complex.

Trading systems designer Perry Kaufman devised an ingenious way to achieve this adaptiveness for trading purposes and called it the *adaptive moving average*. It's abbreviated KAMA, for *Kaufman's adaptive moving average*, while other versions of the adaptive moving average are usually named just AMA or have the inventor's initial, like Richard Jurik's JAMA and Alan Hull's HMA. The aim of all adaptive moving averages is to reduce lag while not sacrificing the smoothness of the average. To see the arithmetic behind the adaptiveness, search on the Internet for "adaptive moving average." You'll get plenty of hits, including the observation at www.investopedia.com that research shows adaptive moving averages don't add all that much, but are still useful when used with other indicators.

Wild and woolly moving averages

In 1960 Chester Keltner devised a classic moving average system in *How to Make Money in Commodities* (Keltner Statistical Service). It starts with a 10-day moving average of the high, low, and close, with a channel on either side made from the 10-day moving average of the high-low range. You buy when price breaks the upper band and sell when it breaks the lower band.

Another technique to modify the moving average is the triple exponential smoothed average, devised by Jack Hutson and nicknamed TRIX. Hutson is the author of *Charting the Stock Market, The Wyckoff Method* (Technical Analysis, Inc.).

The TRIX process is too complicated and lengthy to discuss here, but it entails a smoothing constant that has the effect of suppressing minor-change prices and emphasizing big-change prices. TRIX removes a great deal of the lag inherent in the moving average and works more like a momentum indicator than a regular moving average (see Chapter 13 for more on momentum).

As you should have started figuring out by now, moving averages are a fertile field for plowing by the computationally ingenious.

Choosing a moving average type

Traders debate which type of moving average is the best. Figure 12-3 shows examples of the four main moving averages I discuss in this chapter, which doesn't come close to exhausting all the possible modifications.

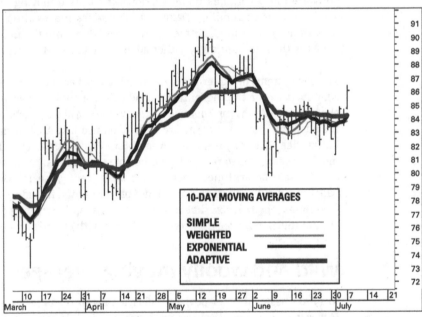

FIGURE 12-3:
Types of moving averages.

© John Wiley & Sons, Inc.

Each version of moving averages has strengths and weaknesses. The weighted moving average is the most sensitive to the latest price moves, followed by the exponential moving average. Notice that the KAMA is the best at chopping off the spiky outlier prices that make the price series noisy. That means it works best at reducing whipsaw losses, too. But it gives a value of zero to the breakaway gap like the last bar on this chart. In a trend reversal like the one depicted on this chart, that's a drawback. You enter the new trend later than if you used a nonadaptive technique, but as a reward, you don't get many false signals.

TIP

Don't invest the moving average with supernatural powers. It's only arithmetic. A moving average can't capture every important move and, in fact, rides roughshod over some important chart events, like breakaway gaps. The moving average is a repackaging of the price series, not the price series itself.

Using Multiple Moving Averages

You like a short moving average because it responds quickly to new conditions, and you like a long moving average because it reduces errors. So why not use both of them? Or three — a short-, medium-, and long-term moving average? You can, and the following sections can help you.

Putting two moving averages into play

Instead of looking for the price to cross a single moving average, you look for a shorter moving average (say 5 days) to cross a longer moving average (say 20 days). When you use 5 and 20 days, you chart a one-week moving average against a one-month moving average.

REMEMBER

The two moving average crossover trading rule is clear: Buy when the shorter moving average crosses the longer moving average on the upside. You sell when the shorter moving average crosses the longer moving average on the downside.

You're free to use any parameter set in the two moving average crossover model. You could use 3 and 30, or 15 and 24, or any other number set at all. Before getting into how to customize the two moving average model, look at Figure 12-4, which shows the same security and time frame as in Figure 12-1, only this time with two moving averages, the short one at 5 days and the longer one at 20 days. You buy when the short-term moving averages crosses above the long-term moving average, and sell when it crosses below. Again, the arrows mark the buy/sell crossovers.

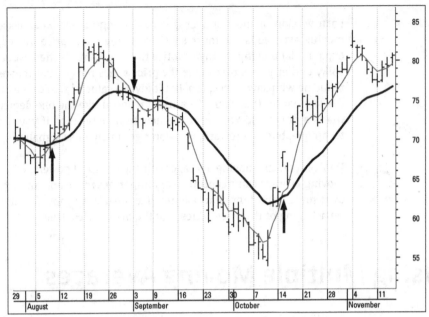

FIGURE 12-4:
Two moving
average
crossover model.

You may notice the similarity of the buy/sell arrow placement on Figure 12-4 to those in Figure 12-1. But you can also see that the outlier problem on the first chart is absent from this chart. The outlier is still there, but the short-term moving average is clearly below the long-term moving average, so you don't care. You hardly see it. On the right-hand side of the chart, some prices close below the short-term moving average, and again, you don't care. The short-term moving average remains nicely above the long-term one, and in fact, you can see a fair amount of daylight between the two moving average lines.

TIP

The more open space — daylight — you see between two moving averages, the more confident you can be that the signal is correct and will continue. When the two moving averages converge (as they do near the outlier, for example), you have less confidence that the signal is going to last.

If you trade the two moving average model, your gain is $25.31 on an initial capital stake of $70.61, or 36 percent, as shown in Table 12-3. This gain is considerably less than the 61 percent you can make by using the moving average level rule, shown in Table 12-2, but consider the advantages of the two moving average crossover:

>> You can *see* the crossover. You still may want to add a filter, such as waiting a day or two after the crossover to put on the trade or qualifying the crossover by a percentage amount.

>> The two moving average crossover is more reliable than the single moving average because it is less sensitive. It lags more but is wrong less often. *You're swapping risk for return.*

>> You have fewer trades and therefore lower brokerage expense. In the crossover of the moving average and price, you have ten trades (five in and five out), whereas in the level rule and two moving average crossover, you have six.

TABLE 12-3 **Hypothetical Profit from the Two Moving Average Crossover Rule**

No. of Days	Action	Price	Profit	Buy-and-Hold
25 days	Buy	$70.61	$3.59	$70.61
	Sell	$74.20		
43 days	Sell	$74.20	$7.60	
	Buy	$66.60		
29 days	Buy	$66.60	$14.12	$80.72
	Mark-to-market	$80.72		
Total			$25.31 (36%)	$10.11 (14%)

Trying the three-way approach

If two moving averages are good, three must be better. For example, you could plot the 5-day, 10-day, and 20-day moving averages on a chart, and you would consider a buy/sell signal to be confirmed only when both the 5-day *and* the 10-day cross the 20-day moving average. If you're always a buyer and never a short-seller, you can add a qualification that a sell signal occurs when the 5-day moving average crosses *either* of the other two moving averages.

REMEMBER

This approach is the belt-and-suspenders school of trading, where you're willing to accept a lot of delay in entering a new trade in exchange for hardly any wrong signals. The three moving average model has one very useful feature — it keeps you out of a trade if the price movement stops trending up or down and starts going sideways, or if it becomes very choppy and volatile, so that you would need an exceptionally long moving average just to see the trend.

In the conventional two moving average model, you're always in the market. When you sell, you not only get rid of the security that you bought, but you also go short. But when the security enters a sideways or choppy period, you're going to get chopped up on whipsaw losses. The three moving average model overcomes that problem by refusing to give you a confirmed signal. You stay out of the security and out of trouble.

In Figure 12-5, the first arrow on the left marks where the short-term moving average rises above the medium- and long-term moving averages. The arrow in the center marks where the short-term moving average crosses below the medium-term moving average — and you're out. You don't enter short at the same time as in the two moving average case. If you had entered short, you'd have been whipsawed several times over the next few weeks. Look at how choppy the prices became, up and down by large amounts over a short period of time. Finally, near the end of the chart, the short-term moving average crosses above both of the other moving averages, and you get a buy signal.

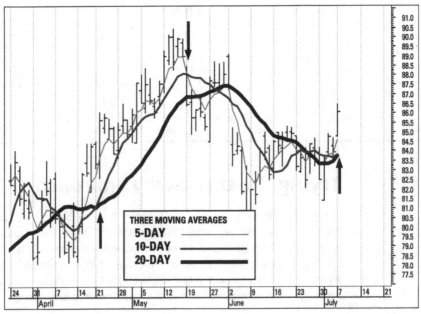

FIGURE 12-5:
Three moving average model.

© John Wiley & Sons, Inc.

Throw them all at the wall and see what sticks

A wild idea is to put many, many moving averages on a chart in what is named a moving average *ribbon* (see Figure 12-6). Your software may contain this option. You'd order up a 5-day, a 10-day, a 20-day, a 30-day, up to eight or ten different parameters. If you use a different color for each moving average, you end up with a rainbow. As the ribbon widens, you can easily see the averages are *diverging*, meaning the shorter moving averages are outrunning the longer ones, which is good because it suggests rising robustness in trendedness.

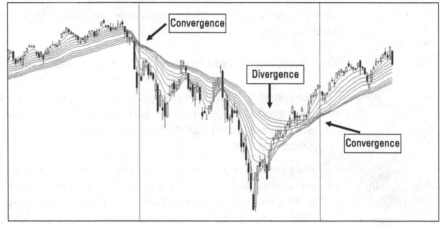

FIGURE 12-6:
A moving average ribbon.

The moving averages contracting to practically a single line is considered convergence, defined in the next section, and therefore the trendedness is fading. You can make a simple trading rule to buy or hold the security only when the current price is above all the ribbons. Otherwise, it's fairly difficult to invent buy/sell trading rules with a ribbon, but the convergence and divergence aspect is really quite useful and the thing looks gorgeous on the screen.

Delving into Moving Average Convergence and Divergence

When the price crosses over a moving average or one moving average crosses over another, you have a chart event with an embedded trading rule. But the crossover is a blunt instrument. You can often see a crossover coming, but if you're following rule-based discipline, you're impatiently waiting for the actual crossover.

If you look at any two moving average crossovers, you see that at a turning point, the short moving average converges to the price and the long-term moving average converges, a bit later, to the short-term one. When two things converge, they get closer together. By the time the crossover actually occurs, the price peak (or trough) has already passed.

Similarly, after a crossover, the two moving averages diverge from one another, meaning they get farther apart. Wouldn't it be nice to quantify the convergence and divergence? Then you'd have a measure of market sentiment. You could say that sentiment is turning against the current trend when the moving averages are converging and market sentiment is confirming the current trend as the moving averages diverge. You'll always appreciate any indicator that makes the supply and demand dynamics crystal-clear.

Here are the convergence and divergence basics you need to know:

REMEMBER

>> **Convergence:** When two moving averages converge, the trend may be coming to an end. *Convergence* is therefore an early warning. Because moving averages are always lagging indicators, measuring convergence is a way of anticipating a crossover.

At a peak, one way to look at the price convergence is to say that short-term demand is faltering — traders are failing to produce new higher closes. The trend is still in place, as shown by the long-term moving average. At a price bottom, you can interpret the short-term moving average falling at a lesser pace as selling interest (supply) falters.

>> **Divergence:** Conversely, when you can see a lot of daylight between two moving averages, they're *diverging*, which means the trend is safe from a crossover, at least for another few periods. In practice, abnormally wide divergence tends not to be sustainable and can be a warning of prices having reached an extreme ahead of reversing.

Calculating convergence and divergence

Calculating and applying convergence and divergence is a little tricky. To calculate convergence and divergence, you simply subtract the long-term moving average from the short-term one. That sounds backward, but stop and think about it for a minute. If the price and moving averages are rising, the long-term moving average is a smaller number, say $10, than the shorter-term moving average, say $15. The short average minus the long average equals $5. Now the price passes its peak and falls. The short-term moving average loses steam and the next day it is $13, while the long-term moving average is still climbing. Today's price drop is a drop in its bucket. The long-term numerical value is $12. Now the difference is only $1. From $5 to $1 is convergence.

The inventor of the moving average convergence-divergence indicator (MACD), Gerald Appel, designed it to use exponential moving averages of 26 and 12 days, although the MACD is a model into which you can insert any moving average that suits your fancy and is effective on your charts. You can easily fiddle with the parameter set in your software to seek better numbers, but be forewarned, you'll be hard-pressed to find a better set than the Appel 26/12 that works well over long periods — by which I mean decades.

Figure 12-7 shows a 12-day and 26-day moving average in the top window. In the bottom window is the result of subtracting the 26-day moving average from the 12-day moving average, which is the convergence-divergence indicator. When the indicator line is rising, the two averages are diverging. When the line is falling, the averages are converging. At zero difference between the two averages, you have the crossover. You can verify this crossover by checking the actual moving averages on the price chart.

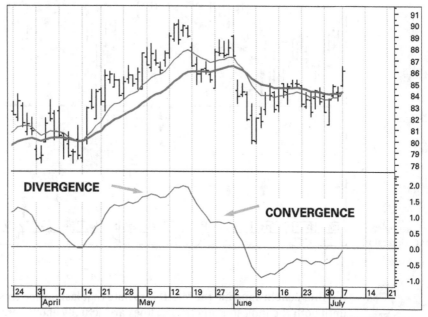

FIGURE 12-7:
Convergence and divergence.

© John Wiley & Sons, Inc.

Creating a decision tool

So far all you have is an indicator line. To transform it into a trading tool, you need to give it a trigger. Appel designed the trigger to be a moving average of the indicator, superimposed on top of the indicator. Normally, it's a nine-day exponential moving average. Figure 12-8 shows the full MACD indicator.

The arrows again show where you would buy and sell. In the MACD indicator window, notice that the crossover of the trigger and the MACD indicator occurs earlier than the crossover of the two moving averages in the top window. Looking from the left, the MACD tells you to buy two days earlier than the moving average crossover. The real benefit comes at the next signal — the exit. Here the MACD tells you to sell over two weeks ahead of the moving average crossover, saving you $4.68, or almost 5 percent. Finally, at the right side of the chart, the MACD tells you to reenter, while the moving averages are still lollygagging along and haven't yet crossed. Actually, you get a crossover of the indicator line about two weeks earlier, but here I waited until there was some daylight between the two lines.

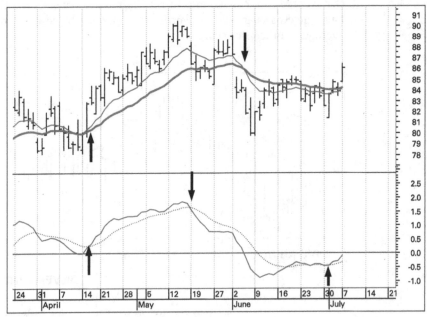

FIGURE 12-8:
MACD indicator.

A refinement in applying the MACD is to note that last upside crossover but to wait until both the indicator and trigger lines are actually above zero to make the buy trade.

TIP

Interpreting the MACD

You may find it hard to read the MACD indicator, except when the trigger is actually crossing the indicator line. You're not alone. Another way of displaying the MACD, in histogram format, is much easier on the eye, as shown in Figure 12-9.

Here each bar in the histogram represents the difference between the two moving averages on that date. You don't use the trigger line in the histogram, because you can choose by eye how fast the histogram bars are closing in on the zero line, or diverging from it. At zero, the two moving averages have the same numerical value — they have zero difference between them. As the bars grow taller, the difference between the two averages is increasing (divergence), and this movement favors the trend continuing. When the bars stop growing and start to shrink, the two moving averages are converging — watch out for a signal change.

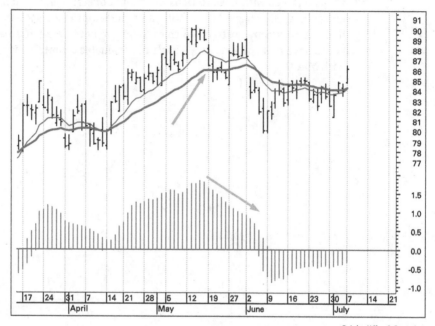

FIGURE 12-9:
MACD histogram.

REMEMBER

The histogram format gives you more flexibility in interpretation, but in the process, takes away a guide — the trigger. You're using your eye rather than a number.

When the bars are upside down (below zero), the signal is to sell. What do you do when the bars become less negative? This indicator means selling pressure (supply) is running out of steam. Technically, you don't get a buy signal until the bars are actually over the zero line, but it's up to you whether to act in anticipation that it will cross the line. Notice that in Figure 12-7, the trigger line does signal a buy on the last day, while on the histogram format in Figure 12-8, the bar isn't quite up to the zero-crossover level. This minor discrepancy is inherent in the calculation method of the software used to make this chart.

REMEMBER

The MACD seems to have predictive power because it gets you out of the trade ahead of the big breakdown, more than two weeks before the shorter moving average crosses the longer moving average to the downside. It also saves you from the gap. The MACD is quicker on the trigger than the moving average crossover, but it's still a lagging indicator. In a wild new move, it lags like any other indicator based on moving averages. Having said that, the MACD is one of the most reliable indicators you'll ever find.

I find it telling that of the dozen or so books Appel wrote, a pamphlet from the 1990s reissued with Edward Dobson in 2008, *Understanding MACD* (Traders Press), is a skinny paperback — and still commands a price of $50, and that's second-hand. A new copy costs more than $200 for fewer than 100 pages. How many books have that track record? That's how valuable a contribution Appel has made with MACD.

Chapter **13**

Measuring Momentum

O ne of the biggest problems in technical analysis is detecting when a trend is about to end rather than just putting in a minor pullback. Momentum is the single best tool for doing that. *Momentum* is the speed of a price change and it's just about the easiest indicator of all — you divide today's price by the price *x* number of days ago. Over time, if the price is rising at a good clip, the momentum number keeps getting bigger, and so a graphic representation on the chart shows a rising line. Momentum refers to the *change* in the price level rather than the level itself. Arithmetically, prices can still be rising but if they're rising at a slower pace, the line flattens out. When prices start falling, the momentum number gets smaller and smaller, and so the line on the chart is a falling line.

That's basic momentum. But it gets more complicated than the original simple formula. For one thing, you want to measure acceleration and deceleration and not just eyeball it on the chart. Measuring is named *rate-of-change* and delivers numbers. In addition, you want to get rid of noise and want to see momentum in the context of the price range. Some more arithmetic is going to be needed.

Momentum can come in some interesting packages. Think about the moving average convergence-divergence (MACD) indicator in Chapter 12 — all its raw material consists of moving averages, but in the end, what you get is a depiction of how the price is changing. Therefore, MACD is really a momentum indicator.

REMEMBER

Most momentum indicators were designed to evaluate the strength of a trend already identified by other indicators, such as the moving average crossover (refer to Chapter 12) or slope of a standard error channel (see Chapter 11). Some traders may use one of the momentum indicators as the ruling indicator on which the trading decision is based, but more often momentum is used as a confirming or secondary indicator (see Chapter 16 for more on ruling versus secondary indicators).

Whether momentum is a leading indicator is debatable. How can any number based on past prices be leading? It can't. And yet traders, acting as a group, respond in reliably predictable ways to certain stimuli. When traders are using a momentum indicator to identify an overbought/oversold condition and a majority of traders judge that the overbought/oversold criterion has been met, you can expect them to obey the trading rule embedded in the criteria. If the security is deemed overbought by a momentum indicator, traders will sell. If it's deemed oversold by a momentum indicator, traders will buy. It's astonishing how often momentum indicators turn out to be right in calling a trend reversal long before other indicators. But beware a mystical interpretation! Momentum identifies when the crowd is becoming more bullish, and traders naturally want to join the crowd. Momentum identifies when bullish sentiment is decelerating and traders want to protect themselves against a possible pending loss. When momentum flips to negative, traders want to join the crowd that is clearly exiting. There's nothing mystical about it — it's crowd-following.

This chapter explains the various forms that the momentum concept takes, ranging from the simple to the complicated.

Doing the Math: Calculating Momentum

Momentum is a fancy word that is often misused in technical talk. In physics and classical Newtonian mechanics, momentum has a specific mathematical definition and can be measured with precision. In technical analysis, sometimes that precision is mistakenly transferred to the human behavior behind price moves.

At its most simple, momentum is mass times velocity (think of a truck accelerating down a hill — it will take a big wall or countervailing force to stop it). But market prices aren't physical objects, whether atomic particles, billiard balls, or runaway trucks. Metaphors that make market prices comparable to physical objects — mass might be viewed as volume traded, for example — are still metaphors, not scientific measurements.

Many top writers and system designers are engineers who transfer concepts and formulas wholesale from their fields. This is a useful starting point but confers a false sense of scientific objectivity to the idea of momentum in securities prices. The momentum measured in market prices arises from human behavior and is categorically different from the kinds of changes observed and measured in physical objects. A runaway truck can be stopped by specific and measurable mechanical means. The only mechanical way to halt a runaway price series is to close down the exchange on which the security is trading.

In addition, price momentum can be changed, and dramatically, by a one-time external event (flash crash in the index, war, and so on). That's the point of a shock — you don't know it's coming ahead of time and you don't know what influence it will have on prices. (Chapter 3 discusses these contingencies.) A flock of birds flying into an airplane will affect momentum in a specific and measurable way. The equivalent of a crow flying into market prices has an unknown effect that can be measured only afterward. In addition, a crow flying into one market (the dollar/Swiss franc) will have one effect, but a crow flying into a different market (the Shanghai stock market) will have a different effect because the participants in each market have different characteristics. In the following sections, I explain many of the most often used momentum indicators, starting from the simplest and intuitively easy to grasp to the horribly named stochastic oscillator.

Simple momentum

This simple version of momentum is a powerful indicator but has fallen out of favor in recent years as more complex and targeted momentum indicators came into fashion.

Everything you really need to know about momentum is that it compares the price today with the price some number of periods ago. This is the same lookback period I talk about in the chapter on moving averages (Chapter 12). You can choose any lookback period when calculating momentum indicators. In this section, I use 5 days, but you usually see 12 or 14 days — the standard parameter used in most software. Why 12 or 14 and not 10 or 15 (two or three trading-day weeks)? Because the inventors of these indicators found 12 or 14 to be the most efficient lookback period.

Although you can use the subtraction method, whereby you subtract today's price from the price some number of periods ago, today nearly everyone uses the method of *dividing* today's price by the price x periods ago.

In Figure 13-1, the momentum indicator using the division method crosses into negative territory (meaning that the latest price is lower than the price five days before) and does the crossover one day before the price opens gap down (see Chapter 7 on gaps). A little later the momentum indicator reaches the positive-negative line but fails to hold it for longer than a day. Finally, momentum crosses above the line while the price is still falling. But sure enough, momentum accurately forecasted a price rise. Three days later, the price matches a previous high and breaks out to the upside.

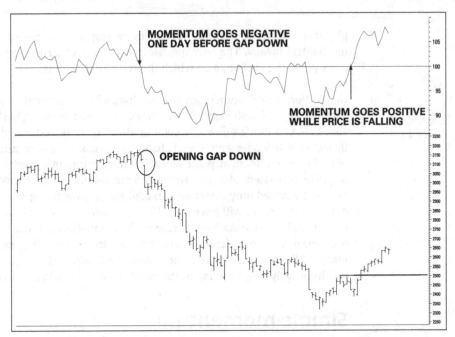

MOMENTUM GOES NEGATIVE
ONE DAY BEFORE GAP DOWN

MOMENTUM GOES POSITIVE
WHILE PRICE IS FALLING

OPENING GAP DOWN

FIGURE 13-1:
Momentum
predicts price
change.

© John Wiley & Sons, Inc.

Using the rate-of-change method

In practice, the momentum indicator most traders use today fancies up the simple version by converting it to a percentage rate of change. Here's one calculation method (of many available):

1. Today's close minus the close x days ago

2. Divide the result in Step 1 by the close x days ago

3. Multiply the result in Step 2 by 100.

The result is information presented in context rather than just the difference between the two prices. If today's price is equal to the price five days ago, the result now reads 100, meaning that the new price is equal to 100 percent of the price five days ago, which is the same as saying that there is zero change between the two prices.

Stop and think about the arithmetic for a minute. In simple momentum, you measure how fast you're going, assume $1 per day. If today the price is $15 and five days ago it was $10, the momentum value is 15/10, or 1.5. Now add another day's worth of price data at the constant speed of $1/day. The simple momentum indicator yields 16/11, or $1.45. This is terrible — the momentum indicator is falling and yet the security is still rising at the same $1 per day.

THE DIFFERENCE BETWEEN MOMENTUM AND MOMENTUM INVESTING

Momentum is an arithmetic calculation technical traders use to identify the speed or change in speed of a trend. *Momentum investing,* on the other hand, entails buying a security just because it's going up without actually measuring the rate of change or considering any other factors. The idea behind momentum investing is that a security that's already rising will continue to rise at least a little longer. This idea sounds like Dow Theory — prices move in trends — but it's incomplete and gives people the wrong idea about the meaning of the word *momentum* to real technical traders.

In the late 1990s, momentum stocks included Internet, telecom, and high-tech stocks that rose on the exuberance of the crowd to valuations many times any reasonable estimate of value. A momentum strategy came to be summed up in the phrase: "If it's rising, buy it."

However, to buy a security just because it's rising isn't momentum-based technical analysis because the momentum trader has no systematic entry and exit criteria. To hijack a hot-button word like *momentum* is a silly effort to dress up an undisciplined approach to trading and obscures a really important use of momentum, using the relative momentum of two or more securities (named *comparative relative strength*) to pick the one that has the best chance to deliver a gain. To choose a security from the universe of securities on the basis of comparative relative strength is a legitimate methodology and one of seven core concepts in William O'Neill's "CANSLIM" approach to stock-picking, beyond the scope of this chapter but worthy of your attention.

Worse, how can you judge the momentum number of $1.45?

But in the price rate-of-change method, your first reading is 15/10 = 1.5 divided by 15 = 0.10 times 100 = 10. The next day, assuming the same $1 rise, you get 16/11 = 1.45 divided by 16 = 0.0909 times 100 = 9.09 percent. The numbers are different but the conclusion is the same — the price may be *rising,* but it's not *accelerating.* In fact, it's decelerating, and by making the indicator a percentage change, you're measuring the rate of deceleration. Yesterday, when the price was at $15, momentum was 10 percent and now it's 9.09 percent. Ah, momentum is falling by about 1 percent. This is a more useful number than $1.45.

REMEMBER

The momentum indicator can move up or down only if the price is accelerating or decelerating. The momentum indicator can flat-line while the price is still moving if the *relative* pace of change is the same.

The percentage rate of change delivers a frame of reference that allows you to judge whether a move is a huge change over a short period or a minor event hardly worth considering. Simple momentum and price rate-of-change look almost identical on a chart, but having those percentage numbers on the vertical axis of the rate-of-change versions allows you to measure the move. If the price is higher today than ten days before, the indicator delivers a positive number. If the price is lower today than ten days before, it will be a negative number — but now you know by what amount in percentage terms.

Say you see a 30 percent move over ten days. It's up to you to decide how to judge it. If it's abnormally high for your security, which typically doesn't reach a speed of more than 30 percent in any ten-day period before pausing or retracing, you can use momentum as a leading indicator. When you see the indicator reach the 30 percent mark, you expect traders to do what they've done in the past: Cause a price pullback by taking profit. You can exit early, join them at the same time, or wait it out, depending on the other conditions on the chart and your trading plan.

By observing momentum over time, you can discover the maximum speed that your security is likely to reach in a specific period of time, like ten days. You may, of course, choose three days, or five days, or any other number of days. Most charting software allows you to backtest historical data to find the optimum number of days that would have generated the most profit when using rate of change as a buy/sell indicator.

Pondering the Trickier Aspects of Momentum

When you see a momentum indicator on a chart, your eye automatically tries to line it up with the price move. Usually the most noticeable thing about a price series is its direction, so you may think you see a correlation between the indicator and the price. Often this observation is true and useful, but sometimes it's an illusion and may lead you astray. To help you avoid mistakes, I describe some of the trickier aspects of momentum in this section.

REMEMBER

The momentum calculation displays speed. When your momentum indicator line is horizontal, you may think that momentum has stopped. This isn't so. *Acceleration* has stopped.

Smoothing price changes

When you look at Figure 13-1 earlier in this chapter, you probably notice that the momentum indicator looks a lot like the price series, only smoother, and with the indicator's highest highs and lowest lows a day or two off the price's highest highs and highest lows.

REMEMBER

Yes, indeed. Momentum sometimes mirrors the price move. This reflection is because, like a moving average, the momentum indicator is tracking the close relative to the close a certain number of days back. The more days you put in your lookback period, the smoother the momentum line. Unlike the moving average, momentum doesn't include all the closes of the days in-between, and by omitting that extraneous information, you get a smoother line.

However, if you have a one-day price spike, you may see a jump in momentum, but ten days later you're going to see a sudden drop in the momentum indicator, too, as that spike gets excluded from the data series. This type of situation is when it pays to look at the price bars and not just the indicator. If the spike was a one-day anomaly, the information you think you're getting from momentum can be misleading.

Momentum isn't a trend indicator like a moving average, and yet it seems to track the trend. How can this be? The answer lies in the nature of price moves, which are caused by human beings and all their emotions. When a price starts to rise, traders jump on the bandwagon and cause the price to move to higher prices at a faster pace. So it's not surprising that the slope of the price move often steepens at the same time as the slope of the momentum indicator. When traders stop adding to positions, closes may still be higher, but by less than they were at the beginning of the move. The trend remains in place and is still delivering profits to you, but at a slower pace.

Filtering momentum

A smooth line is visually more helpful, but you may want momentum to be more responsive to price changes. Therefore, you could shorten the number of days in the comparison from ten to (say) three. A three-day momentum indicator is more sensitive, but it also crosses the zero/100 line repeatedly when the price isn't trending, or is trending only slightly, generating small whipsaw losses. You can also get whipsaw losses when the price is only putting in a small pullback and not reversing at all.

REMEMBER

The standard solution to whipsaws is to filter the signal. Instead of making the zero/100 line the buy/sell rule, you can dictate that the indicator has to rise (say) 2 percent over the zero/100 line for a buy and fall 2 percent under it for a sell. You can also delay accepting the buy/sell signal for one or more days. You can backtest both kinds of filters by using historical data.

Depending on the security, upmoves and downmoves aren't ordinarily symmetrical in size, duration, or speed. Sometimes your security has upmoves that accelerate strongly but decelerate in a sloppy, slow manner. Remember, every security has its own habits.

For instance, if a security usually delivers a momentum reading of plus 130 to minus 130, this reading means that the price tends to speed up or slow down by not more than 30 percent over the course of any 10-day period. Some securities are like old Chevy pickups — their momentum lumbers from plus 120 to minus 120 over many months, while other securities are sprightly Aston Martins that zip between plus 150 and minus 150 in a few weeks.

Many commentators speak of a *momentum cycle* as though it were a scientific fact of life. It's not, but you must make up your own mind on whether price cycles are real, and if they *are* real, whether they're useful to your trading. Sometimes you can see an eerie regularity in the momentum indicator, especially in longer time frames (like weekly and monthly data).

Applying Momentum

The trading rule for momentum is simple: Buy when the indicator crosses above the zero line and sell when it crosses below the zero line. The *zero line* is the level at which the current price is equal to the price *x* number of days ago. When the momentum indicator crosses above zero, the price trend is upward, and the indicator is signaling you to buy. When it crosses below zero, the trend is downward, and the indicator is signaling you to sell.

However, because momentum measures the rate of change and not the price itself, it has some peculiar properties, which I discuss in the following sections.

Discovering divergence

Momentum can be a confusing indicator, because your eye is accustomed to interpreting a line that is pointing upward as having to do with the dollar value. But in this case, this upward line refers only to the speed of the price change. The distinction is driven home when you have a price that is rising while momentum is falling.

Divergence (see Figure 13-2) refers to momentum that moves in the direction opposite to the direction of the price trend. Divergence also refers to momentum higher or lower, but less high or low than a previous peak or trough, while the price trend is making a new higher high or lower low. Technically, they're both going in the same direction, so it's a misnomer to call it a divergence, but when momentum falls proportionately short of the price move, you can think of it as a failure to confirm.

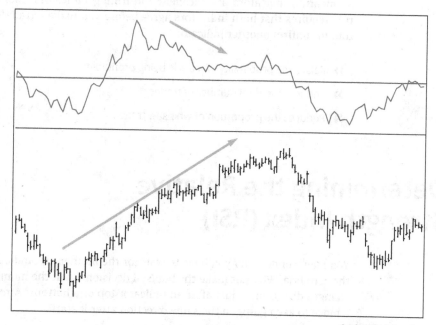

FIGURE 13-2:
Momentum and price divergence.

© John Wiley & Sons, Inc.

In Figure 13-2, the price is making a series of new highs, but about midway through the rise, momentum stops making new highs and starts going in the other direction. Then it flattens, meaning that the new price gains aren't as robust as the older price gains. Notice that momentum crosses the buy/sell midline on the very next day after the highest price high. Here is an ideal case for using momentum as a buy/sell indicator in its own right. To sell when momentum crosses the buy/sell line, you exit near the peak.

TIP

Volume can be a useful adjunct to momentum-price divergence. As I note in Chapter 11 regarding breakouts, as a price trend is peaking, you usually see an abnormal rise in volume. A volume spike often foreshadows the end of a strong trend. If you have both spiking volume and momentum-price divergence, get ready to bail out — the end of the move is nigh.

Confirming trend indicators

A change in momentum is a reliable guide to a change in price trend. A new uptrend is almost always preceded by rising momentum. Most of the time, momentum peaks ahead of the price peak, generating divergence in the direction of momentum and price — a valuable warning that you should be getting ready to exit.

Momentum indicators are excellent confirming indicators, too. A confirmation rule requires that both indicators agree before you make a trade. Using momentum to confirm another indicator

>> Raises the probability of a trade being profitable

>> Reduces the total number of trades

>> Reduces the proportion of whipsaw trades

Determining the Relative Strength Index (RSI)

You may wonder why you have to wait for the momentum indicator line to cross the zero line. Why not make the buy/sell decision when the momentum indicator changes direction — just after an indicator top or a bottom? After all, you expect a move to keep going in the same direction after it starts.

A technical trader and one of the pioneering founders of modern technical analysis, J. Welles Wilder, Jr., answered the question. He pointed out that you want to make the trading decision at the change of direction only by ensuring that the *average* upmove is greater than the *average* downmove over a certain number of days (or the other way around for a sell signal). In other words, the average momentum is relatively higher (or lower), hence the name *relative* strength. Be sure to differentiate between the *internal* relative strength I'm talking about here and a different measure, *comparative* relative strength between two securities. Don't fret — if you order your software to load relative strength and in error click on comparative relative strength, your software will chide you by asking you to name the other security. It's easy enough to start over.

REMEMBER

The relative strength index (RSI) is much faster than momentum in signaling an impending price change, making RSI a good tool for timing profit-taking, especially if you're using a shorter-term version (like 5 days rather than the standard 14 days). However, the RSI falls short in the reliability department when it comes to buy/sell signals. For that reason, traders use RSI more often as a confirming indicator, while they use other indicators to obtain the buy/sell signal.

In the following sections, I outline how you can do the RSI math and visualize it on a chart. Plus, you can also discover some of the nuances of using the RSI.

Calculating the RSI

The RSI measures the relative speed of price changes. The RSI uses averages over several days rather than single price points. However, it uses the ratio method, like momentum. To calculate RSI, you first calculate relative strength (RS) over a specific number of days. The calculation looks like this:

$$RS = (\text{Average of Close} - \text{Previous Close on Up Days}) \div (\text{Average of Previous Close} - \text{Current Close on Down Days})$$

$$RSI = 100 - (100 / (1 + RS))$$

Reversing the order of Close/Previous Close on Down Days eliminates negative numbers and delivers absolute values. This arithmetic process creates an *oscillator* that is limited to a range of zero to 100. When the indicator is at or near zero, it means that the security is fully oversold. When it's at 100, the security is overbought.

An oscillator is the result of converting the highest and lowest numerical values of an indicator to +100 for the highest and –100 (or zero) for the lowest, so that you can see when price changes are nearing extremes and thus identify overbought or oversold conditions.

The RSI and most oscillators rarely go all the way to zero or 100 percent, but rather vary between the 30 and 70 percent mark of the entire range. In some instances, you may find that the 20 to 80 percent mark is better, or even 10 to 90 percent.

The RSI, like most oscillators, is limited by one of its arithmetic components, the high-low range over *x* periods. You may have a 75-day uptrend, for example, that has five or six sell signals generated by an RSI that is using 14 days as the base range. They're false signals if you're a long-term trend-follower, but splendid opportunities to goose return if you trade in a shorter time frame.

Picturing RSI

In Figure 13-3, the RSI is shown in the top window, with two momentum indicators in the second window (a raw momentum indicator and a smoothed one containing more days), and the price chart itself in the main window. The gray trendlines are hand drawn, just for orientation.

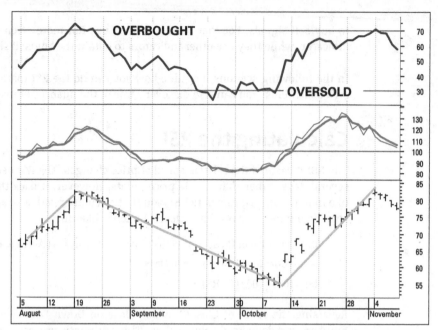

FIGURE 13-3:
Relative strength
index (RSI).

On the left of the chart, as the price is rising, the RSI and momentum rise, too. RSI, however, hits and surpasses the 70 percent limit and starts turning down the very next day after the highest close. Momentum also turns down, but it doesn't cross the center sell line for another two weeks. The RSI then falls to the bottom of its range at an index reading of 30 percent.

Because you're using averages, the indicator has a normal range of between 30 and 70 percent of the maximum range, although touches of the maximum extremes do occur as follows:

» **Overbought:** When the RSI is at or over the 70 percent level, the security is considered overbought. As I describe in Chapter 2, an overbought condition is when the security has moved by what traders in that security consider an extreme, so traders want to take profit. You can automatically sell when the security becomes overbought (when it crosses the 70 percent line), or you can use the line as a confirming indicator with other indicators.

In Figure 13-3, using the crossover of the 70 percent line as a sell signal in its own right is the correct trading action.

» **Oversold:** When RSI hits the 30 percent level, the security is considered oversold. A security is oversold when everyone who was going to sell has already sold, and the security is now relatively cheap (inviting buyers back in).

But notice that the RSI in Figure 13-3 first hits the oversold level about two and half weeks before the price itself actually makes its lowest low. That's because the price was making new lows, but the 14-day *average* downmove was getting smaller each day — the downmove was decelerating. In *this* instance, the RSI was giving a premature signal and it would've been better to consider crossing the oversold line as a warning rather than a sell signal.

WARNING

When trends are strong, securities can remain overbought or oversold for long periods. However, a divergence between the price and the indicator is a warning sign that the price move may be coming to an end. In Figure 13-3, for example, the RSI serves as a sell signal at the overbought level, but doesn't provide an equally clear buy signal when it first meets the oversold level. Instead of reversing smartly, the RSI indicator meanders down around the oversold line for several weeks. So, on one occasion it's a buy/sell signal, and on the next occasion, it's a warning.

In the place on the chart in Figure 13-3 between the overbought and oversold areas, the indicator is going sideways near the 30 percent line and the price is still falling. By analyzing the *internal dynamics of the price* (the ratio of average up days to average down days), the RSI indicator tells you not to sell the security short at this point, even though the price is still falling, because it is about to reverse to an upmove. If you're a buy-only trader, hang on. Your chance is coming. Finally, you can see that an upmove starts again and hits the overbought level on the right-hand side of the chart in Figure 13-3. Again, the RSI peaks on the same day as the price high. Notice that momentum peaks a week earlier, but it hasn't crossed the buy/sell centerline before the chart ends.

Filtering RSI

Tushar Chande, author of *The New Technical Trader* and *Beyond Technical Analysis* (John Wiley & Sons, Inc.), has probably done more tinkering with momentum indicators than anyone else on the planet. The Chande momentum oscillator calculates the difference between the sum of all recent gains and the sum of all recent losses and then divides the result by the sum of all price movement over the period, with a default period of 20 days. The oscillation range is plus-100 to minus-100. The security is considered overbought when the indicator is above plus-50 and oversold when it's below minus-50. Most software packages apply a nine-day moving average to act as a buy/sell signal line.

The Chande momentum indicator differs from the RSI because it includes up and down days in both the numerator and denominator (hence the need for minus-100). By refining the strength of a move against all price movement over the period, a strong upmove appears earlier than in RSI and likewise, a strong downmove appears sooner, too. This may be only a day or two, but hey, a day or two can mean a lot.

ANOTHER WAY TO FILTER MOMENTUM

Welles Wilder (see the average true range in Chapter 7) invented a different momentum-filtering technique. Larry Connors and Linda Raschke recommend it in *Street Smarts: High Probability Trading Strategies for the Futures and Equity Markets* (M. Gordon Publishing Group). This filter is fairly complex, so hang on to your hat.

You start with what Wilder named "average directional movement," defined as Plus Directional Movement (+DM) when the current high minus the prior high is greater than the prior low minus the current low. You get a Minus Directional Movement (–DM) when the prior low minus the current low is greater than the current high minus the prior high. Note that in both calculations, a negative number is considered a zero. ADX is really a trend filter rather than a momentum filter, but it serves the same purpose — to filter out minor pullbacks.

Another Chande momentum indicator is named Aroon, meaning *dawn* in Sanskrit. Aroon comes in two lines, one depicting how many periods since the most recent high (the up line) and one measuring how many periods since the most recent low (the down line), generally over 20 periods and both converted to an index basis. When Aroon Up is over 70 and staying there, the uptrend is okay. When Aroon Down is below 30, the downtrend is dominant. Aroon is meant to be a confirming indicator, but you could also use the crossover of the two lines to signal buy or sell.

Using the Rest of the Price Bar: The Stochastic Oscillator

A lot can be going on in other parts of the price bar, such as closes near the high versus closes near the low. When the close is near the high and each high is higher than the day before, you not only have an uptrend, but an uptrend that is accelerating. In a rally, you expect prices to close near the high of the daily high-low range. In a sell-off, you expect the price to close near the low of the daily high-low range.

Two relationships are particularly important: The high-low range over *x* number of days, and the relationship of the close to the high or the low over the same *x* number of days. (If you use the low, the resulting indicator is named the *stochastic oscillator*, and if you use the high, the indicator is named the *Williams %R*, after its inventor, Larry Williams.) In the following sections, I outline how to use the stochastic oscillator as an indicator.

No indicator name is worse than this one. The word *stochastic* refers to randomness, which of course is the exact opposite of what you're trying to achieve in applying technical concepts — finding order. It gets worse — the first component of the indicator is named the *%K*, because that was the letter of the alphabet assigned to the list of experimental formulas by its inventor, George Lane. The second component of the indicator is called *%D*, for the same reason. %K is called the fast stochastic and %D is called the slow stochastic, as you can discover in the next section. The good news: %K and %D appear only in the stochastic oscillator and aren't used anywhere else in technical analysis.

Step 1: Putting a number to the fast stochastic %K

The %K indicator takes the difference between today's close and the lowest low of the past five days and divides that by the widest high-low range of the past five days. I discuss this normalization formula in Chapter 12. The ratio is then multiplied by 100 to make it an oscillator that ranges between 0 and 100, again with a normal spread between 30 and 70 percent or from 20 to 80 percent. Five days is the standard parameter used for the indicator, although you can use software to find a number of days that better fits your particular security.

The %K indicator shows you how much energy the price move has relative to the range. If today the closing price is higher than it was yesterday, it's farther away from the lowest low than it was yesterday, too. If neither day put in a new high or low, the high-low range usually remains the same. Arithmetically, therefore, today's %K is a higher number than yesterday's, and the line on the chart has to rise, as follows:

$$\%K = (\text{Current Close} - \text{Lowest Low}) \div (\text{Highest High} - \text{Lowest Low}) \times 100$$

But here's a brainteaser: What about the case in which the high-low range over the past five days is $5 to $12 and today's price is $12? If today's close is $12, the highest high, the top part (numerator) of the ratio is today's close ($12) minus the lowest low, $5, or $7, exactly the same as the five-day range, or the bottom part of the ratio (denominator). As you probably discovered in grade school doing fractions, $7 divided by $7 is 1, and if you multiply it by 100, your oscillator reading is 100. The indicator is telling you that the price is as high as it gets relative to the range.

And a lot of good that does you! You already know that the price made a new closing high today. When that happens, the %K gives a reading of 100 percent, which by definition is an *overbought condition* — even if the price is still trending upward! This is exactly what happens in the section of the chart in Figure 13-4 marked by an ellipse. You see that the price has moved smartly up, with several gaps to boot. When the %K indicator (the thin line) reaches 100 percent, it's telling you that the security is overbought. If you used the %K line alone as a buy/sell indicator, you might sell at this point — and miss out on another $10 rise in the security.

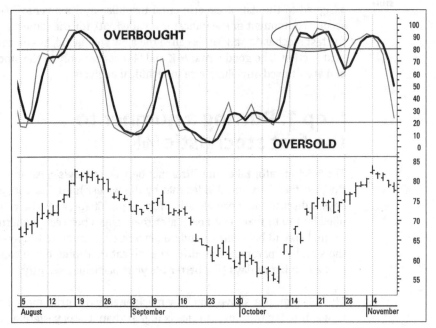

FIGURE 13-4:
Stochastic
oscillator.

WARNING

The stochastic oscillator gives a false overbought or oversold reading at a new highest high or lowest low, because the highest high or lowest low is then used in both the numerator and denominator of the ratio. Therefore, the stochastic oscillator works best in a sideways price movement. This is also true of the Williams %R, which is essentially the same indicator, only upside down. If you trade the Japanese yen, the stochastic oscillator is wrong a great deal of the time.

Step 2: Refining %K with %D

In the stochastic oscillator, the *crossover line,* which tells you whether to buy or sell, is named %D and is formed by a short-term simple moving average of %K (the higher line in Figure 13-4). A moving average always smooths and slows down the price series so %D is sometimes called the *smoothed indicator* as well as the "slow" indicator. When you put the two indicator lines together, you get crossovers of the first indicator line by the smoothed shorter-term indicator line that give you exact buy/sell signals.

You can calculate %D with the following formula:

%D = Three-Day Simple Moving Average of %K

When %K crosses above %D, it's a buy signal, and the other way around for a sell signal. It's convenient when crossovers occur promptly at overbought or oversold levels, but you'll see plenty of crossovers that occur when the security isn't over-bought or oversold. Note that you can add numerous fancy modifications to the stochastic oscillator, including a slowing factor in %K. And as with any indicator, you can change the number of days in the lookback period.

Fiddling with the stochastic oscillator on the chart

You can sometimes see meaningful patterns on a chart of the stochastic oscillator. For example, see Figure 13-5 that shows some of the nuances of the stochastic oscillator. The stochastic oscillator shows a series of three higher highs in the indicator that have %D rising over %K in right crossovers (to the right-hand side of the peak), implying hidden power is in the upmove on the left-hand side of the chart that can't be discerned from just looking at the prices themselves.

But look again. Under the first bump up in the stochastic, only two days have lower closes (and one duplicate close). You could also draw a support line under the lower closes or series of "knees," as Lane called them. As it happens, this time the final downside crossover beats the break of the support line by five days, but that isn't always the case.

You can become obsessed with the stochastic oscillator. Aficionados study charts for divergences, like when the price hits a new low but the stochastic oscillator fails to confirm and in fact shows a higher low. This type of situation is what you can see in Figure 13-5 and is named a *bullish divergence.* Similarly, a *bearish diver-gence* is when the price is making a higher high but the stochastic forms a lower high. The point is that momentum isn't confirming the price action.

After looking for divergences, traders then move on to pinpointing the number associated with the divergence. Is it above or below the midpoint at 50 percent? A bullish divergence over the 50 percent line is favorable. In a very real sense, the stochastic oscillator is bar reading on steroids.

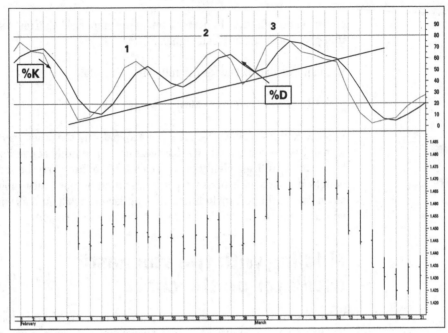

FIGURE 13-5:
Bullish
divergence.

WARNING

The stochastic oscillator became fabulously popular in the 1990s as technology permitted the spread of short-term swing trading to the general public. "Trade like the professionals!" was the sales pitch, and an accurate one, too, in the sense that professionals are heartless about not holding a security that isn't performing. The fad for this indicator, however, resulted in some technical writers making exaggerated claims for it. The stochastic oscillator has some serious drawbacks, such as having almost no trend identification capability and often signaling a premature exit.

REMEMBER

Don't use the stochastic oscillator in a strongly trending market. When your security exhibits an abnormally long period of trendedness, you can get jumpy wondering how long it will last. However, this type of situation is when the stochastic oscillator isn't useful and can be downright dangerous, as in Figure 13-6. The stochastic oscillator rises up from the oversold level in the oval and a little later the price rises over the hand-drawn resistance line. Surely this is a buy signal! But the price turns around after only a few days and puts in a lower low. If you're a very short-term trader, you may have been able to eke out a small gain from the buy signal, but not from this instance of the stochastic oscillator alone.

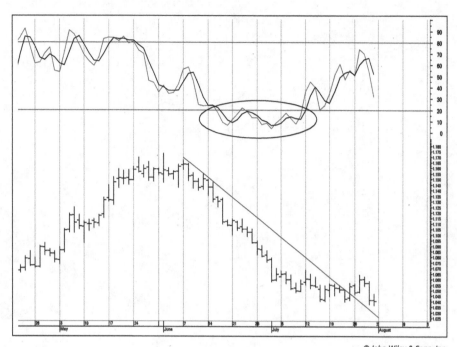

FIGURE 13-6:
Stochastic oscillator in error.

Chapter **14**

Estimating Volatility

Volatility is a measure of price variation, either the total movement between low and high over some fixed period of time or a variation away from a central measure, like an average. Both concepts of volatility are valid and useful. The higher the volatility, the higher the risk — and the opportunity.

A change in volatility implies a change in the expected price range yet to come. A volatile security offers a wide range of possible outcomes. A nonvolatile security delivers a narrower and thus more predictable range of outcomes. The main reason to keep an eye on volatility is to adjust your profit targets and your stop loss to reflect the changing probability of gain or loss.

In this chapter, I describe three ways you can measure volatility and discuss their virtues and drawbacks. Then I describe the most popular way traders incorporate consideration of volatility into their trading plans — the Bollinger Band. I also introduce another kind of band — the average true range band.

WARNING

Volatility comes in two flavors, historical and implied. Historical volatility refers to price variations in the recent past, and that is what I describe in this chapter. Implied volatility is a different kettle of fish. Implied volatility is a term used in option analysis and not covered in this book.

Catching a Slippery Concept

Volatility is a concept that can easily slip through your fingers if you aren't careful. Just about everybody uses the word volatility incorrectly from a statistician's viewpoint — and even statisticians squabble over definitions. To the mathematically inclined trader, *volatility* usually refers to the standard deviation of price changes (see the "Considering the standard deviation" section). Standard deviation isn't the only measure of volatility, but it suffices for most technical analysis purposes. In general usage, volatility means variance, and that's how I use it in this chapter.

Variance is a statistical concept that measures the distance of each bar between the high and low from the mean (such as a moving average). You calculate variance by taking the difference between the high or low from the average, squaring each result (eliminating the minus signs), adding them up, and dividing by the number of data points. Squaring magnifies wildly aberrant prices, so the bigger the variation from the average and the more instances of such big variations in any one series, the higher the volatility.

Traders don't use variance as a stand-alone measure or indicator, and it's not offered in most charting packages. Why? Because variance isn't directly useful as a separate measure from the standard deviation, which is essentially the square root of variance. Don't panic at the thought of square root or any other statistical measure in technical analysis. Your software will supply the indicators that incorporate variance, and you don't have to know how to calculate the indicators in order to use them effectively.

REMEMBER

Time frame is everything. How you perceive volatility depends entirely on the time frame you're looking at. Failure to specify a specific time frame is why you see so many conflicting generalizations about volatility. The period over which you measure volatility has a direct effect on how you think about volatility and, therefore, what kind of a trader you are. Your trading style isn't only a function of what indicators you like, but also of how you perceive risk. Two traders can use the same indicators but get different results because they manage the trade differently by looking at volatility differently (scaling in and out, choosing a stop-loss level, and so on).

In Figure 14-1, your eye tells you that the low-variance prices on the left side of the chart are less volatile and therefore less risky to trade than the high-variance prices on the right side of the chart, even when the high-variance prices are in a trending mode. And that's the point about volatility — it describes the level of risk. High variance means high risk. In the following sections, I go into more detail about the nature of volatility, including both high and low levels.

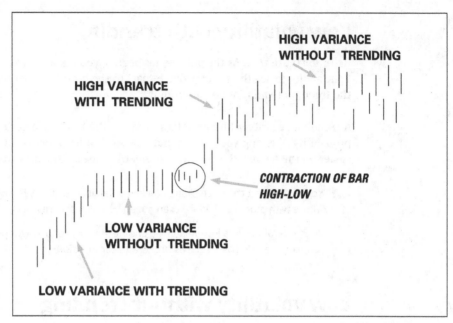

FIGURE 14-1: Degrees of volatility.

© John Wiley & Sons, Inc.

How volatility arises

Think of volatility in terms of crowd sentiment. Volatility rises when traders get excited about a new move. They anticipate taking the price to new highs or lows, which arouses greed in bulls putting on new positions and fear in bears, who scramble to get out of the way in a cascade of stop losses. The start of a new move is when you get higher highs (or lower lows). Volatility tends to be abnormally low just before a turning point and abnormally high just as the price is taking off in the first big thrust of a new trend. It's also, however, a sad fact of trading life that sometimes volatility is high or low for no price-related reason you can find. (Refer to Chapter 4 for more about this pesky noise.)

REMEMBER

High volatility means trading is riskier but has more profit potential, while low volatility means less immediate risk.

Volatility isn't inherently good or bad. Stability of volatility over time is a good thing because it allows you to estimate maximum potential gains and losses with greater accuracy. Every security has its own volatility norm that changes over time as the fundamentals and trader population changes. Sometimes you can impute a "personality" to a security that is really a reflection of the collective risk appetite of its traders.

Low volatility with trending

Refer to Figure 14-1. As the price series begins, you instantly see an upward trend. Your ability to see the trend is due in part to the orderliness of the move. You see the trend, not variations away from it.

REMEMBER

A trending security with low volatility offers the best trade because it has a high probability of giving you a profit and low probability of delivering a loss. It's also easier on the nerves. Here's why low volatility means the best trade:

>> You can project the price range of a low-volatility trending security into the future with more confidence than a high-volatility security.

>> You generally hold a low-volatility trending security for a longer period of time, reducing trading costs such as brokerage commissions.

Low volatility without trending

A security that's range-trading sideways with little variation from one day to the next is simply untradeable in that time frame. You have no basis on which to form an expectation of a gain, and without an expectation of gain, you shouldn't trade it. You can reduce the time frame (from one day to one hour, for example) to make visible and tradeable the minor peaks and troughs.

TIP

If a price is trading sideways without directional bias but the high-low range of the bars contracts or widens, now you're cooking with gas. Range contraction and expansion are powerful forecasting tools of an upcoming breakout. You can start planning the trade. In Figure 14-1, every bar is the same height except the ones in the circle, which are narrowing. The drop in high-low range and therefore in volatility often precedes a breakout, although you don't know in advance in which direction unless you also have a reliable pattern (refer to Chapter 9), including candlesticks (see Chapter 8).

High volatility with trending

WARNING

You may think that the degree of volatility doesn't matter when your security is trending, but an increase in volatility automatically increases the risk of loss. You may start fiddling with your indicators to adapt them to current conditions. Tinkering with the parameters of indicators *when you have a live trade in progress* is always a mistake. A better response to rising volatility is to recalculate potential gain against potential loss (as Chapter 5 discusses).

High volatility without trending

When a security is range-trading, it's called a trader's nightmare. When it's range-trading with high volatility, it's a horrible nightmare. The right section of the price series in Figure 14-1 shows this. In this situation, the range is so wide you can't identify a breakout; you see spiky one- and two-day reversals as bulls and bears slug it out, making it hard to find entries or to set systematic stops.

TIP

The solution to high volatility in a nontrending case is to stop trading the security or to narrow the time frame down to an intraday time frame. Often you can find tradeable swings within 15-minute or 60-minute bars that don't exist on the daily chart.

Measuring Volatility

Volatility is the degree of variation of a price series over time. You can measure volatility in plain or fancy ways. In financial analysis, volatility usually means one thing — the standard deviation, which I discuss in the "Considering the standard deviation" section later in the chapter. Before tackling that, look at other useful measures of volatility.

Tracking the maximum move

REMEMBER

One way to measure volatility is to capture the *largest* price change over *x* number of days — the *maximum move*, also called *gross move*. You subtract the lowest low from the highest high over 10 days or 100 days or some other number of days. You use the resulting maximum move to set a profit target *(maximum favorable excursion)* or worst-case stop loss *(maximum adverse excursion)*.

In Figure 14-2, the top window shows the highest high in a rolling 30-day period minus the lowest low in the same 30-day period — the maximum move. Notice that at the beginning and middle of the chart, you could make as much as $30 in a 30-day period in this security, but then the volatility of the price change tapers off to under $10 by the end of the chart. At that point, you're taking less risk of a catastrophic drop in the price over any 30-day period, but your profit potential has just been cut to one-third of its previous glory, too — the usual trade-off between risk and reward.

FIGURE 14-2:
Thirty-day
minimum and
maximum of a
stock.

WARNING

Volatility changes. Projecting the volatility of the last 30 days to the next 30 days is to assume conditions will not change — but conditions *always* change. Projecting a straight line or channel carries small risk. Projecting volatility carries such high risk that it's foolhardy.

Maximum move and trend

In Figure 14-2, seeing the connection between the 30-day maximum move in the top window and the prices in the bottom window is hard. The straight line starting at the middle of the bottom window is the linear regression (see Chapter 10). The line slopes upward means the price is in a slight uptrend, but at the same time, volatility is on a downtrend. This is a good combination for you; trendedness is delivering new profits at an ever-lower risk of a big one-period loss. But remember, low volatility precedes a breakout, so it may not be a good deal for long.

REMEMBER

The *price* trend can differ in size and slope from the *volatility* trend. Sometimes they're in sync, rising or falling together, or they can move in opposite directions. Knowing something about the trend in the maximum move doesn't necessarily tell you anything about the trend in prices, and vice versa. In other words, volatility is often independent of price trendedness.

Maximum move and holding period

In Figure 14-3, the orderly price series has a net change from the lowest low to the highest high (A to B) of exactly the same amount as the disorderly price series below it. But obviously the disorderly series implies a greater risk of loss *if you have to exit before the period ends.* The trendedness of each security is the same, as shown by the identical linear regression slopes.

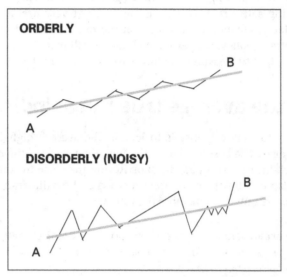

FIGURE 14-3:
Orderly and disorderly price series.

WARNING

Figure 14-3 illustrates that measuring the maximum high-low range over a fixed period of time fails to capture the risk of holding a position *during* the period, so don't write your expected holding period in stone.

Considering the standard deviation

Maximum move as previously discussed measures the gross low-to-high move over a period, but the bottom chart in Figure 14-3 exhibits a different kind of volatility that isn't captured by the maximum move. The disorderly price series has the same degree of trendedness and the same low-to-high outcome over the period, but it's obviously a riskier trend. What is the right way to express that riskiness?

The answer is the standard deviation. The *standard deviation* is a measure of the dispersion of prices away from the average. The wider the spread, the higher the standard deviation. The concept is in the same statistical family as standard error, which I introduce in Chapter 11. The standard deviation is measured from a moving average and measures the actual variance of each price away from the centerline.

I bet you were expecting a chart showing standard deviation right about here. Well, charting software does offer it, but it's not very useful as a stand-alone measure. Hardly anyone actually looks at the raw standard deviation on a chart, because better applications exist, including Bollinger Bands (See the section "Applying Volatility Measures: Bollinger Bands" later in the chapter.)

Using the average true range indicator

Another way to view volatility is to look at the average high-low range over *x* number of days. The best version of the high-low range is the *average true range (ATR)*, which incorporates gaps by substituting the close for the gapped high or low. See Chapter 7 for the calculation method and for illustrations of expanding and contracting ranges. Remember the following:

>> **Range expansion:** The highs and lows are getting farther apart; volatility is rising. Range expansion provides a bigger profit opportunity and an equivalent increase in risk of gain or loss.

>> **Range contraction:** The highs and lows are moving closer together, and you may think that risk is lower, too. But this is true only up to a point — the point of a breakout.

In Figure 14-4, the ATR indicator in the top window starts falling after the one-day big-bar rise that marks the beginning of the support line. You don't know whether you can draw the support line until afterward, but you can see the ATR indicator failing to match that spiky high and continue to fall. The price is rising, but the indicator is falling. And as usual, a divergence between indicator and price is a warning sign. Sure enough, right after the highest high, you get a series of lower highs and can draw a resistance line (see Chapter 10). Pretty soon the price breaks under support.

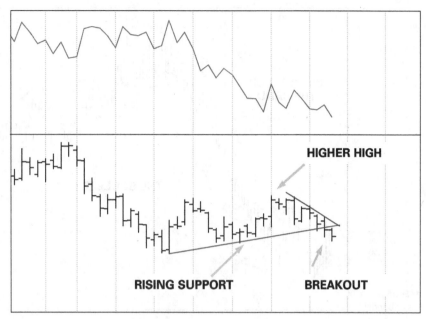

FIGURE 14-4:
Average true
range indicator
(ATR).

Labels in figure: HIGHER HIGH, RISING SUPPORT, BREAKOUT

Applying Volatility Measures: Bollinger Bands

The most popular volatility measure is the Bollinger Band (see Figure 14-5), invented by John Bollinger. He charted a simple 20-day moving average of the closing price with a band on either side consisting of two standard deviations of the moving average, effectively capturing about 95 percent of the variation away from the average.

You use Bollinger Bands to display the price in the context of a norm set at the 20-day moving average, which is the number of days that Bollinger's research showed is the most effective in detecting variance in U.S. equities. The bands display *relative* highs and *relative* lows in the context of the moving average — they're adaptive to the price by the amount of the standard deviation. The bands are, so to speak, moving standard deviations.

REMEMBER

The price touching or slightly breaking the top of the band is a continuation signal. Often the price continues to *walk up* or *walk down* the band, as shown in Figure 14-5. A Bollinger Band breakout is just like any other breakout — you expect the price to continue moving in the same direction as the breakout.

FIGURE 14-5:
Bollinger Bands.

© *John Wiley & Sons, Inc.*

At some point, every price thrust exhausts itself. Bollinger Bands display the end of the upmove in two ways:

>> **The price bar stops hugging the top band in an upmove, and slides down to the center moving average (or farther).** In Figure 14-5, the retreat to the moving average occurs at the ellipse. As a general rule, the failure to make a relative new high signals the end of the move, although this time, the bulls made a second effort to keep the rally going. In this case, the price was forming a double top (see Chapter 9).

>> **The bands contract.** When the bands contract, the range is narrowing. Traders are having second thoughts. They aren't willing to test a new high, but they aren't willing to go short and generate new lows, either.

TIP

The narrowing of the trading range is named the *squeeze* and implies an impending breakout. Figure 14-5 displays a reversal, but a reversal isn't the inevitable outcome. Breakouts can occur in the same direction as the original move, too. In this case, the downside breakout of the bottom of the band occurred unusually quickly after an upside breakout of the top band.

WARNING

A rapid break of the opposite band is sometimes a head fake. In the case of a downside move like the one in Figure 14-5, traders could have been overly exuberant in taking profits after such a big run up to the high. See the upward pullback from the downmove in the two circles. Sometimes pullbacks keep going, and the price resumes the uptrend — although hardly ever after breaking the bottom band like this one. To detect head fakes, use Bollinger Bands with other confirming indicators, especially momentum indicators like the relative strength index and MACD (refer to Chapter 12).

Applying Stops with Average True Range Bands

Bollinger Bands aren't generally used to set stops. The bands are equidistant from the moving average, so an upside breakout has the same statistical strength as a downside breakout. When you have a strongly trending security, you can't make a reversal move face a tougher breakout test — but logically, you should. I call it a "prove it" test. Given that false breakouts are so common, this reason makes it necessary and sufficient for you to consider another type of band, as observed by system designer Steve Notis. (The Notis PBS software is no longer available, but if you're computationally competent, you can reproduce it in your charting software.)

REMEMBER

To use a band for a stop, you want the band to be asymmetrical, so that in an uptrend, a downmove has to be more severe than recent upmoves to trigger your stop. But you can't filter Bollinger Bands. Instead of using the standard deviation to form the upper and lower bands, you can use a version of the average true range (ATR). You can adjust the ATR as follows so that a breakout proves that it's statistically significant:

>> **Uptrend:** Widen the distance of the lower band from the average.

>> **Downtrend:** Widen the distance of the upper band from the average.

The greater width of one of the bands from the center moving average separates corrective moves from real reversals. This move can become labor intensive, not least because before you can widen either band you must be sure of the trend direction. ATR doesn't give you a read on directional volatility like standard deviation.

In Figure 14-6, the price makes a bottom on the left-hand side and starts an upmove. The centerline is a moving average of the *median price,* or the average of the high, low, and close. The bands are formed by taking a moving average of the ATR and adding and subtracting it from the moving average.

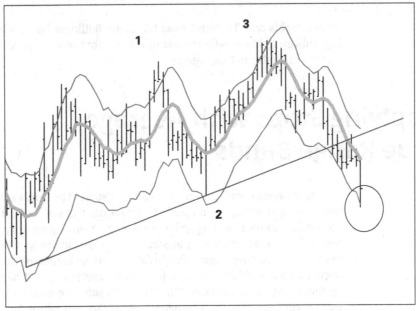

© John Wiley & Sons, Inc.

FIGURE 14-6:
Average true
range band.

This process creates an ATR test that a breakout has to pass to qualify as a true breakout. When the price starts a new uptrend, the price breaking the upper band confirms that you have identified the trend correctly.

A downside breakout has to pass a bigger test in an uptrend. Accordingly, you widen the lower band by adding a percentage of the ATR to it. On the chart in Figure 14-6, the lower band is 50 percent wider than the upper band (it is 150 percent of the ATR). The last bar on the chart breaks the band, just after the support line is broken. This is no mere retracement! You have a double breakout of the trend (support) plus a volatility breakout (ATR band).

As with Bollinger Bands, a breakout above the upper band signals continuation, but because breakouts are a sign of abnormally high volatility, you can usually count on a pullback to the median. A longer-term position trader would buy at the left-hand low and hold the break of the support line. A swing trader, on the other hand, would sell at breakout "1" and go short the security to the touch of the support line at point "2." Now he becomes a buyer again to point "3," where high volatility again triggers a short position that he holds to the break of the support line or final ATR band breakout.

Few traders would use the ATR breakout alone as the sole deciding factor. On Figure 14-6, I put only a support line, but in practice, you would be looking at other indicators. I didn't do the profit-and-loss arithmetic in this case, but it's pretty clear that a swing trader using volatility would have made a series of gains that collectively added up to a higher profit than the trend-following buy-and-hold trader.

Chapter **15**

Ignoring Time to Create Better Timing

Timing is important. It counts in cooking, romance, and a thousand activities. It counts so deeply in technical analysis–based trading that the word "timing" appears in the titles of many articles and books. So why throw time out the window in constructing charts?

The answer is that important price moves can happen at any time. The time of day (or night) is irrelevant. What's important is the price move. With some important exceptions, like the daily close or the month-end, price moves based on changing sentiment occur independently of time. They depend on the news and Events that drive supply and demand.

You can divorce indicator signals that direct your buy/sell timing from conventional time constants. You don't really care at what hour a breakout occurs; you care far more about whether it's a true breakout you should trade or a false one you should ignore. By removing time, you get some amazingly good results, as this chapter explains.

Focusing on Tick Bars: In the Spirit of Ignoring Time

Before diving into the two methods that ignore time entirely, I first need to discuss tick bars, which I mention in passing in Chapter 6 on reading basic bars. Tick bars don't ignore time. The bottom horizontal x-axis on the chart looks the same as on any standard chart. But tick bars are in the spirit of the methods that do ignore time, because they exist only when a minimum number of trades have taken place. Not enough trades, no tick on the chart.

You get a tick entry on the chart only when a minimum number of trades has been achieved — however much time that takes. You get to define the number of trades in your software. The virtue of tick bars is that they display raw supply and demand when those characteristics are big enough to deserve notice.

If you set your custom tick size too big, whole days can go by with no entry on your tick chart. You'll still see regular bars and regular volume on a regular chart, but there wasn't enough true interest, as evidence by the number of trades, to generate an entry on the tick chart. In practice, a bunch of days with no tick entries means you set the threshold too high.

REMEMBER

When you set the tick threshold properly, a series of rising ticks with each tick representing a large number of contracts or shares means the professionals are buying. After all, only the professionals (hedge funds, fund managers, mutual funds, and so on) have the capital to buy large number of shares, not the retail amateurs (you and me). The tick chart is a way to incorporate volume into the price bar — through the back door.

Another virtue of tick bars is that when trading volumes are low and you're getting few ticks, you have a built-in method to suppress your perception of volatility. Remember that volatility indicators are built on a comparison of today's price versus the price a specific number of periods ago. You can get a misleading high volatility reading on very little price action in a sideways market. By compressing low activity periods, you're diluting them and avoiding the dreaded whipsaw loss.

WARNING

Not every software package contains a decent tick bar capability, and even if your software does allow you to draw tick bars, you may have to fiddle for some time before you get one. Be sure to label it in a large font to avoid confusing it with a regular chart. As with the other time-independent charting methods, though, you can apply all the same indicators and patterns to tick charts.

Narrowing the Focus to the Move Itself: The Constant Range Bar

Momentum is one of the only indicators that can honestly be said to *lead* price action (refer to Chapter 13). Furthermore, as I discuss in Chapter 14, the average true range is a highly useful concept to detect a change in sentiment in the form of volatility as it widens and narrows like a pig in a python.

If you put these two observations together, you get a *constant range bar,* also referred to as a *momentum bar* or *Mbar,* a newish development in technical analysis that looks only at momentum and only in the form of a range. More than one analyst claims to have invented constant range bars. The copyright on range bars belongs to technical designer Danton Long, who introduced them in 2003 and also invented several other original indicators (including a stop). Parallel invention or not, they're available on only a few platforms, including TD Ameritrade, TradeStation, and CQG, plus some other broker platforms.

These sections take a closer look at constant range bars and how you can use them to make money trading securities.

Defining a constant range bar

Like point-and-figure charting, which I describe in the "Catching the Big Kahuna: Point-and-Figure Charts" later in this chapter, the *constant range bar* takes only price into consideration and simply ignores time. The constant range bar displays the high-low range as a bar and then only if a minimum range parameter is met, like 10 points. If the price doesn't move those 10 points, no bar. This wipes out all the noisy price actions that aren't useful.

REMEMBER

Constant range bars, like tick bars and point-and-figure charts, eliminate noise and show only meaningful price moves.

Constant range bars are also named momentum bars because you get a bar only if the price has moved out of its last range. What you're looking for is a mini-breakout from one range to another. Making each bar the same height serves that purpose — the range of each bar is literally constant. (This can take a little getting used to.) Obviously you can't use standard bar-reading techniques (see Chapter 6) on constant range bars. And because it's the bar range that is constant, each bar can cover any amount of time at all, from minutes to weeks. Constant range bars have you in the market only when there is a trading opportunity, regardless of the calendar.

REMEMBER

Range bars are open to applying other indicators, including especially support and resistance and channels. Look online, especially at YouTube videos, for more information about range bars. Just beware of puffery.

Identifying what criteria are needed

The following conditions have to happen for a constant bar to happen:

>> **A high-low range at a certain minimum number:** In this sense, the constant bar is a kissing cousin to the tick bars that I describe in the previous section. Each bar represents a block of trades having the same range, specified by you. In other words, each bar is exactly the same height, and you get a bar only if the price has moved at least one tick from the previous bar, no matter how long that takes and regardless of volume. When a price is moving sideways in the same range, the result is a large expanse of empty spaces.

>> **A distinct change from the previous one:** In other words, a meaningful gap has to occur outside the high-low range of the existing bar. It's usually set at one tick but can be set to a higher number of ticks, which makes sense when you consider that you're trying to identify change. A new constant range bar has to open outside the previous bar's range for change to be meaningful.

>> **A close at the high or the low:** This criterion is a little harder to grasp, but it also makes sense in the context of identifying meaningful change in momentum.

Say your security has an average true range of 120 points. In order to determine whether something significant is happening, you could decide to set your constant bar range at 50 percent of the average true range, or 60 points. Your constant range bar chart is going to place a new bar only if it opens (say) 20 points away from the last constant range bar and contains at least 60 points between the low and the high.

It could take a few hours (or days or weeks) for a new bar to appear, meaning the constant range bar methodology chart has winnowed out a ton of noise and is giving you pure signal. You haven't wasted time and risked whipsaw losses trying to trade a sideways-moving price. Instead you could be looking at some other security that does have a chance of a significant move.

Catching the Big Kahuna: Point-and-Figure Charts

Point-and-figure (P&F) charts have been around for more than 100 years and are probably available on all charting software. More than likely, floor traders in the 1870s invented P&F as a pre-electronic way to record the relevant price moves instead of every tiny fractional change. P&F charting strips away time and displays only significant prices on the chart. *Significant* prices are those that exceed the high or low of a recent trading range by a specified amount. You ignore minor moves — literally. You don't even record them on your chart. The result is filtered price action. You don't see a price move in the opposite direction of the current trend until it meets your own definition of meaningful, raising confidence in the accuracy of a reversal signal.

You can also easily identify patterns on P&F charts, especially support and resistance, and therefore, breakouts of support and resistance. P&F charts look very different from standard bar charts, but after you get used to them, you may find their directness and simplicity addictive. P&F is the easiest of all the technical concepts, and as Jeremy du Plessis points out in *The Definitive Guide to Point and Figure* (Harriman House), the only computational method that is unique to financial prices. Engineers and scientists use measures like standard deviation, but they never use P&F. Also, P&F is the only major technique to ignore volume altogether.

REMEMBER

P&F and constant range bars emphasize a shift in the price *range* as the basis of trading decisions, which is in keeping with the idea of measuring crowd behavior (check out Chapter 3). The purpose of the display method is to filter out irrelevant prices to isolate the trends.

P&F analysis is suitable for trading that has a medium- to long-term holding period — weeks and months. The only way to know whether P&F charting is right for you is to try it out on your chosen securities and see what gains you would've made, how many trades it requires of you, and so on.

Visualizing What's Important

Technical indicators aim to identify trend-tuning points and, if a trend exists, how strong it is. But all charts contain a lot of data that isn't meaningful — it's filler or noise. The standard bar chart has an entry for every day, even when nothing interesting happened. What if you could isolate just the juicy nuggets of price information and forgo the noise?

Displaying the price only when it makes a significant move is the essence of P&F charting. If nothing noteworthy happened on a particular day, you put nothing on the chart. Because chart events like a breakout or reversal often follow real-world events (breaking news, for example), you can consider the P&F chart to be event-driven.

The P&F method of displaying data takes time to get used to. Some people think that it looks weird, while others take to it like a duck to water. Stick with it, though, and you can easily get the hang of it.

Putting each move into a column

In P&F charting, you put a price entry on the chart only if the price is higher than the previous high by a certain amount or lower than the previous low by a certain amount.

When a price is going sideways — not making a new high or low — nothing is happening in the security, and you enter nothing on the chart.

For a new high that is higher than the previous high, you enter an X. For a new low that is lower than the previous low, you enter an O. You place the Xs and Os in a column that represents a continuous move, either up or down. The P&F chart contains alternating columns of Xs and Os, where each column is a move. A column of Xs is an upmove and a column of Os is a downmove. Each X column is reserved for rising prices and each O column is reserved for falling prices.

Say you're considering a security whose price has been rising. The high today is $9. You start a new chart and enter an X next to the $9 label on the vertical axis, as I've done in Figure 15-1. The next day, the price high is $10, so you enter an X *in the same column* at the $10 level. When the high reaches $12 the next day, you add two Xs to denote the move from yesterday's $10 to today's $12. You keep adding Xs in the same column until the price climb ends. In the example in Figure 15-1, the price stops climbing at $13. You see a column of Xs that represents the price rise from $9 to $13 in a single move.

When the upmove is over and the price makes a new low below yesterday's low by a specific amount, you *must* start a new column, using an O and placing it at the dollar level of the new low. (I tell you more about this topic in a minute in the "Defining box size" section; for now, consider that the new low suffices to consider that the upmove is over.) Figure 15-1 tells you that the new low came at $10. You now expect the next entry to be another O where the question mark is placed on the chart. Whatever happens next, the formation of a new column alerts you to a change in the price dynamics.

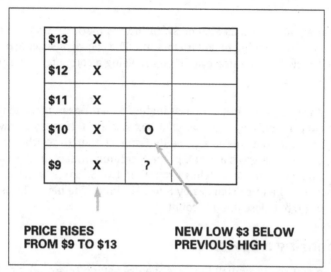

$13	X		
$12	X		
$11	X		
$10	X	O	
$9	X	?	

PRICE RISES FROM $9 TO $13

NEW LOW $3 BELOW PREVIOUS HIGH

FIGURE 15-1: P&F chart format.

REMEMBER

Each column on the chart represents an upmove or a downmove, regardless of time. On a daily chart, a column can represent 2 days, 10 days, 100 days, or any other number of days. You start a new column only when the last directional move is over. On the chart in Figure 15-1, you have an upmove from $9 to $13 and thus five Xs, but that doesn't mean it took 5 days. It may have taken 30 days because on days showing no new high, you skipped over that price data and didn't make a chart entry.

Most P&F charts exhibit dates at the bottom of the chart along the horizontal axis. These dates aren't spaced evenly at regular intervals because they're there only for convenience — in P&F charting, the date is irrelevant and only price action matters.

Dealing with box size

The *box size* is the minimum amount that the security needs to move above the recent highest high (marked by the last X) or below the lowest low (marked by the last O) before another entry is made on the chart. The following sections discuss how to get the box size right in P&F charting.

Defining box size

The horizontal axis suppresses dates and compresses time, but the vertical axis is spaced in the conventional way. In the days when traders used actual graph paper, they filled in the little boxes of the grid with the Os and Xs set at some appropriate dollar amount, such as $.50 or $1. In futures markets, traders use the number of points corresponding to dollar amounts. The choice of spacing on the vertical axis is still called the *box size*, even if you're using a computer program and not actual graph paper.

When your security has a highest high of $10, for example, and it regularly varies by $.50 per day, you might set your box size at $1. If today's new high is $12, you acknowledge that this is a price extreme — four times the usual daily trading range — and deserves a new X in the X column. In fact, in this case, the new high is a full $2 over the last high, so you fill in two $1 boxes with the X notation. What happens if the price changes by $.98? Nothing. The new price is close to the box size of $1, but close doesn't count.

Choosing a box size

When you select a small box size, you're asking to see a lot of detail, including small retracements. By increasing the box size, you're filtering out filler data, just like when you make a rule that requires a price to cross a moving average by *x* percent (see Chapters 12 and 13 for a discussion of filtering).

TIP

The smaller the box, the more sensitive the chart is to price changes. The bigger the box, the less sensitive the chart is. If you're averse to risk, you may prefer a small box size. If you want to see the big picture, you prefer a bigger box. Table 15-1 contains the standard box-size guidelines.

TABLE 15-1

Approximate Guidelines for Box Size

Security Price	Box Size
$5–$20	$.50
$20–$100	$1
$100–$200	$2
$200–$300	$4
$300–$400	$6

WARNING

If you leave a charting program in default mode, the program will adjust the box size to fit the screen, which may result in some unhappy outcomes. You could get a box size of $0.67 or some other arbitrary number. Box size is too important to leave to a program if only because other traders are using a standard round-number box, like $.50 or $1. Besides, the software, whether your own or on a website, adjusts box size to accommodate the amount of data you select, so you get different P&F charts (and hypothetical trading decisions), depending on how much data you display. The software uses the box size that fits the highest range in the data series in order to get everything on one chart. But the trading range of any single security changes over time, and you want to take note of that rather than let the software obscure the changing range. If you use P&F charting software, fix the box size so you know whether the range is expanding or contracting.

Adding the reversal amount to the picture

The purpose of the box size is to note a significant change in price. But how do you know how far a price has to move below the X (upward) column to warrant starting an O (downward) column? For that, you establish a second criterion, the *reversal amount*. The traditional reversal amount is three boxes. If your box is $1 and you're now in a rising X column, you have to get a new low that is $3 lower than the low today to start a new O (downward) column.

TIP

You can backtest a variety of box sizes and reversal amounts to arrive at the best numbers to use for any particular security. As a general rule, though, P&F chartists recommend sticking to the three-box rule for reversals and adopting different box sizes for chart entries, depending on the absolute level of the prices.

WARNING

A box size of $4, the appropriate box for a security selling over $200, with a three-box reversal, works out to $12. If you have 100 shares, you would exit on a reversal of at least $1,200, which is a fairly hefty sum of money. If you use the three-box reversal as a stop level, you have to accept that big a loss when the price goes against you. If you judge that $1,200 is too big a loss to take on a single position, you can trade a smaller number of shares (an odd-lot) or switch to a cheaper security.

Drawing the daily chart

In practice you'll use software to draw P&F charts. But to understand the process, imagine for a minute you're doing it by hand. To draw the chart, every day you check the highest high and lowest low of the day. Is the price higher than the previous high by $1? If so, enter another X above the last X in the column. Is the low lower than today's low by $1? Enter nothing. By $2? Again, enter nothing. By $3? Aha! That's three boxes worth, the reversal amount, and you start a new column, entering the O at a level $3 below the last X. Because it's a reversal, now you expect the next entry to be one box lower. The next day, is the low price lower than yesterday by $1? If so, enter another O. If it's higher, it has to be higher than today's high by $3 to abandon the falling-price O column.

TIP

If you see a lot of reversal columns that contain only one entry, chances are your box size is too small — or your reversal amount is wrong.

REMEMBER

What if you get a new high by one box and on the same day, also get a new low by the reversal amount — three boxes? This is an *outside* day (see Chapter 7). The new low trumps the new high, and you should start a new column of Os. After all, you're looking for a threat to the trend (and your pocketbook). A new low by the reversal amount constitutes a serious threat.

Applying Patterns

Patterns pop out on P&F charts. Some of the most common patterns include support and resistance, but also simple patterns like double and triple tops and bottoms appear. These sections show how to use them.

Support and resistance

P&F charting offers two versions of support and resistance: The horizontal historic-level version and the conventional version that slopes along a series of highs or low. Here I talk about both types.

Horizontal support and resistance

Traders remember the highest high ever or the lowest low in the past three months as benchmarks when the price approaches the same level. In P&F charting, the horizontal line that you draw to mark the top or bottom of columns becomes a kind of recent-history support or resistance. Therefore, you often get a series of columns that all end at a floor or a ceiling, regardless of whether they're Xs or Os. Floors and ceilings are very handy both for spotting a breakout and setting a stop.

In Figure 15-2, the top-left chart shows a breakout X above the resistance line. Using conventional charting, you wouldn't have known that line was there unless you were on the lookout for historic highs and lows. But P&F chartists draw them all the time to denote where supply becomes abundant or demand falls short, halting a price rise.

Conventional support and resistance

On a standard bar chart, you draw a support line along a series of lows or a resistance line along a series of highs (see Chapter 10). These lines almost always have a slope that describes the trend and are hardly ever horizontal except in a consolidation. You can draw sloping support and resistance lines on P&F charts, too.

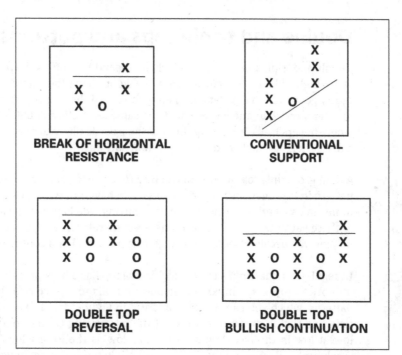

FIGURE 15-2:
Patterns on
P&F charts.

© John Wiley & Sons, Inc.

REMEMBER

You trade P&F support and resistance the same as you do when using conventional support and resistance — a breakout to the upside triggers a purchase and a breakout to the downside triggers a sale. As with conventional support and resistance lines, don't erase a support line after it's broken — it has a good chance of becoming the new resistance line. An old resistance line may become the new support line, too.

Because a P&F chart filters out noisy prices and compresses time, your chart often displays authentic long-term support or resistance that you'd miss on a regular daily bar chart. You may also see *triangles*, which are support and resistance lines that converge. Chapter 9 covers triangles.

The top-right chart in Figure 15-2 shows a conventional support line. You could have a conventional (sloping) resistance line, too. Notice that if your boxes are perfectly square, you can draw a 45-degree line and extend it out into the future by starting with just two columns when one of the columns is one box higher or lower than the other. The 45-degree technique allows you to start a support or resistance line more simply and sometimes earlier than in conventional bar charting. The upward-sloping 45-degree line is named a *bullish support line,* and a downward-sloping 45-degree line is a *bearish resistance line.*

Double and triple tops and bottoms

Double and triple tops are formed when demand falls off as the price nears a previous high. When bulls fail to get a breakout above the established high, it's a pretty good sign that sellers are happy to unload the security at that price. When you get more than one low at about the same level, it's a double or triple bottom, where buyers think it's a bargain, and the price is likely to rise. See Chapter 9 for a discussion of double and triple tops and bottoms.

REMEMBER

A double or triple top or bottom can be either a reversal pattern or a continuation pattern in P&F charting, depending on the behavior of the opposite-direction columns. In conventional time-based bar charting, you have to wait for confirmation of these patterns — chewing up time. P&F, therefore, can speed up the process of helping you decide whether you're getting a reversal or a continuation.

TIP

In regular bar charting, a confirmed double top has a high probability of resulting in a price drop. A qualified double bottom leads to a price rise. They're reversal patterns, which you can see in chart form in Figure 15-2. In P&F, however, chartists find that in an uptrend of Xs, if the intervening Os are on a rising line (the lowest low in the last O column isn't as low as the lowest low in the previous O column), a double top may turn into a triple top and then an *upside breakout* — in other words, a continuation pattern. This configuration is shown in the fourth pattern in Figure 15-2. If the opposite-direction columns are horizontal, though, the traditional reversal interpretation is probably correct.

Projecting Prices after a Breakout

P&F chartists forecast prices after a breakout by using the box count, either vertically or horizontally. However, vertical projections work more often than horizontal projections. The following sections discuss how to make your own forecasts based on P&F chart breakouts.

REMEMBER

In P&F charting, you buy when the new price surpasses the highest X in the previous X column, and you sell when the new price surpasses the lowest low O in the previous O column. When the price surpasses a previous high or low, you have a breakout.

Using vertical price projection

Say that your security has just made a double or triple top breakout like the one in Figure 15-2. You want to know how high the price will go. Or your security has fallen to a new low but is now rising up off it. You want to know the potential gain if the bottom is really in and the upmove continues. You know that the price will retrace to the downside over the course of the move, and you don't want to mistake a retracement for the end of the trend. If you have faith in the forecast, you decide to ride out the retracement.

P&F chartists create forecasts in each case with an ingenious version of momentum. Here's how you can do it:

1. **Find the bottom of the last X (upward) column if you have an upside breakout (or the bottom of the lowest X column if you suspect a reversal to the upside).**

2. **Count the number of boxes in the column (say four boxes).**

3. **Multiply the number of boxes by your reversal amount (see the reversal amount section earlier in the chapter), say the standard three.**

   $4 \times 3 = 12$

4. **Multiply that product by the box size, say the standard $1.**

   $12 \times \$1 = \$12$

5. **Add the product to the lowest low in the starting column to get your new price target.**

   If the lowest low was $10, you add $12, and your price target is now $22.

Figure 15-3 shows a sample vertical P&F projection.

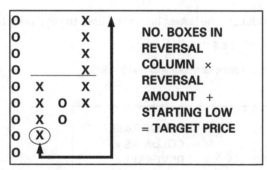

© John Wiley & Sons, Inc.

FIGURE 15-3:
Vertical
projection.

The price objective is only a guide. The actual new high may fall short of $22, or it may be a great deal more than $22. You don't automatically sell at $22 if the price is still making new highs. But you may want to evaluate the risk-reward ratio in terms of the price projection (the reward) and the lowest low in the starting column (where you may place your initial stop). As I discuss in Chapter 5, you always want to manage the trade so that the expected gain from a trade is higher than the worst-case loss you allow.

TIP

To estimate how far a downmove may go, reverse the process. You start from the highest-high box before the downmove column begins, count the boxes, multiply by three, multiply again by the box size, and voilà! You have an estimate of where the drop may stop.

Applying horizontal projection

You use a horizontal count to project the ending price of a breakout after a period of consolidation. Say the price has been going mostly sideways for some period of time. Yes, it has alternating X and O columns, but your eye can detect a base, or bottom formation. (For a downside breakout, you need to see a top formation.)

Figure 15-4 shows a base forming after a five-column downtrend ahead of an upside breakout. To calculate the projected price, follow these steps:

1. **Identify the number of columns in the base, which is the sideways period before the breakout, and exclude the breakout column.**

In this example, say you identify five columns.

2. **Multiply by the number of columns in the base by the reversal amount you choose — say the standard three-box reversal.**

$5 \times 3 = 15$

3. **Add the product to the lowest low in the base to get a price target.**

Say the lowest low is $10.

Now you have a price target of $10 + $15 = $25.

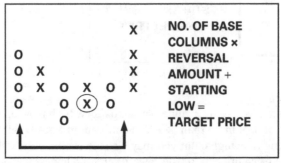

FIGURE 15-4:
Horizontal
projection.

Combining P&F Techniques with Other Indicators

The innate simplicity of P&F charting is appealing, but you can add value to decision making by speeding up the buy/sell signal or seeking confirmation or lack of confirmation from other indicators. Because other indicators are time based, how can this merger be done?

Here's how you can use P&F charting along with other indicators:

>> **Moving averages:** You use the price at the center of each column in calculating a moving average in P&F charts instead of the usual method of averaging prices over a fixed number of periods. Thus you're using the average price per reversal. If the moving average shows that you had a downtrend and now you get a new column of Xs that rises over the moving average, you have more confidence that the Xs really do imply a rising trend and thus a safer buy signal.

>> **Parabolic stop-and-reverse indicator:** The parabolic stop-and-reverse (SAR) indicator delivers a speedier reversal than waiting for a new column of Xs or Os. The parabolic SAR has the advantage of tightening your stop as the momentum of a price move decelerates.

>> **Bollinger Bands:** Data displayed in the P&F format can't display momentum and thus overbought or oversold, a shortcoming that can be partly addressed by applying Bollinger Bands (refer to Chapter 14). If your columns of Xs persist in pressing against the top of the band and sometimes breaking it, you have confirmation of the uptrend. When the next column of Os crosses the centerline (a simple moving average) to the downside, you expect a swing all the way to the bottom band.

Finally, Bollinger Bands are wide apart when volatility is high, and they "squeeze" narrower as volatility dissipates and prices become congested. In a congestion, P&F prices are in a series of short columns that you can't trust to deliver a reliable buy-or-sell signal. When you see the short columns together with the narrow Bollinger Band, you can guess that the market is fickle — it's not trending, and you should go find something else to trade.

Chapter **16**

Combining Techniques

I f trading with one indicator is better than trading with none, two indicators works even better. A second indicator offers *confirmation* of the signals you get from the first indicator. The confirmation principle is well-established as a core concept in technical analysis and a perfectly logical safeguard against the unhappy fact that any single indicator will be wrong some of the time. It's conceivable — but less likely — that two indicators together will both be wrong at the same time. You can add as many indicators to your charts as you can hold in your head or program into your computer, but experience shows you tend to get diminishing returns from a third and fourth indicator, and by the time you get to five and six indicators, you're more likely to get conflicting signals than added clarity.

This chapter surveys some combinations of techniques and offers guidance on the process of putting techniques together to forge a systematic approach to trading. Adding indicators multiplies the difficulty of the trading decision, but can pay off in terms of reducing uncertainty as well as increasing the gain/loss ratio.

Adding a New Indicator: Introducing Complexity

A single indicator (like the popular 20-day moving average) will improve your gain/loss ratio. But because even the best indicator fails sometimes, it's better to create a trading rule that uses a second indicator, filter, or pattern to provide confirmation.

But which two indicators should you choose? Or should you choose three, or four, or more? Because technical analysis has produced thousands of stand-alone indicators and patterns, the number of possible combinations and permutations is humungous. By the time you add time constraints, such as "Buy 30 minutes after the open (or high or low or close) if x, y, and z occur," the number of potential trading rules can be in the millions.

REMEMBER

Adding a new indicator piles on complexity and can get tricky. When you combine indicators, they often contradict one another. One indicator says buy, whereas a different indicator says sell. This conflict is common. Worse, one indicator will always issue a buy or sell signal before the second one. A large portion of the gain to be had from a new move comes in the first few periods, so if you wait for confirmation from an additional indicator, you're giving up potential profits in return for the comfort of expecting fewer false breakouts.

The price of your security, for example, crossed above its moving average and you bought it. The trend has been in place for a while. Now a momentum indicator like RSI or MACD is signaling that the security is overbought and will retrace. You don't know if the retracement will be minor or become a full-blown reversal. You know that the moving average lags the price action — no help there. Do you accept the sell signal from momentum, which is more likely to have some leading character?

No single correct answer exists. Sometimes momentum indicators are wrong, and the retracement doesn't occur at all, leaving you with the problem of where to reenter your trend, which is running away without you. But even after the most exhaustive backtesting and observation, you're still wrong some of the time no matter which decision you make. The purpose of combining indicators is to improve the odds of being right about the next price move, but you'll never be right 100 percent of the time.

REMEMBER

The only way to know whether two or more indicators work well together is to backtest them together, with the trading rules meticulously stipulated. Testing a single indicator is easy. Testing multiple indicators and rules for various contingencies is hard work and often raises more questions than it answers. And many people don't have the time or aptitude for backtesting. In that case, at the least take the time to observe the indicators on the chart and estimate how well they work together. After reading the following section and some practice, you should be able to see matching signals, divergences, support and resistance, and patterns. Expert traders say, "Trade what you see on the chart," and it's good advice.

Choosing primary and secondary indicators

Some technical analysts say you must choose a primary or *ruling* concept. Any confirming indicators you add are secondary; their purpose is to validate the signal generated by the ruling concept. I call them *validator* indicators.

Say you're using a classic moving average crossover as the ruling concept and add one of the momentum indicators as a validator. Now suddenly the momentum indicator is flashing a warning signal. What do you do? If you take the trade the momentum indicator is telling you to take, you're dumping your ruling concept in favor of a secondary one. To override your ruling concept is like abandoning your date at the prom when you restore original wording: see a prettier girl.

TIP

You need to plan ahead of time what exceptional validator indicators you'll obey over your ruling concept. You have dual goals here, and they conflict — to validate your ruling concept indicator and the trading plan you built on it, but also to make money. From a trading plan point of view, if you obey the validator concept, your stop will be set in the wrong place because it had been set based on the ruling-concept *plus* the validator, not the validator alone.

There is a solution. You should already know from your backtests or practice trading the probability of the validator alone. Say the validator is right 55 percent of the time and returns 40 percent when it's right — over many hypothetical trials. The ruling concept is right 75 percent of the time and returns 20 percent when it's right. Simply multiply. Switching to the validator delivers 22 percent while sticking to the ruling concept delivers 15 percent. If the validator is correct this time, your gain will be higher if you dump the ruling concept. I've found in my own trading that obeying the validator yields a higher return that waiting for the validator to confirm the ruling concept. It's jumping the gun, to be sure — and it violates the confirmation principle that two indicators are better than one. However, this is a very common outcome. One indicator will always contain more lag than the other one — that is, be slower at generating a buy/sell signal.

You just have to remember to change your stop and target at the same time, and you need to remove this trade from your combined-indicator track record and account for it separately. Again, this record-keeping is tedious but essential if you want to trade systematically and not by the seat of your pants.

Inserting unexpected validators

Say you're using arithmetic indicators like moving averages and momentum as your ruling and validator concepts. You don't use candlesticks (see Chapter 8) or patterns (see Chapter 9), although you know about them. As your chart is accumulating ever more price bars as time goes by, suddenly you see one of those special candlesticks or patterns. It's rare for you see a pattern. If you can see it without even looking, everyone else trading this security must see it, too. And you don't want to be too far out of step with the crowd that trades this security.

For example, you're using a two-moving average concept as the ruling concept and one of the momentum indicators for confirmation. You don't use candlesticks or patterns, but out of the blue you spot a bearish candlestick, like a hanging man (see Chapter 8), that is a big warning. You decide to exit early even though your indicators aren't signaling a sell and your stop is still far away. Is this the right decision? In the majority of cases, yes, you should obey the hanging man. But then you need to remove this trade from your track record that is measuring the gains and losses from the central two-indicator system.

Figure 16-1 shows another example. In this case, you're using the Donchian 5/20-day moving average crossover (buy when the 5-day crosses above the 20-day and sell when it falls below the 20-day). You get a sell signal. A little later, the price bounces and you get a buy signal followed in a few weeks by another sell signal — a whipsaw. But before then, you can't avoid noticing the double top, even though pattern recognition isn't one of the indicators in your toolkit. But it's the gorilla in the room on this chart, so you run right out and research it. The rule in double-top analysis is that after the confirmation point is reached, the price often pulls back above it before resuming the downtrend, giving you a better opportunity to go short. This time you follow the double-top rule and avoid the moving average-generated whipsaw. Pattern recognition served you well.

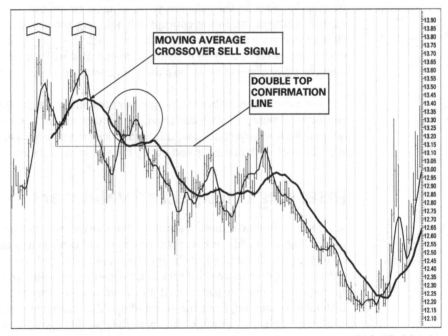

FIGURE 16-1: Trade what you see.

© John Wiley & Sons, Inc.

WARNING

A wide knowledge of indicators can help make your trading more adaptive and flexible. But it's human nature that when you have a hammer, everything looks like a nail. Beware of imagining double tops on every chart after the successful trade exemplified in Figure 16-1 and beware of believing that every double top delivers this outcome. A series of successful trades on a single indicator doesn't make it a magic indicator that always works. I can't say it often enough — no indicator works all the time.

Studying a classic combination

Choosing your indicators can make all the difference. You start with a classic moving crossover, but you know it entails late entries and lower profits because moving averages are lagging. To improve the moving average system, you add two additional indicators:

>> You want to enter earlier, so you add a momentum indicator.

>> You want to exit closer to the high, so you also add an overbought indicator (a sentiment indicator).

This is a classic beginner's trading system that tends to be reliable and consistent in terms of delivering profits and reducing the number of losses. In Figure 16-2, the main window shows the primary trading concept, a moving average crossover. You buy when the 5-day moving average closes above the 20-day moving average (the thicker line) and sell when the price closes below the thinner 5-day moving average. To identify the entry sooner, you jazz it up by adding a momentum indicator at the bottom of the chart that tells you when momentum is on the rise, giving you an earlier entry than the moving average by three days. At the top is a different momentum indicator (relative strength) telling you when the price is coming down off an overbought level. This gives you an exit one day earlier.

Using the moving average alone makes you a profit of $2.51 in three weeks, but when you accelerate the entry and exit by using the additional indicators, you boost profitability by over 50 percent, as shown in Table 16-1.

At a glance, the case in Figure 16-2 demonstrates a successful integration of three indicators that accelerates entry and exit and makes you more money. But in reality, it's seldom this neat and tidy — or clear. Here are some examples of problems that can arise when you combine indicators.

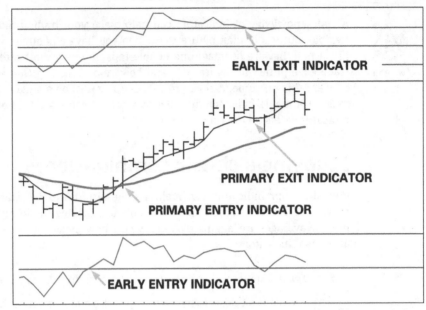

FIGURE 16-2: Confirming indicators.

EARLY EXIT INDICATOR

PRIMARY EXIT INDICATOR

PRIMARY ENTRY INDICATOR

EARLY ENTRY INDICATOR

© John Wiley & Sons, Inc.

TABLE 16-1   **Indicator Trading Results**

Indicator Trading Rule(s)	Buy	Sell	Profit
Moving average concept	$64.35	$66.86	$2.51
With momentum and relative strength	$63.38	$67.32	$3.94

Trading decisions multiply exponentially

Indicators add up arithmetically, but trading decision complexity multiplies exponentially. For example, what if the momentum indicator gives you a false reading? Indicators are wrong a lot. In the example in Figure 16-2, the early entry worked, but plenty of times it doesn't. You need an exit strategy — a stand-alone stop-loss rule — for that early entry when it's incorrect. The best rule for this type of situation may be to exit when you lose a specific dollar amount or percentage of capital at stake.

Concepts can mirror each other

The purpose of using multiple indicators is to get confirmation that a signal is likely to be correct. Obviously, if you're using a momentum indicator, you don't get independent confirmation from another momentum indicator because they're both using the same conceptual principle.

In the case of Figure 16-2, the confirming indicators look almost identical. And they are! Technical writer Tushar Chande studied the correlation among various momentum concepts. He found that momentum and the relative strength indicator shown on this chart (Chande's own version) are more than 90 percent correlated, meaning they move in lockstep. (See Chapter 13 for a discussion of all the guises momentum can assume.) You aren't really getting a third viewpoint, so to speak, when two of the indicators are basically measuring the same thing if in slightly different ways.

Concepts sometimes clash

Two or more concepts don't always play well together. For example, see Figure 16-3. The stochastic oscillator, momentum, and MACD are all used to improve the timing of entries and exits. On this chart, you have a sell signal from the moving average crossover. You use a trailing stop loss based on the average true range (refer to Chapter 5). It gets hit. Should you exit? Silly question! Of course you should exit. You should always follow your stops.

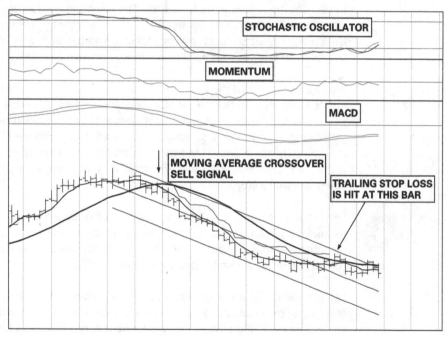

FIGURE 16-3: Conflicting signals.

© John Wiley & Sons, Inc.

But after the exit, now what? Look at the stochastic oscillator. It says not only should you exit the short position, but you should buy. The two moving average crossover doesn't confirm, and momentum in the next window is wavering around the center buy/sell line and doesn't deliver a hard decision. MACD in the next window has a crossover to the upside but the entire indicator remains under the bull/bear line. This situation suggests a trend change might be coming (or might not).

Reconciling clashing, or *divergent,* indicators can be solved, at least in part, by either exiting and waiting, or adding another indicator, such as the linear regression channel, Bollinger Band, or ATR band so see where the current price fits into the bigger scheme of things.

TIP

When looking at multiple indicators, add up the ones that say buy, the ones that say sell, and the ones that say "stay out" or are hard to read, and go with the course of action that has the *preponderance of evidence* on its side, to borrow a phrase from the legal profession. You seldom have a trading decision that is proven beyond a reasonable doubt, and so preponderance of evidence is the reasonable course when divergence appears.

Oddball combinations aren't that odd

In practice, no combination is oddball. Any combination that works on *your* securities in *your* time frame is acceptable. I know one trader whose setup consists of the divergence of support and on-balance volume in a very short time frame (minutes, in fact). It's 90 percent reliable — amazingly good.

Moving averages and momentum are basic indicators that many traders use and aren't beginner's indicators at all. But some traders use other indicators altogether, such as combining pivot point lines with candlestick interpretation to get viable trades, complete with stops. Other traders use Fibonacci counts to figure out where the price lies in the wave continuum. Even traders who know Fibonacci counts are unproven may use Fibonacci or Gann retracement levels to figure where to place a stop.

TIP

Use the KISS approach — keep it simple, stupid. Especially if you're a novice at technical analysis, don't add too many conditions and try to account for every contingency. And of course you're either backtesting or practice-trading first (right?), in order to obtain your expectancy reading.

You can easily discover how some of the big names in technical analysis conduct their work; technical analysts are unusually generous in disclosing their ideas. In addition to the books written by well-known analysts, you can find an overview in the classic *New Thinking in Technical Analysis, Trading Models from the Masters,* edited by Rick Bensignor (Bloomberg).

Sailing into Outer Space

If you research trading systems or regimes for sale, you will see some wild and crazy stuff. Here are two system designs that should entrance you in addition to the more conventional methods previously described.

The Conquistador

The core concept is to buy a security — the Conquistador was designed for currency futures but can be applied to other securities — when indicator conditions are met in three time frames. In other words, you get confirmation not from a second indicator of a different statistical nature, but from the same indicator viewed from a different angle. The Conquistador was devised by one of the pioneers of technical analysis, Bruce Babcock, author of numerous books, including *The Dow-Jones Guide to System Trading,* and later refined by another super-smart designer, Nelson Freeburg, publisher of *Formula Research* newsletter.

The system is simple: You buy when

>> Today's close is over the 10-day moving average **and**

>> Today's 10-day moving average is over the 10-day moving average ten days ago **and**

>> Today's close is above the close 40 days ago.

Sell conditions are met when the closes and averages are below the benchmarks. Trailing stops are applied using the average true range principle, like the Chandelier exit I discuss in Chapter 5. There is a whisper of ichimoku thinking in the Conquistador. Refer to Chapter 18 and see if you can spot the similarities.

The virtue of the three-timeframe confirmation is that you're out of the market in sideways range-trading conditions. Because you aren't looking at any of the momentum indicators, you can't be tricked into seeing trend strength emerging — you have to wait for it to be proved. The virtue is also the drawback; you'll be out of the market a lot of the time. Experts disagree on how often securities are trended versus untrended. If you use the three time frame method, you can calculate the trendedness of your securities.

Wave with relative strength

Prices clearly move in waves, whether you accept various wave theories or not (like Elliott Wave, discussed in Chapter 17). You'll quite often see waves within a channel, like the standard error channel that I discuss in Chapter 10. On many occasions, a tidy wave-like set of price moves appears that peaks out at or near the top of the channel and bottom out at or near the bottom. How do you know you have arrived at a top or bottom? Enter the relative strength index (RSI) as Figure 16-4 shows.

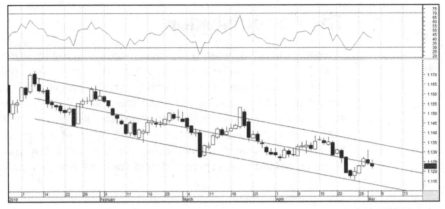

FIGURE 16-4:
Informal wave with RSI.

© John Wiley & Sons, Inc.

In Figure 16-4, the RSI has been modified from the default of 14 days to 9 days. Why 9? Because that's the average number of days between a high and a low over the past year in this particular security. When the RSI indicator is peaking, the security is overbought. It's time to exit and either go short or wait for the indicator to show the security is oversold.

WARNING

This is an exceptionally pretty chart. Pretty charts don't come along all that often. This security also spends a fair amount of time going sideways. And because RSI is like all oscillators, valuing today's price in in the context of recent prices (in this case, 9 days versus the software's default parameter of 14 days), it can be misleading and result in whipsaw losses. For RSI to work properly as it does in this chart, you need the channel to have some directional slope.

Enhancing gains with selective timing

In practice, you can enhance profitability by scaling into the trade, or adding to your position as additional indicators confirm the trade and your gains start accumulating. Say you have $5,000 to place on your security and five indicators. You start by placing a portion of that capital ($2,000) when the first two indicators signal buy. Then you place additional lots of $1,000 as each of the next three benchmarks is reached until you have 100 percent of the capital allocated to the trade. One commonly applied idea is to scale in after the price tests support and bounces off it to the upside.

When you get your first indication that the trend is ending, you exit all at once. Scaling in but exiting all at once is a controversial money management technique, although many gurus claim it's the secret of their success. But before rushing out to use this idea, consider that the signals that affirm continuation are second-tier validator signals (or they would have come first). Often they aren't actually buy/sell signals in their own right, although you feel comfort that they provide confirmation. And don't forget that scaling in gradually and exiting all at once gives you an arithmetic headache calculating the actual win-loss ratio and thus the new, ongoing expectancy. It's just arithmetic, but time-consuming.

Trading with Limited Expectancy: Semi-System, Setup, and Guerilla Trading

If you're going to be a system trader, you need to know the expectancy of your system — and you need to trade the backtested securities all the time using the exact indicators that generated your gain/loss history. System trading is the pinnacle of high-end, disciplined trading found among some sophisticated individuals, small firms, and hedge funds. But not everyone has the resources, including patience, to engage in full-bore system trading.

Instead of an arithmetically precise expectancy, you may find that limited expectancy is good enough. You still have to sit down with a piece of paper or a spreadsheet and perform the expectancy calculation, even if you used indicators not in your usual toolkit on some trades or applied nontechnical judgments. Nontechnical judgments are called *discretionary*. Among professionals, discretionary managers outnumber system managers by a large amount. Discretionary managers cherry-pick trades, add or subtract technical indicators, consider nontechnical factors, and are vulnerable to emotion — the very thing you're trying to avoid. By definition, you can't backtest discretionary trading systems. But you can determine expectancy with any trading history, even if it's not exact.

Discretionary trading can be successful and the limited expectancy you get from a discretionary trading history may be valid because humans *learn*. Popular author Malcolm Gladwell (*The Tipping Point, Outliers,* and other best-sellers, Hachette Book Group) writes that expertise arises from a minimum of 10,000 hours of practice at a specific task. This is why occasionally adding an extra indicator or overriding an indicator signal may be the right thing to do in terms of making a profit and avoiding a loss. After all, your goal is to make money, not to have a beautiful system.

In fact, at an extreme of nonsystematic trading, some successful traders don't use predetermined indicators applied on a chart; rather they study the chart and see what their experienced eye may detect. By sheer force of having observed the prices of a single security all day, every day for many years, the trader gets a feel for the price action. After spotting something, the trader draws the indicator on the chart to validate what he saw. Sometimes he makes a decision based on a candle pattern, and other times he decides based on a classic pattern like head-and-shoulders, a breakout accompanied by a volume spike, or any of a dozen other combinations. But note the intuitive trader hardly ever makes a trading decision on a single indicator. Theoretically he could go back and define exactly what were the bases of the judgment calls — the trading decisions — but it's not a system per se. Estimating positive expectancy from a few ad-hoc indicators takes year of practice, and I don't recommend it for the newcomer.

So should you build a trading system? If you want reliable and consistent results over a long period of time, yes. But you must be prepared to invest a lot of time and computational capital performing backtests and determining your risk-reward preferences. I know more than one academic who backtests an ever-evolving system for decades to contain every possible contingency — but never actually places any trades.

You should always start with a set of concepts that embody at least two indicators, especially if you're a beginner. But you don't have to stop there. To combine discretion with indicator-based trading, your options include semi-system trading, setup trading, and guerrilla trading.

Semi-system "discretionary" trading

In semi-system trading, you have an indicator system that generates buy/sell signals and you know the associated expected gain/loss from the system, but you cherry-pick the trades and change the buy/sell signal using nonsystem indicator or factors from outside the system altogether (such as fundamentals). Generally, cherry-picking is used to avoid losses when a buy/sell signal is weak, or a big news event is pending that experience tells you means the average range will likely expand (and raise the risk of your stop getting hit). You enlarge your stop to be greater than usual to get past the Event without having to exit on a normal-sized stop.

Logically, you might better have more indicators, or different indicators, than to fiddle with the proper application of your system. But adding or changing indicators to get new win/loss stats is tremendously time-consuming. Besides, the right thing to do if you're fiddling with a system is just to get out — go square — until you feel higher confidence.

This brings up an important point about backtesting or practice-trading testing. To test properly, most software requires you to be in the market long or short on specific indicator readings. You have to work quite hard to embed squaring rules where you have no position. Your software wants you to have a position! The very nature of a buy/sell system is that it contains a bias to be in the market all the time. To be square is to be indecisive, and the very nature of a buy/sell system is to deliver a trading decision.

Combining indicators to create a buy/sell system is fairly easy, but it's devilishly hard to fold in squaring rules. Some systems are buy/sell only with no squaring rules for exactly this reason — it's so hard to build them. In the absence of squaring rules, though, you're at risk of overtrading — swinging at every ball that comes over the plate but hitting only a small percentage and counting on the occasional home run to generate your good win/loss stats.

The squaring problem has another pernicious aspect — reentering in the same direction after your stop has been hit, which is called the *continuation rule* problem. Should the rules for reentering in the same direction trade be the same or different from a first-time entry? Traders and statisticians alike quarrel about it. Allowing yourself discretion in this circumstance is a key reason system traders slip into discretionary trading in the first place. Most discretionary traders probably started out intending to be pure system traders but then encountered contingencies not really covered by the system, like the continuation problem (Chapter 3 discusses contingencies in greater detail.) A surplus of contingencies is probably why academic system-builders can never finish their systems and start actually trading.

Solving the squaring problem — setups

Setup trading is a popular form of swing trading that many self-styled gurus are marketing today. You identify a specific bar configuration, trade it, and get out. One of the latest additions to this genre is trading penny stock-pot stocks on a single candlestick. Because most pot stocks don't have earnings or other fundamentals, traders are flying on rumor and blind faith. Often rumors suffice. The pot-stock strategy is to wait for a giant white candlestick that was triggered by an announcement or a rumor, buy as soon as possible, and exit with a gain in short order, sometimes the same day, before the penny stock falls back. Promoters advertise that a 12-cent pot stock rose to 30 cents before falling back to 12 cents, which is a 150 percent gain. Dozens of penny pot stocks do the same thing. The calculation is absolutely correct. And so is the methodology. It's still technical analysis, if a terribly risky version without a second validator indicator.

Because you're in the market only to take advantage of the setup configuration, you no longer have to worry about being square; being square is your natural state of affairs, and you're square most of the time. Instead of having a buy/sell system, you have a strategy of trading only the *setup*. The big white pot-stock candlestick is a setup.

A *setup* is a particular configuration of bars, usually with one or two other confirming conditions like a pattern or an indicator, that delivers an expected outcome in a high proportion of trades. Candlestick trading can be considered setup trading, too (see Chapter 8).

A simple but effective one-rule concept is to buy when the price moves above the range established in the first *x* number of minutes of trading. Say the first half hour of trading from the open generates a range of $5 to 5.50. As soon as the price hits $5.75, you get in. Where do you get out? That depends on how much you want to take home. It could be a few minutes or a few hours, but your intent is to exit the same day. That's because you're deducing that a big move in the first few minutes will be followed by an additional move in the same direction — demand rises on rising prices — but you don't have an equivalent sell signal. You know to sell when you have hit some predetermined profit.

Fund manager Toby Crabel, the author of *Day Trading With Short Term Price Patterns and Opening Range Breakout* (Traders Press), originated this concept, which is also referred to as a *volatility breakout*. Crabel calls this strategy the opening range breakout. With the opening range breakout, you can improve the odds of getting a successful trade by adding one or more confirmation validators, such as:

>> The preceding bar was an inside day or doji (refer to Chapter 8).

>> The *x*-minute opening range over the past three to ten days was narrowing (see Chapter 14).

>> The opening is a gap from the day before (see Chapter 7).

Figuring out why setups work

Setups generally win by entering very early in a move, unlike systems based on indicators that await confirmation from always-lagging indicators. Setups usually have catchy names (like *pinball* and *coiled spring*). Do these setups work? If you identify the setup correctly, yes, the price does often behave in the predicted manner. Unfortunately, analysts don't have statistics on exactly what percentage of the time they don't work, but experienced setup traders say that setups work often enough that early entry delivers the edge.

One benefit of setup trading is that you can be out of the market until you spot a setup situation. You take no risk when you're out of the market. Many setup trades are *intraday*, where you enter and exit the trade on the same day. Other setup trades are more long-lasting because they lead to authentic trends that you stick to until your exit rules or stop is hit. In the next section, I describe some aspects of trading setups. For more on setups, see Timothy Knight's *High Probability Trade Setups* (John Wiley & Sons, Inc.).

Getting an efficient entry

A setup identifies the conditions that precede and accompany a price move, giving you a head start in entering a trade. When you correctly identify the setup, the price goes in your direction immediately. And when a strong move begins, the first few minutes, hours, or days can account for 25 percent or more of the total move. That's the thrust or impulse aspect of new moves.

REMEMBER

The key to setup trading is early identification of a trading opportunity and thus early entry. As a general rule, your goal as a setup trader is to take a profit bite out of a move without necessarily having a position over the entire move, like a system trader.

Using ruthless exits

Efficient entries and ruthless exits are the hallmark of setup swing trading, but being quick on the trigger doesn't imply that the trader is a wild-eyed risk taker. Quite the opposite. Risk management is the key feature of setup swing trading and thus may be appropriate for beginners. You must

>> *Never* give up profits by sitting out a retracement (as you often do when trend-following).

>> Absolutely, positively use stops and keep them updated. All good traders use stops — if you can't bring yourself to obey stops, setup trading isn't for you. In fact, any trading isn't for you.

>> If the setup succeeds, you keep moving your stop to secure each new level of gain. Generally you hold until the price moves against you by some specified amount, usually a dollar amount. Sometimes setups are so short-lived that an initial stop is all you need and you aren't in the trade long enough to use a trailing stop. Setup trading can be hit and run.

Setup drawbacks

The term "day trading" is often associated with setup trading. For setup trading to highjack the term day trading isn't strictly accurate. You could be a system trader on a day-to-day basis.

Setups may sound ideal for a newcomer to technical trading, especially the part about being out of the market a lot of the time, but setups have their own drawbacks. The top one is that setup trading requires intense concentration. In system trading, you can place your orders and walk away — your stop and profit-target orders will keep you safe. But setup trades must be watched. Remember the following:

» A setup that you like may not appear every day or even every month. With a small universe of securities, you'd have to memorize a dozen setups if you want to be in the market much of the time. If you like only one or two setups, you have to monitor a large universe of securities.

» If you focus on setups to the exclusion of all the other technical concepts, you're at a loss for what to do when setups don't appear.

» To find your favorite setups, you have to scan a list of securities, and the best setups may appear in securities that you wouldn't touch with a bargepole on a fundamental or value basis.

» Setups require intense concentration and often the ability to trade actively during market hours. If you have a day job, this task can be impossible.

Guerrilla trading

Guerrilla trading is setup trading on adrenaline. Trades are very short term, usually lasting only a few minutes and targeting only a few points of gain — but repeated over and over during the same session so that a few points per trade can add up to quite a lot over the course of the session. Because targets are tight to the entry, stops are even closer and often hit on pure randomness.

Guerrilla trading is often concentrated around earnings announcements, as in the case in Chapter 4, or around scheduled news releases where the trader pounces on the market response. The guerrilla trader cares nothing about what the fundamentals mean, or about cycles, trends, or even indicators — the only indicator he needs is an initial price response that he can ride for a few minutes. In the normal course of every response to a news event, prices wax and wane, so the guerrilla trader can often do the same trade repeatedly on the same news. All that is needed is speed and an itchy trigger finger.

Chapter **17**

Judging Cycles and Waves

S tock and commodity market prices often move in a regular and repetitive manner that looks like a series of ocean waves on the chart. Each wave in a series of waves has a specific height and length, and when those are the same or nearly the same from wave to wave — or waves are consistently proportional to one another — the pattern is called a *cycle*. Some market price cycles follow economic developments, and some patterns that look like cycles follow some other organizational principle, like the lunar cycle. In some cases, analysts can find a strong correlation with numbers series or a connection to some other cause that is unseen and unproved.

This chapter describes some of the more prominent ideas about waves and cycles developed over the years, with some theories going back centuries. You should suspend disbelief and give the various theories a chance, including the increasingly popular Elliott Wave theory I cover at the end of the chapter. If you're lucky enough to get a feel for cycles and waves, you'll be adding another dimension to standard indicator-based technical trading.

Defining a Cycle and a Wave

In economics and finance, cycles all look alike and start with a continuous line that begins at a low, forms a semispherical bump, and returns symmetrically to the same or near the same low, over and over again, over time. A *cycle* is made up of waves, and the *wave* is modeled on the sine wave as Figure 17-1 shows. You see this pattern all the time in music and electrical energy, not to mention the ocean tides.

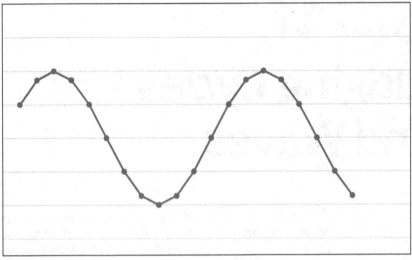

FIGURE 17-1:
A sine wave.

As applied to financial markets, the core concept is that human behavior forms and repeats in specific recurrent patterns. Whether the impulse for financial market prices to form cycles is inherent in the universe or arises from some unexplained aspect of crowd behavior, nobody knows.

Think of the following to differentiate between cycles and waves:

>> Cycles have a repetitive character. Not only will prices surge and retreat, but they'll also surge and retreat in a more or less orderly manner so that you can count the periods between them and use that count to project the next surge and retreat.

>> Waves, on the other hand, can be big or small, short-term or long-lasting, choppy or orderly. You don't know when a wave begins how far it will go. Market waves aren't like the ocean tides.

Cycle theorists (and physicists) speak of their cycle components as waves. You can have waves without a cycle, but you can't have a cycle without waves.

Just as you try to attribute supply and demand dynamics to the shape of indicators, you can consider a bigger form of crowd behavior when looking at cycles and waves. Refer to Chapter 2 to read about George Soros's reflexivity feedback loop. This idea postulates that expectation of a market price move causes crowd behavior that validates the very price behavior that was expected. If and when the crowd is disappointed because an intervening Event has now changed conditions, a new expectation gets a grip and the crowd causes that expectation to come true, too. This causes an up-and-down pattern that can have the appearance of regularity — otherwise known as *cyclicality*.

Starting with economics

The economic *cycle* is the process by which an economy (and the businesses in it) expand, reach a peak, and then contract and go into recession. They do all this in a wavelike pattern around a growth trend. Economists have been trying to pin down the economic cycle for more than two centuries. So far there have been the following:

>> A super-long cycle, the Kondratiev wave of 45 to 60 years

>> The infrastructure cycle of 15 to 25 years

>> The business cycle of 5 to 7 or 7 to 10.5 years

>> The inventory cycle (another business cycle) of about 40 months devised by Joseph Kitchin in 1927

All are still in use today. Some traders who write newsletters and blogs feature these economic cycle theories as the basis of their trading decisions.

Economic cycle theories can be based on data like the number of ships leaving a harbor each week, the unemployment rate, the rising and falling cost of commodities like cocoa, salt, and coffee, or a thousand other data points. One of the off-putting aspects of cycles is that there are so many of them. They overlap, they offset, they last too long for practical application. But hang on. Consider that in the 19th century, the Rothschilds had minions to plot many cycles from data series going back hundreds of years. They were seeking the confluence points where a preponderance of overlapping cycles hit a top or a bottom at the same time. The confluence points comprised a buy/sell indicator for the securities the Rothschilds were trading. The Rothschilds' secret cycle technique, which clearly was working for them, sparked a small industry of cycle-seekers starting around 1912. It has never stopped. It's interesting that at least one of the Rothschild companies still uses cycles and has still kept their exact nature a secret.

Moving on to magic numbers

Looming over the cycle question is the issue of whether some giant mystical order in the universe dictates financial price movements. One of the best explanations of specific numbers that reveal the mystical order of the universe is in Tony Plummer's *The Law of Vibration: The Revelation of William D. Gann* (Harriman House). This book attributes regular rhythms and recurring patterns to a "sacred geometry" that reveals the "deep structure" of the universe. Maybe there are gravitational waves from outer space affecting trading crowd behavior. Einstein predicted these cosmic ripples almost a hundred years ago and their existence was proven only in the last decade.

Other number-based cycle theories include Elliott Wave, which I describe in the last section of this chapter, and a lesser known theory based on the number embedded in *pi*, which I don't cover. I call these specific number "magic numbers" because the theorists who propose them consider the numbers to have magical properties that somehow determine future prices in securities markets.

Using cycles

Market cycle analysis is far more complicated — and contentious — than applying indicators. Just about every technical analyst will use an indicator for the same purpose, but put a group of cycle theorists in a room and you will get a fist-fight. Every cycle theorist can show you charts of his cycle-based predictions overlaid on actual prices to demonstrate his theory works — but with a lot of adjustments and exceptions, and each theory involves different numbers — 4 days (no, 5), or 20 days (no, 22). If the experts can't come up with something reliable on cycles, why bother?

The answer is easy: Indicators fail sometimes, so any extra help you can get from elsewhere can add to your trading edge, whether volume, market sentiment, fundamentals, seasonality, or cycles.

Opinion is divided about whether cycles are an integral part of technical analysis. Cycles fit into the technical universe because they're couched in price terms alone without reference to fundamentals. Some technical analysts embrace a cycle theory alone, some modify a cycle theory with other indicators, and some dismiss all cycle ideas out of hand as crackpot, requiring too much effort or not useful. *You don't need to embrace a cycle theory to become a skilled technical analyst. You can safely ignore cycle theories altogether.* But you should know about the existence of cyclical theories to be able to evaluate assertions and promotions. Besides, cycle theories are fun.

Cycle material is far more complex than standard indicators. You'll have to accept (or overlook) some wild-eyed, mystical, and possibly fruitcake ideas. But don't dismiss cycles out of hand. Several big-name traders, including authors Toby Crabel, Larry Williams, and Jim Rogers, embrace some aspects of cycle theory. You don't have to believe in some hidden order in the universe if you are lucky enough to get a feel for cycles.

A full review of cycle theories is beyond the scope of this book. I do a quick review of some of the major ideas that are in vogue today. You'll likely notice that many of the theories were first invented by guys from many generations back. Don't let that bother you. Remember, the essence of market movements doesn't change. Traders respond to a giant breakout today exactly the same way they behaved in 1900 or 1930 or 1990 or will in 2020 or 2030. The technology to keep track of price changes and to manipulate indicators has advanced tremendously from the days of colored pencils and chart paper, but the humans behind the price moves don't change.

Cycling with Supply and Demand — The Pragmatic Mr. Wyckoff

You don't need to attribute an unidentified mysterious natural law to the cyclical appearance of chart prices. Just take a leaf from one of the earliest technical analysts, Richard Wyckoff, a stock market guru in his day (1910s–1934). He attributed the cyclical appearance to plain old supply and demand. See `www.stockcharts.com/school` for more on Wyckoff.

You can find many books, websites, and YouTube videos on the Wyckoff technique. Wyckoff wrote a number of books and newsletters, including *Stock Market Techniques* (self-published, 1933). A good introduction is *Charting the Stock Market, the Wyckoff Method*, edited by Jack Hutson (Frasier Publishing).

What Wyckoff brought to the table was a combined technique approach that is clean and logical. He started with a plain-vanilla bar chart. To that he added a point-and-figure chart that filtered out noise and delivered pure signal. Then he moved on to identify and measure waves, but not the wave of an individual security. Instead he calculated an average of the leading securities in a sector or the market as a whole, such as the five stocks in the Dow 30 that have the most volume or the biggest price changes. The wave group needs to be revised fairly often as conditions change. This process is to follow the *smart money,* meaning the big institutions that really do drive price changes.

A Wyckoff wave isn't a geometrically predestined wave or cycle like the Gann or other versions that I discuss in this chapter. Instead, it's formed by identifying four market sentiment turning points or phases:

>> **Accumulation:** The upmove analysts identify with higher highs and higher closes, driven by demand, and can draw a support line under

>> **Markup:** Where the price breaks out above recent ranges and eventually tops out

>> **Distribution:** Also known as supply, where those holding the security can't get rid of it fast enough

>> **Markdown:** When the security becomes oversold

See Figure 17-2. Note that because you don't know the duration of any of these waves, you really must use stops.

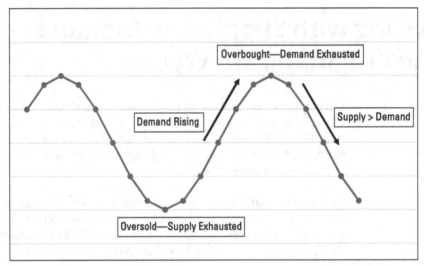

Overbought—Demand Exhausted

Demand Rising

Supply > Demand

Oversold—Supply Exhausted

FIGURE 17-2:
The Wyckoff
Model.

© John Wiley & Sons, Inc.

Finding Universal Harmony — Hurst's Magic Numbers

J. M. Hurst identified what he named 20 "natural harmonic" arithmetic wavelength relationships among cycles, including 60 minutes, 160 minutes (not 120), 1 day, 5 days, 40 days, and so on up to 17.93 years. Make note of that 17+ year number. You're going to see it more than once, which is a little spooky.

Hurst was an American engineer who was among the first to apply computer-based analysis to masses of price data, a scientific approach appreciated today. But how do you use the wavelengths? Hurst assumes that even though cycles are profoundly influential, they don't *dictate* the exact price moves. More than one will be operational at any one time. The way to identify an uptrending cycle is to add the slope of the five longer-duration cycles above the one on which you're working.

So if you're considering a 20-day cycle, you add up the slopes of the 40-day, the 80-day, the 20-week, the 40-week, and the 18-month cycles. You're looking for a confluence of all the cycles to identify a turning point, although you may have to shift some cycles to make them fit the larger cycle. This seems to be similar to the secret Rothschild system of waiting for cycles in various commodities and economic indicators to line up to deliver buy/sell signals.

Although Hurst's book, *The Profit Magic of Stock Transaction Timing*, is out of print, you can find it secondhand. You can also consult many newer books, websites, and YouTube videos about the Hurst methodology. You can also find Hurst software (`http://sentienttrader.com`).

Looking to the Moon and the Stars

Many cycle concepts rely on astronomical analysis, which I discuss in the following sections. Astronomy is the science of the moon and stars, something humans have been studying for thousands of years.

Examining the lunar cycle

Don't laugh (or turn the page) — the moon influences market sentiment. Here are a couple of theories.

Lunar cycle theory

The *lunar cycle theory* holds that equities perform better (go up) starting a few days after a full moon. Falling market prices occur a few days after a new moon. Using the Chinese lunar calendar, major market crashes tend to occur about three days before a new moon and often in the eighth and ninth Chinese lunar calendar (September or October in the West). As it happens, the U.S. crashes in 1929, 1987, and 2008 did occur in September or October, and the more slow-moving crash in 2000 occurred in October to December. However, this theory doesn't account for crashes in other countries or other asset classes. It's also out of line with the U.S. market crash in December 2018.

The moon rotates around the earth every 29.53 days. Adjusting for weekend and holidays, you expect to see a major security index cycle every 20 days or so. And academic research using fancy statistical techniques prove those 20-day cycles do exist with some regularity in many countries.

Saros cycle

Another lunar cycle idea pertains to the Saros cycle, or the way the moon revolves around the earth in an elliptical pattern, causing *supermoons* (when the moon is closest to the earth and appears to the naked eye as far bigger than usual) and eclipses. Eclipses are associated with some notable financial events, including the Tulip Mania crash in 1637, the 1979 dollar crisis, and the 1997 emerging markets crash. And yet eclipses of one sort or another occur about four to seven times per years in one place or another without affecting financial markets, and no specific financial cycle theory is associated with the Saros cycle.

The Saros cycle is 18 years, 11 days, and 8 hours. That's interesting because more than one nonlunar cycle analyst has come up with a U.S. stock market cycle that's roughly the same amount of time, including one that is 17.6 years, the Balenthiran cycle. This cycle consists of a bull run of 17.6 years containing 5-year uptrends and two midcycle corrections of about two years each. Notice that Hurst data-mining that I discuss earlier has a cycle lasting 17.93 years.

Adding more celestial bodies

One lunar cycle system that has befuddled generations of technical analysts is The Delta phenomenon promoted by Welles Wilder in his book *The Delta Phenomenon or The Hidden Order in All Markets* (The Delta Society). Wilder was one of the top pioneers in technical analysis and much respected. He invented the relative strength index (RSI), the average true range (ATR), average directional index (ADI), and the parabolic stop-and-reverse indicator. The original offering of the secret formula in the 1980s was for $35,000 to join the Delta Society, which still exists today. Now you can get the original book for less than $50.

The Delta phenomenon identifies turning points using the confluence of a 4-day, a 4-month, a 1-year, a 4-year, and a 19-year cycle. The supposed hidden symmetry of the market is disclosed when you see the confluence of the short-term delta (every four revolutions of the earth) and the intermediate delta (every four revolutions of the moon around the earth) and the medium-term delta (the complete tidal cycle) and the long-term delta (every four revolutions of the earth around the sun). The final superlong delta is the "total interaction" of the sun, moon, and earth every 235 months, or 19 years and 5 hours. I can't make it work, but perhaps you can.

Including the sun

Sometimes you can see what looks like dark spots on the sun. They're called sunspots and are caused by a change in temperature that is caused in turn by a change in magnetic force. Sunspots last anywhere from a few days to a few months. How many sunspots are visible changes according to a roughly 11-year solar cycle. If you conduct an Internet search for the term sunspots, you can find a chart showing the regularity of sunspots over the past 400 years.

Linking sunspots with economic and stock market activity goes back as far as 1730, when a rise in sunspots is seen as increasing human excitability and causing rallies. In the 1930s and again in 1965, analysts found a strong correlation between a rise in sunspot activity and U.S. stock market performance, specifically that stock market rally peaks consistently precede sunspot cycle maximums. From 1750 to 2000, the sunspot cycle was 11.7 years. In the 20th century, the average sunspot cycle was 10.3 years.

Figuring out what's (maybe) wrong with astronomy cycle theories

Anything that helps you understand market sentiment can be useful, no matter how outlandish. The earth, moon, and sun have changing electromagnetic effects that may very well affect the electromagnetic human brain, which generates about the same amount of power as a lightbulb. Astronomy isn't entirely preposterous as a factor in market prices. Or maybe it's just a coincidence that market events seem to line up with astronomical factors. Correlation is not, after all, causation.

One drawback to linking market price moves to astronomical events and cyclicality is that society is changing. The sun, moon, and stars exhibit regularity over fixed time frames, but human economies are, on the whole, accelerating. In the 19th century, the railroad was the big new invention and was the central focus of stock markets across the world for about a hundred years. Compare railroads to cellphones. Cellphones, first invented in 1973, took off in 1991. With the introduction of 3G in 2001, cellphones have undergone a technological revolution in less than 20 years, or five times faster than railroads. If the pace of technological innovation drives an economy, logically the pace of market responses to the change in economic conditions should speed up, too. Can you still forecast major tops and bottoms at 10- or 11-year intervals, or 17-year intervals, or 80-year intervals, or any other interval based on past correlations that might be accidental or coincidental in the first place? Remember, statistical excellence requires at least 30 trials or instances, and heavy-duty science like taking a rocket to the moon and back calls for a minimum of 200.

Following the Earth's Axis: Seasonality and Calendar Effects

Where you *can* get the hundreds of trials preferred for statistical evidence is the seasons. Every year has four. You aren't surprised to hear that heating oil futures go up as winter heads for Chicago. The prices of agricultural commodities rise and fall with the seasons. *Seasonality* is the term used for the natural rise and fall of prices according to the time of year.

Oddly — very oddly — equities and financial futures exhibit a similar effect: They change according to the time of year. The changes are regular and consistent enough to warrant your attention.

Differentiating between seasonality and calendar effects

Seasonality used to be a term applied to agricultural prices, and *calendar effects* was a term applied to equities. Today they're used interchangeably. You can discover the seasonality characteristics of any given stock by using *seasonality trackers* on various websites, including the following:

>> **Thomson Financial Seasonality Tracker:** This site (https://charts.equityclock.com/thomson-reuters-corporation-tsetri-seasonal-chart) is the best known. Plug in your own stock ticker symbols to get a chart showing ups and down attributable to seasonality.

>> **Time and Timing:** Another excellent site is www.timeandtiming.com, which covers all the top futures contracts (interest rates, currencies, metals, oil and gas, and agricultural commodities). In addition to vast amounts of historical comparisons, you can find trading ideas that worked in the past, complete with average gain, win-loss ratio, and so on.

The most well-known calendar effects

In equities, you have probably heard the adage, "Sell in May and go away." This advice comes from work on calendar effects by Yale Hirsch and his son Jeffrey Hirsch, who tested the correlation of stock indices with the time of year in their annual *Stock Trader's Almanac* (John Wiley & Sons, Inc.). The rule is called the *best six months rule*.

Hirsch discovered that nearly all the gains in the S&P 500 are made between November 1 and April 30. This rule isn't true without exception, but it's true for most years since 1950. When April 30 rolls around, you sell all your stocks and put the money in U.S. Treasury bills. Come November 1, you reenter the stock market. If you had followed this rule every year since 1950 and also modified the exact timing a little by applying the moving average convergence-divergence indicator (check out MACD in Chapter 12), a starting capital stake of $10,000 in 1950 would have ballooned to $2,846,350 by April 2018. On average, you would've been invested only six and a half months each year — and remember, when you're not in the market, you're not taking market risk.

Other calendar effects include

>> **January Barometer:** When the S&P 500 is up in January, it'll close the year higher than it opened. Since 1950, this rule has an accuracy reading of 86.8 percent.

>> **President's Third Year:** Since 1939, the third year of a presidential term is always an up year for the Dow except once in 2015. In fact, the only big down year in the third year of a presidential term since the Panic of 1907 was 1931.

>> **Presidential Election Cycle:** Wars, recessions, and bear markets tend to start in the first two years, while prosperity and bull markets tend to happen in the second two years. Since 1833, the last two years of a president's term produced a cumulative net gain in the Dow of 742.5 percent, while the first two years produced 332.2 percent.

Hirsch and others have discovered many other calendar effects. Hirsch's annual *Stock Trader's Almanac* publishes the probability of any of the three major indices (Dow, S&P 500, and Nasdaq) rising or falling on any day of the year. The almanac bases this information on what has happened in those indexes on those dates since January 1953.

Using seasonality and calendar effects

Paying attention to calendar effects can help improve your market timing. When you're sitting down to make a trading or investment decision, you can avoid a costly mistake by consulting the calendar not only for the specific security, but also for the index to which it belongs. Calendar effects are certainly more than a curiosity, although a wild rally isn't going to stop solely because it's May 1. But because so many traders and money managers know about calendar effects, they're to some degree a self-fulfilling prophecy.

Examining Big-Picture Cycle Theories

This section deals with the grand, big-picture cycle ideas as a stand-alone section because they're pervasive — and controversial. No big-picture theory has been proved by statistical measures. To be fair, no theory has been disproved, either.

TIP

Technical analysis is a sufficiently crowded field already. Why make things more complicated than they have to be? You can use simple techniques to make profits and avoid losses. Do you really need to know the secrets of the universe, too?

You'll want to decide at some point whether to pursue any of the big cycle ideas. Some smart and successful people in the field believe them. Those who don't are mostly too polite to ridicule the ideas. You'll also run into critics who mistakenly think that all technical analysis involves cycle ideas.

To be sure, some of the cycle schools of thought contain mystical overtones and unproven claims about how the world works, such as "the trading crowd is only the instrument of bigger forces at work." The core idea is that market trading is essentially an irrational process — you're trying to follow the irrational crowd and that makes you irrational — but the crowd is, unknowingly, following some hidden universal laws.

REMEMBER

Because these ideas can never be verified, some critics unfairly color the whole field of technical analysis with the charge of supernatural voodoo. Empiricists cast doubt on these theories because they're not proven. Economists in particular frown on many cyclical theories because they lack a theoretical basis. Economists do observe business cycles — several of them — but they overlap and don't appear regularly. Still, market cycle theories are correct some percentage of the time, and most technical traders are reluctant to level the charge of crackpot against cycle theories. You're welcome to research cycles online at sites like `www.cycles researchinstitute.org`.

One of the most prolific cycle writers was Edward R. Dewey, whose books include *Cycles: The Science of Prediction* and *Cycles: The Mysterious Forces that Trigger Events* (Simon and Schuster). Right off the bat are the words "science" and "mysterious" in his titles, something the 21st century mind rebels against. One of Dewey's findings was a 40-month market cycle. Remember, this was during the 1930s and 1940s. Earlier but evidently unbeknownst to Dewey's traders was the same finding of a 40-month stock market cycle in the United Kingdom and the United States over the period from 1890 to 1922. At one point an outfit named the Foundation for the Study of Cycles determined a cycle of 40.68 months over the entire history of U.S. stock prices (ending in the 1960s).

What are you to make of these findings? Some people have an innate ability to grasp these findings and apply them usefully in their trading. Others, and I am in this second group, find the ideas interesting in a general way but not relevant and useful to my own trading.

Shining a Spotlight on the Magnificent Mr. Gann

If you spend more than a few minutes researching technical analysis, you can't avoid running into a reference to W.D. Gann (1878–1955). In addition to writing numerous books about technical analysis, he also wrote many other books (see the nearby sidebar).

Gann covered the waterfront of themes in this chapter. He discovered a set of commodity cycles of 20, 30, 45, 60, 84, and 90 years. He used astronomy. He discovered magic numbers. He applied geometry to charts to derive shorter-term cycles. I cover only a few of Gann's ideas in the following sections.

For example, Gann discovered repetitive price behavior using spirals, angles, and a hexagonal chart that traders use today. The spiral chart uses as anchoring points the two equinoxes and the two solstices, whereas the hexagonal chart uses planetary positions. Your charting software won't include these methodologies. If you like them, you'll have to buy Gann software or look online for it.

Applying core Gann concepts

What most standard software does include is the Gann angle and Gann fan. A Gann angle is a line connecting one unit of price change to the next unit. The best angle is one unit of price change over one unit of time, or 45 degrees. You expect the price to move the same one unit over the same length of time going forward. Other versions include 2x1 (price changes by two units per one unit of time) and other multiples up to 16x1.

TIP

When you're using the slope of a support line or standard error channel — in other words, the *degree of steepness* — to gauge the robustness of the trend by eye, remember the 1x1 Gann angle. You'll find that a flattish slope (like 25 degrees) means the trend is weak, and a too-steep slope (like 70 degrees) means it's flaky and prone to correction, but the 45 degree angle is just right to predict continuation of your trend with some confidence. It's the Goldilocks slope.

Gann used the 45 degree angle as the starting point of an additional eight lines spaced at specific intervals off the starting point, forming a *Gann fan*. The starting point is a top or bottom on the chart extended out by hand to the next low or high, and the fan lines represent alternative support and resistance lines. It's likely that later techniques using geometrics similar to the Gann fan (Andrews pitchfork and speed resistance lines, not covered in this book) were based on this 1935 work by Gann.

Celebrating Gann's 50 percent retracement rule

One of Gann's more lasting contributions to technical analysis is the 50 percent retracement rule. Gann discovered that retracements in the securities he was trading at the time tended to occur at one-half of the original move from the low to the high. To illustrate, say the price moved from $10 to $30. At $30, the crowd decided that the security was overbought and started to sell. The ensuing price decline, the retracement, stops near 50 percent of the original $10 to $30 move, namely $20. Figure 17-3 shows the 50 percent retracement case.

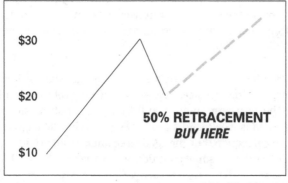

FIGURE 17-3:
Gann 50 percent retracement rule.

© *John Wiley & Sons, Inc.*

In fact, Gann said that the most profitable retracement is a 50 percent retracement. The area around 50 percent is a danger zone, because the price can keep going and become a full-fledged reversal around there (in which case you lose all the gains). But it's the best place to reenter an existing trend (with an exit planned just below using a stop-loss order in case it doesn't work). If the trend resumes, Gann wrote that it will then exceed the previous high, which gives you an automatic minimum profit target. This observation may be the origin of the phrase, "Buy on the dip."

Gann also saw retracements occurring at the halfway point of a move, such as 25 percent (half of 50 percent), 12.5 percent (half of 25 percent), and so on. Statisticians can't offer proof that retracements occur at 12.5 percent, 25 percent, or 50 percent with more frequency than chance would allow. The absence of statistical proof in a field populated by mathematical sophisticates is puzzling at first.

But when you ask a statistician why not just run the numbers and test the hypothesis, the statistician will point out that defining the low-to-high original move and then defining the stopping point of a retracement is a computational nightmare. No matter what definitions you give the software, another analyst is sure to want to refine them in some other way. You'll see studies, for example, showing that the actual percentage change of many retracements isn't precisely 50 percent, but rather in a range of 45 to 55 percent. And it's possible that because so many technical analysts know about the Gann 50 percent rule, it tends to become self-fulfilling.

REMEMBER

A critical point about the 50 percent retracement rule is that you may think you want to exit to protect your profit at the 50 percent level. If you bought the security at $10 and it rose to $30, but has now fallen to $20, shown in Figure 17-1, you want to sell at $20 to hang on to the gain you have left. But if the 50 percent retracement rule works this time, you'd be getting out exactly when you should be buying *more* (adding to your position), because a resumption of the trend at the $20 level almost certainly means that the price will now go higher than the highest high so far, $30.

Another puzzle: A 100 percent retracement, a price that goes from $10 to $30 and back to $10, will often form a *double bottom*, a bullish formation. When the price peaks twice at the same level, you have a *double top*, a bearish formation. (See Chapter 9 for more details on these formations.)

Embracing the Most Popular Wave Idea — The Elliott Wave

By far the most popular wave idea for several decades now is the Elliott Wave theory. A trader named Ralph Nelson Elliott believed that man's behavior, including his behavior when trading in the stock market, revealed similar characteristics as the Fibonacci sequence and could, therefore, be charted to predict future behavior. Elliott observed that securities prices appear in a wavelike form on charts, hence the name of his forecasting method, *Elliott Wave*, which I discuss in these sections.

CONNECTING THE ELLIOTT WAVE TO FIBONACCI

The foundation of Elliott Wave theory is the Fibonacci sequence of numbers. A 13th-century Italian mathematician named Fibonacci discovered a self-replicating sequence of numbers with curious properties. It starts with 1, 1, 2, 3, 5, 8, 13, 21, 34, 55, 89, 144, and so on to infinity. After the first few numbers, the sum of two adjacent numbers in the sequence forms the next higher number in the sequence. Most important, the ratio of any two consecutive numbers approximates 1.618 or its inverse, 0.618. One to 1.618 is named the "golden ratio."

Nature offers many examples of this ratio: daisy petals, ferns, sunflowers, seashells, hurricanes, whirlpools, and atomic particles in a bubble chamber. And many of man's works purportedly embody the Fibonacci ratios as well: the pyramids in Egypt, the Parthenon in Greece, and Cézanne's choice of canvas shape, although some mathematicians dispute some or all of these. In fact, many of the named instances of the golden ratio in nature, anatomy, art, and architecture don't pass the test. A good example is the shell of the chambered nautilus, which supposedly obeys the golden ratio, but look it up — nautilus shells' average growth ratios of 1.24 to 1.43 are quite far from 1.618.

Of course, critics point out that many other events in nature, architecture, and human behavior follow a sequence of 2, 4, 6, 8, and so on. The number 11 can be considered magic, not to mention pi (3.14159), used to calculate the circumference of a circle. Prime numbers, which are numbers divisible only by themselves and one (3, 5, 7, 11, 17, and so on), are important numbers. In fact, many other self-replicating number sequences exist. In short, scientists say that to attribute human behavior to any single number sequence is ludicrous, or at least not plausible.

Historically, the golden ratio initially arose from Euclid, who was fascinated by the pentagon, which has five sides — and yet five is not a magic number.

Looking closer at the Elliott Wave

The basic idea of the Elliott Wave is that all price movements have two segments:

» The *impulse wave* is the way the crowd wants to take the price in a trend. Considering that the right way to look at price developments is through the lens of crowd psychology, impulse is an excellent choice of words. Each impulse wave has five parts: three waves that go in the trend direction, alternating with two that go in the opposite direction.

» In a correction, each *corrective wave* has three parts: two that go against the main trend and one that goes with it. If a bull market reaches a new high in five waves instead of three and also goes down in five waves instead of three, you're witnessing the beginning of a major bear market.

You'll often see three clear waves up, although sometimes a move has more upwaves than three, as in Figure 17-4. The three-waves rule is only the model of how markets move, not a rigid orthodoxy.

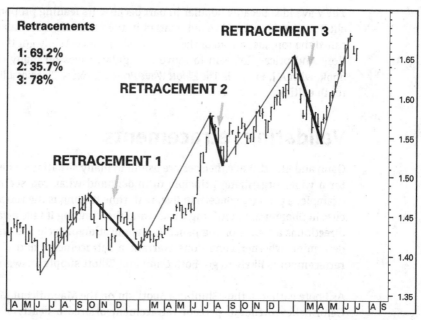

FIGURE 17-4: Wavelike appearance of a trend.

© John Wiley & Sons, Inc.

Elliot Wave practitioners are the first to admit that calling corrective waves is tricky, much harder than seeing impulse waves. Experienced practitioners advise against straining to make a correction "fit" the Elliott Wave model. A correction often also just keeps on going, whereupon it isn't a correction but a true reversal and thus a new trend in the opposite direction.

Counting waves can be an elaborate and time-consuming process, and miscounting as prices evolve can result in losses and having to start all over again. If the wave idea appeals to you, be prepared to devote a lot of time to it. If you choose not to count waves, you can still benefit from the observation that trends start with an impulse wave that then retraces in the opposite direction before the trend resumes. "Buy on the dip" isn't bad advice when you're sure that you have a trend.

Figure 17-4 shows a security with four waves and three corrections (69.2 percent, 35.7 percent, and 78 percent). Notice that none of the percentage retracements qualifies precisely as a Gann or Fibonacci number, although you might stretch the point and say that 68 percent isn't all that far from 62 percent (Fibonacci) and 78 percent is fairly close to 75 percent (Gann). Most traders acknowledge the wave-like movement of prices even if they don't try to count them according to the Elliott Wave principle.

The wave idea became popular in part because its leading proponent, Robert Prechter, called for a massive bull market in 1982 that did materialize — and then he called the top, just ahead of the 1987 Crash. That certainly got the market's attention! And prices do seem to move in regular waves on many charts. Prechter's book, with A.J. Frost, is *The Elliott Wave Principle* (New Classics Library), now in its tenth edition.

Validating retracements

Gann and Elliott Wave theories are useful in many situations where you're looking for a wider organizing principle to understand what you see on the chart. For example, a primary concern in live, real-time trading is the retracement, as I discuss in Chapter 2. Identifying a trend and then finding it fade away in the opposite direction is a source of anguish. A key application of cycle and wave concepts is to determine whether conditions warrant a retracement, and if so, how far the retracement is likely to go. Both Gann and Elliott supply answers.

As I note earlier in the "Shining a Spotlight on the Magnificent Mr. Gann" section, Gann believed the 50 percent retracement offered a nearly surefire method of entering a new trade after a 50 percent retracement. Fans of the Fibonacci sequence assert that the 38 percent and 62 percent retracement levels occur more often than chance would allow and are reliable retracement ending points to reenter a trade. I've found the 62 percent retracement level in my own trading to be reliable well more than half the time. Here's an issue: If you were to put the main Gann retracement numbers (12.5, 25, 50, and 75 percent) and the main Fibonacci retracement numbers (23.5 percent, 38 percent, and 62 percent) on the same chart of a trend, you'd have so many lines that the next retracement would be bound to hit one of them or a level near one of them.

WARNING

Some advisors using one of the wave or cycle ideas choose to display the retracements that did work while conveniently not mentioning all the others that could have been shown on the same chart. In other words, they're going to be right no matter how the retracement turns out. You may see advertisements and solicitations claiming that the seller has objective methods of forecasting securities prices, and these methods are often based on Gann or Fibonacci "scientific" principles. Beware. By definition, all math is science. If you're going to follow an advisor, put your faith in a consistently winning track record rather than in claims of an inside track to universal truth.

Like all technical methods, applying Gann and Elliott Wave ideas is an art, and constant revision is necessary as prices evolve. Statisticians scoff at magic numbers, but in any particular market or security, if a majority of traders believe that a retracement will stop at 38 percent, 50 percent, or 62 percent after a peak, they can and do make it come about.

The sensible approach to Gann and Fibonacci retracement ideas is to be aware of their influence over some traders. You don't have to believe in cycles, the universal truth embedded in Fibonacci numbers, or that market prices follow a hidden system in order to take advantage of what the crowd is thinking.

Chapter **18**

The Mind-Blowing Ichimoku

chimoku embodies just about every technical concept in this book — trending, support and resistance, pivots, trend reversal, momentum, stops — everything but the kitchen sink. This seems like a lot of performance for a few lines on a chart, but it's all there if you take the time to study it. Ichimoku takes more time than conventional technical analysis, in part because the mindset is less focused on raw supply/demand and fear/greed, and tries to detect value in a more organic way. This entails some tricky arithmetic. You can find out just what you need to know about ichimoku in this chapter.

Taking a Closer Look at Ichimoku

Ichimoku's design is intended to deliver an instant visual snapshot of a price's trendedness — up or down, strong or weak, nearing or at a turning point, and other aspects of the price move. Ichimoku means "at a glance" in Japanese, and that seems like an impossibly tall order. But with a little practice, you can find ichimoku does work to deliver the goods. The following sections can help you get started.

Defining ichimoku and its characteristics

When you first see an ichimoku chart, you'll be tempted to say "at a glance" must be ironic and you're being the butt of a joke. As Nicole Elliott says in her YouTube video, at first ichimoku seems like spaghetti. But stick with it. With a little practice, the "glance" aspect will turn out to be true, and very useful. That's because the raw price lines will fall above or below the clouds, and the clouds form a range of prices that are an estimate of the equilibrium price. This is a sister-under-the-skin of the theory of reversion to the mean that I discuss in Chapter 2.

In a nutshell, ichimoku places a series of specific fixed-number moving averages on the chart, and the crossover delivers the buy/sell signal, as in conventional technical analysis. Ichimoku also projects an arithmetic manipulation of the moving averages into the future to create an area of support/resistance (named a *cloud*) that is self-adjusting because it's based on the moving averages. I describe the arithmetic methodology later in this chapter in the "Building a cloud" section.

Eyeing ichimoku's differences with conventional technical analysis

Ichimoku doesn't offer anything conceptually different from conventional technical analysis, and all the techniques will be familiar to you. Ichimoku, for example, uses the midpoint of the high-low range in its moving averages. (Chapter 7 discusses the high-low range, and Chapter 12 discusses the moving average.) See Table 18-1 for some of these differences.

TABLE 18-1   **Comparing Ichimoku and Conventional Technical Analysis**

Ichimoku	Conventional technical analysis
Uses only candlestick notation.	Uses several varieties of bar notation.
Always uses standard time on *x*-axis.	Has the option of looking at price action regardless of time (point-and-figure, other methods).
Uses midpoint of high-low range.	Uses high and low separately in indicators.
Uses moving average of the midpoints with one using the close.	Uses the moving average of the close.
Delivers self-adjusting areas of support and resistance.	User needs to add support and resistance.
Midpoint methodology entails display of self-adjusting 50 percent retracement.	Fifty percent retracement can be added; not self-adjusting.
Moving averages have stair-step appearance.	Moving averages are smooth.
Momentum is implicit.	Momentum can be explicit.
Projects moving averages forward and backward in time.	Doesn't project moving averages.
Self-contained and self-sufficient.	Can be added to endlessly.

Adapting to new core concepts

To start grasping ichimoku, you have to abandon a few of the core concepts you probably have accepted and buy into some new ones. For example, in conventional analysis, analysts consider the relationship of the close to the high. If the close is at the high, the market is wildly bullish. If the close is at the low, sentiment is seriously bearish, and both of those judgments inform your decision on your next trade. But the ichimoku mindset considers the high and low as *extremes* when what you're seeking is the best expression of sentiment — the average.

In addition, conventional technical analysis uses the close to calculate moving averages (as well as other indicators). Not so in ichimoku, which uses a slew of moving averages calculated on the *average* of the high and low over the period, not the close alone. This makes a great deal of sense if you consider that what you're aiming for in a moving average is the essence of the price change. So, a conventional moving average built on the close will incorporate some of those wildly bullish or bearish price extremes, while the ichimoku technique waters them down by using the midpoint. Think of ichimoku as using *moving midpoints* rather than moving averages based on the close.

A third difference is that ichimoku calculates averages based on past data but then projects some of those lines out into the future. This is such a problem for software designers that it took several years for them to catch up. You may have to buy an add-on to your software program, although many have it built-in by now.

Finally, non-Japanese ichimoku users didn't rename the components but kept their Japanese names, including some that aren't normal usage in English. This is a form of respect for the techniques. Take a deep breath and just master the names. There are only seven.

TIP

The ichimoku open-close averaging arithmetic makes for smoother, less choppy moving averages than averages constructed using just the close. This process delays the crossover signal. This is only one of the reasons ichimoku is an excellent way to avoid whipsaws, something all trend-following suffers from.

Building a cloud: Starting with moving averages

The ichimoku chart consists of a series of moving averages and their attendant crossovers, just as in conventional technical analysis, but by also shifting some of the moving averages forward, the ichimoku chart offers a new feature, an area of support and resistance named a *cloud*.

REMEMBER

Moving averages are the workhouse of technical analysis, but in ichimoku, they have a twist. Not only does the ichimoku calculation methodology apply plain-vanilla moving averages, it also projects two of them into the future to form a cloud and one of them backward in time to nail down perspective, as the following list shows:

>> **Tankan-sen:** This is the highest high plus the lowest low over the past 9 periods divided by 2. *Sen* means line in this context.

>> **Kijun-sen:** This is the highest high plus the lowest low over the past 26 periods divided by 2.

Figure 18-1 shows the tankan and kijun in the regular manner. The crossover of these two lines is a buy or sell signal as in any other moving crossover rule, but with some refinements I describe in this list.

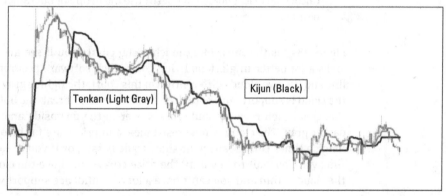

Tenkan (Light Gray)

Kijun (Black)

FIGURE 18-1:
The tankan
and kijun.

© John Wiley & Sons, Inc.

>> **Senkou span:** To most English speakers, the word "span" means the amount of space something covers, like a bridge span or an arch span. A *span* is the distance of something from end to end not interrupted by anything else. It's an uncommon usage to apply the word span to a chart line, but you can get used to it.

The senkou-span has two parts:

● **Part A:** The tankan + kijun divided by two *projected out 26 days*. So, Part A is an average of shorter-term plus longer-term prices projected into the future.

● **Part B:** The highest + lowest price over the past 52 periods divided by 2 and also projected out 26 periods. So, Part B is the average of a full year of the high and low and thus ultra-long-term.

Parts A and B together form the cloud or kumo, as Figure 18-2 shows.

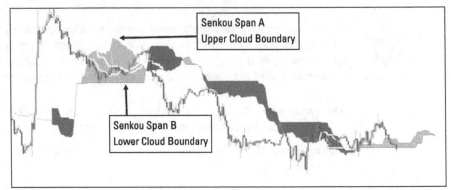

FIGURE 18-2:
Parts A and B of
senkou-span
form the kumo.

Senkou Span A
Upper Cloud Boundary

Senkou Span B
Lower Cloud Boundary

© John Wiley & Sons, Inc.

>> **Chikou span:** Today's close projected 26 periods back in time. This is the only calculation in ichimoku that doesn't use the midpoint but rather the close directly.

Figure 18-3 is the most like the ichimoku charts you'll see and use, although it looks a lot better in glorious living color. Each software program will color each line and the two clouds differently. On this chart, the lighter gray cloud marks that the cloud is support, and note that the price doesn't break the bottom of the cloud. The cloud then reverses and crosses over to the downside and changes color to darker gray. The cloud is now resistance, and prices are far below the cloud for a longish time. This means your short trade is safe, or if you can only buy, it's not time yet. You wait to buy until the price crosses to above the cloud. At that point the cloud is thin and you can't have a lot of confidence support will hold.

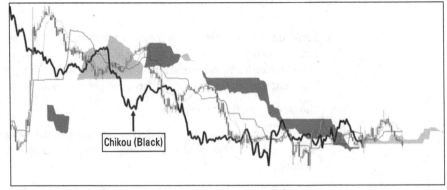

Chikou (Black)

FIGURE 18-3:
Ichimoku series.

© John Wiley & Sons, Inc.

ICHIMOKU'S EMBEDDED MOMENTUM

Ichimoku uses moving averages, but the end result is different from a conventional moving average crossover system (see Chapter 12) in the following ways:

- Ichimoku uses three numbers in its moving averages — 9 periods, 26 periods, and 52 periods.

  The ichimoku moving average uses 26 days because in Japan at the time the technique was invented, trading took place on Saturdays, making 26 days an accurate count for a month. Weirdly, nobody adjusts the ichimoku moving average to match the Western week, presumably because it works well the way it is. And oddly — very oddly — when Gerald Appel devised the MACD in the late 1970s, he also used 26 days as one of the parameters, long before ichimoku became known in the West. He selected 26 days because it was the optimum number over a gazillion trials. (Check out Chapter 2 for more on the law of large numbers.) Elliott notes that when Hosoda wrote down the ichimoku methodology in 1969, computers weren't available to all, and he used dozens of students to do the backtesting work — and validated the 26-day parameter.

- The MACD isn't only a directional indicator, but also a momentum indicator. To the degree ichimoku contains momentum, it's more a suggestion and inference than a direct calculation. Another difference between Appel's MACD and ichimoku — Appel uses a 12-day as the second moving average whereas ichimoku uses 9 days.

Grasping Why Analysts Rely on Ichimoku and Why You Can

Ichimoku delivers a visual impression of trendedness and how strong or weak the trend may be in not one, but two contexts — the upcoming future in the form of the cloud and the perspective of today's price move compared to 26 days ago in the form of the chikou.

In obtaining the senkou spans, you're creating leading edges, which may be considered a form of resistance when the current price is below the cloud. If the current day's candlestick is above the cloud, the function of the cloud switches to support at the top of the cloud and secondary support at the bottom of the cloud. In practice, prices often penetrate the cloud in both directions.

If you think about it for a minute, you can see that a fat cloud means a wider high-low range in recent price movements, or volatility. A fat cloud also implies stronger support or resistance, an insight you don't get from any other support/resistance indicator, although not everyone agrees a fat cloud confers confidence. But experiences suggests a fat cloud implies the probability of a breakout in the opposite direction is low and correspondingly, when the cloud gets really skinny, you need to worry about a reversal.

In Figure 18-2, note that the two spans switch sides a few times and before they do that, the width of the cloud is pared down to nothing. The exact crossover point isn't meaningful or useful for trading purposes but can be interpreted as displaying the actual equilibrium point.

It may seem a little strange to project out old data into the future and by such a long period of time — 26 days. But projection serves the purpose of illustrating where *balance* lies. In the chart in Figure 18-3, the scale is tipping to one side — downward. After a giant rally on the left-hand side, the security slides downward for a prolonged period. The cloud is effective resistance on four occasions. When the price finally does break above the cloud on the right-hand side, the cloud is thin and sure enough, the latest price is testing support at the very bottom of the cloud.

Refer back to Figure 18-1 and the plain vanilla moving average crossover; you'd have had 12 trades. In following just the moving average crossover plus buying or selling only when price is above or below the cloud, the number of trades is pared down to four. In practice, you may use additional non-ichimoku measures for entry and exit, but ichimoku alone reduced the total number of trades and rescued you from moving average whipsaws.

Stay with me — there's more. Finally, add the chikou line, which is today's close plotted 26 days *into the past*. This is hard to understand, but ichimoku traders swear it's the most important thing on the chart. As long as the chikou is above the price bars, you're confident market sentiment is still bullish, and the more space, the better. When it starts poking down into the bars, sentiment is turning negative. Think about downward poking for a minute — it means today's price is lower than prices over the past 26 days. The drop hasn't reached the moving averages yet and thus not the cloud, either, but you can see "at a glance" that sentiment is shifting. This is the sense in which chikou displays momentum. It's not measured in exact numbers like relative strength or MACD — although you could take the exact number from your software data window and do something extra with it. One only slightly goofy thing to do with chikou is to hand-draw the line at the same slope out into the next period.

Ichimoku gives clear signals when prices are clearly trending and a tangle of lines when prices aren't trending. When prices are above the cloud, the top of the cloud is support, and when prices are below, the bottom of the cloud is resistance. What if the chikou line is far above or below both the prices and the cloud? In Figure 18-3, the chikou line is deeply below both prices and the cloud. You may say this is a measure of being oversold and suspect an upside correction could be on the way. Sure enough, the chikou bottoms just past the middle of the chart and prices do indeed surge above the cloud after that. You should buy when the chikou crosses above the close and sell when it crosses below. The chikou plots a possible future that quite often turns out to be correct.

Using Ichimoku in Your Analysis

You can use ichimoku a little or a lot. You are welcome to experiment with ichimoku in setting up your trading rules. Here is some guidance on a few issues.

Venturing inside the cloud

The buy signal in ichimoku is the crossover of the two moving averages with the additional condition that current prices must be above the cloud. When both conditions are met, it's fairly safe to buy. The opposite is true for a downside moving average crossover and prices needing to be below the cloud.

REMEMBER

What if you have the crossover but prices venture inside the cloud? Some analysts say get out until that above/below the cloud condition is met. This squaring rule ensures you're trading only when the trend is very strong. It may also leave you twiddling your thumbs for longer than you like. Other analysts say it's okay to hold a long position with the current price inside the cloud as long as the bottom edge of the cloud isn't broken. In other words, you can use the cloud as a built-in stop loss. If you're long and the price falls to the cloud top, you can have a stop at the cloud top for (say) half your positions. The other half has a stop placed just below the bottom of the cloud. This two-part exit rule has the virtue of being crystal clear and simple, but it's labor-intensive — you have to change the two stops every day. It also has no reference to how much money you are willing to lose. See Chapter 5 for more on stops.

Changing time frames

What about the fractal quality of charts? Can you use ichimoku on a 60-minute chart, or 240-minutes? Yes, the spooky fractal quality still applies. In fact, most retail traders in the foreign exchange (FX) market trade on time frames shorter than one day and were among the first to adopt ichimoku (as they were among the first to adopt all technical analysis when its popularity exploded in the mid-1980s). When you search for YouTube presentations on ichimoku, the vast majority will be showing FX charts. Don't let it bother you — ichimoku is universal and can be applied to any security.

Ichimoku on time frames less than a day, however, tend to have prices much closer to the cloud than the daily time frame. See Figure 18-4, the daily chart. You see a moving average crossover at the arrow, which arrives just after an opening gap down. The price then proceeds straight through the entire cloud in a few days.

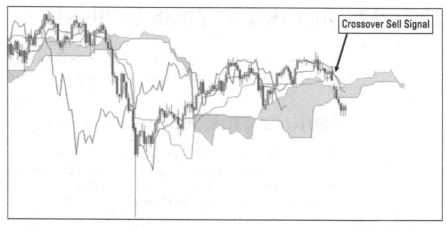

Crossover Sell Signal

FIGURE 18-4: Ichimoku with crossover.

Now look at the same chart on the 60-minute time frame in Figure 18-5. This chart delivers the moving average crossover 10 hours before the daily chart, for an extra 63 points, which is more than half the average daily true range. But after prices have plunged straight through the cloud and out the other side, they start creeping back up — twice. In fact, the second upmove is right at the top of the cloud when the chart ends. How to think about that? The trade is safe on the daily chart — the cloud is far above current prices. But you aren't trading on the daily chart. What else can you consult?

As it happens, you can look at several things:

>> The last two candlesticks are dojis. The doji candlestick means the market participants are deeply uncertain about what's coming next. When in doubt and looking for scraps of evidence, don't neglect candlesticks as a stand-alone sentiment indicator. And this is despite the most recent high exceeding the previous high. Remember, you don't care much about highs or low in candlestick work. You care about the core thrust, not the possibly flaky extremes.

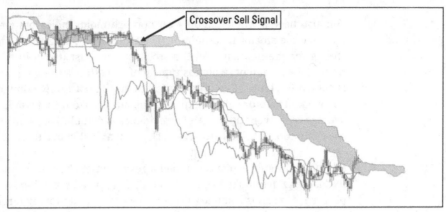

FIGURE 18-5: Ichimoku with crossover on 60-minute chart.

© John Wiley & Sons, Inc.

>> The two moving averages are at about the same value. Sometimes you have to consult your software's data window to be sure.

>> The chikou in the circle in Figure 18-6 is strange and inexplicable, but the current price projected 26 periods back is often a correct predictor. In this case, it's pointing down.

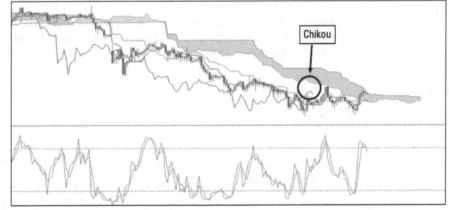

FIGURE 18-6: Ichimoku on 60-minute chart with stochastic oscillator.

© John Wiley & Sons, Inc.

Trading with Ichimoku

You can trade ichimoku as a stand-alone technique. It certainly has all the characteristics you want in a trading guide: direction, momentum, even a built-in stop.

You also have a whole panoply on non-ichimoku indicators you could add. You may like the stochastic oscillator (see Chapter 13), because the heavy trending is ending for the moment and the stochastic is most useful in a sideways, range-trading environment, which is typical of the aftermath of a giant move and what is shown in Figure 18-6. The stochastic in the bottom window is crossing to the downside. Therefore, don't expect an upside breakout that would deliver a moving average crossover buy signal. The evidence is cumulative — ultimate resistance at the cloud top isn't likely to break. The stop at just above there is safe.

Ichimoku doesn't explicitly embed a reversion to the mean concept as I describe in Chapter 2. Ichimoku is more dynamic than mean reversion and also more complicated. A mean is a single number, albeit always a moving target, whereas ichimoku uses multiple means and jiggers them around to push them forward and backward in time. A mathematician could probably tell you in how many ways ichimoku is *not* a reversion to the mean theory.

So now harken to my comment in Chapter 16 that when you're adding indicators to get confirmation of your primary "ruling" indicator, you want something with a different theoretical basis. And a linear regression line bookended with a two standard error channel is mathematically entirely different from ichimoku, as Figure 18-7 shows. Sure enough, most recent prices testing the cloud top are also testing the channel top. A little peek above the lines is acceptable in both cases and doesn't qualify as a breakout.

You can easily add plain old support and resistance lines, too. If you like channels and waves, you can use them in conjunction with ichimoku. Nicole Elliott likes to add Elliott Waves (see Chapter 17).

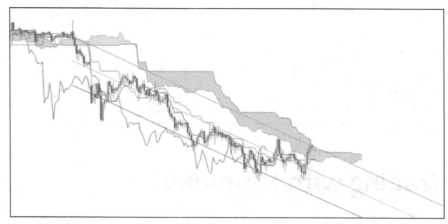

FIGURE 18-7:
Ichimoku on 60-minute chart with standard error channel.

© *John Wiley & Sons, Inc.*

ADDING TRADING RULES

Manesh Patel, in *Trading with Ichimoku Clouds, The Essential Guide to Ichimoku Kinko Hyo Technical Analysis* (John Wiley & Sons, Inc.), adds specific trading rules, some of which are summarized here. You buy when

- Price is above cloud.

- Tenkan crosses above kijun.

- Chikou has lots of space between itself and the price (implies strong momentum).

- Price is at least 50 points away from farther edge of cloud in the opposite direction.

- Entry is less than 200 points from tankan and 300 points from kijun.

Patel also warns that you must adjust your stops every day. Patel shows multiple back-tests of his ichimoku trading plan. In fact, his discussion of backtesting comprises more than 100 pages of a 198-page book. This is an important point: Backtesting ichimoku is hideously complicated and takes some computational skill. Most users won't take the time and put in the effort. But ichimoku is like all other technical analysis concepts — it will fail some of the time, and to prevent getting hosed by the occasional failure, you need to add specific trading rules, like Patel's list. Note you don't change the parameters — the 9-day, 26-day, and 52-day — but instead stipulate the number of points (or dollars) away from the conventional entry/stop/exit points ichimoku dictates to ensure they work the best on your security. Most rules will result in signal delay, as Patel found in his backtests.

5

The Part of Tens

IN THIS PART . . .

Check out how the top traders build their trading plans to suit their abilities and appetite for risk.

Join the experts in applying indicators that most effectively make the most gains and lose the least while doing it.

Review the top resources to get more knowledge about technical analysis and the technical trading mindset.

Chapter **19**

Ten Secrets of the Top Technical Traders

Technical trading can take any number of equally valid forms. The trader who waits for multiple time frame confirmations on three indicators can claim just as much technical validity as the guy with the itchy trigger finger who has to trade every hour. The technical trader is the retired rocket scientist, the self-taught housewife, the cubicle programmer, and the college student. You can't tell from looking at them who is the best technical trader. The technical trader may be sane and reasonable or an outright crackpot, but both types are technical traders. You'll also run into poseurs who claim technical expertise but really only know one or two things, and although those one or two things may work for them, the danger is real they won't work for you. As for the academics with systems perpetually in test mode, they may be technical analysts, but they aren't traders.

Until you put cold, hard cash down on your technical trading ideas, you aren't a trader. You may be the smartest guy in three counties, but if you can't make money trading, you're just a smart guy, not a trader. In fact, the ability to focus is far more important than brainpower in technical trading. Whatever their styles, successful technical traders all have one thing in common — they've built a trading *plan* that uses the technical tools that suit their appetite for risk, and they follow it. A plan contains not only high-probability indicators, but also money management rules. This chapter discusses ten secrets that successful technical traders utilize. Remember them as you start trading.

Appreciate Probability

Technical analysis works because market players repeat the same behaviors, but history never repeats exactly. The probability of any particular pattern or indicator repeating itself — getting the same outcomes — is never 100 percent. If you want to be a technical trader, you have to gather the data from your trades carefully and apply expectancy rules in order to have any hope of long-run success. You must keep track of your win-loss ratio and the other metrics of the expectancy formula in Chapter 5. To trade without having a positive expectancy of a gain is gambling. It's not trading. You may have a slight edge from using a few indicators, but you don't really have control of your trading. Position sizing and other aspects of money management are useful, too, but if you don't have positive expectancy on every trade, in the long run you *will* lose.

Backtesting Matters

You need to examine the trades your indicators would have generated over some period of time — a minimum of six months, and a year is better — to get a fair estimate of the expected gain/loss. You have to write it down and do the arithmetic. Technical analysis entails a scientific mindset and that means keeping records. I keep an Excel spreadsheet on every trade and update it every day. It takes less than ten minutes per day, and it's a small price to pay to know exactly what indicators were working that day and what indicators didn't work. Betting your hard-earned cash on an unproven set of indicators is wishful thinking, not informed trading. Indicators give you an edge, but not a winning lottery ticket.

The Trend Is Your Friend

The single best way to trade is to follow price trends. If you buy when an uptrend is forming and sell when the uptrend peaks, you'll make money over the long run.

REMEMBER

If you can't see a trend, sit back and wait for the trend to appear. Nobody is holding a gun to your head forcing you to trade. To stay out of the market when the security isn't trending is okay — as is getting out of the trade temporarily when a pullback occurs. A security purchase isn't a lifelong commitment. You're not being disloyal or unfaithful to your security if you sell it during a pullback.

It doesn't matter if your security — Apple, Amazon, or whatever —is the best security of all time. The essence of technical analysis is to analyze the price action on a chart to arrive at buy/sell decisions. You determine whether the security offers a trading opportunity by looking at indicators on the chart, not on the fundamental characteristics of the security itself. You're welcome to trade only high-quality names, but in practice, you can make just as much gain from a real dog of a stock as from the market's darlings.

Entries Count as Much as Exits

The buy-and-hold strategy has been discredited many, many times. Buy-and-hold is never the optimum methodology. Look back at the two big stock market crashes in recent history — the tech wreck that started in March 2000 and the financial crisis collapse that started in October 2007. It took 13 years for the S&P to recover and hold a level above the high of March 2000; in other words, if you owned the entire 500 stocks in the S&P, you would have made no net gain for 13 years. Debunking buy-and-hold is why you often see "it's when you sell that counts." But, obviously, when you buy counts, too. You can have a so-so trend identification system, but if you get in at a relative low, you will thrive, whatever your holding period.

Stops Aren't Optional

Stops are different from the embedded buy/sell signals in indicators. A moving average crossover doesn't know how much cash loss you'll be taking as it lolly-gags its way to the sell signal. You have to decide ahead of time how much loss you can tolerate, either in cash or percentage terms, and just accept it when stops get hit (without remorse or anger). A good stop is not so tight that you forego any real chance of achieving the expected gain, nor so loose that you give back a big chunk of previously earned gain. You need to acquire skill at crafting stops that combine your security's behavior patterns with your risk appetite — a double set of conditions.

Don't trade without stops. There are no acceptable excuses for failing to use stops.

Treat Trading as a Business

You should make the trading decision on the empirical evidence on the chart and not on emotional impulse. It's human nature to bet a larger sum of money when you've just had a win. Likewise, you may become timid after a loss.

A good technical trader follows his trading plan and disregards the emotions created by the last trade or by the emotions that swell up from being in *trader mode*. Trader mode can inspire competitive aggression, analysis paralysis, confirmation bias, and any number of other interferences with the rational application of your trading regime. You may not have a full-bore trading system, but you should trade what you do have systematically. A good trading regime uses rules that impart discipline in a conscious effort to overcome the emotions that accompany trading. Trading is a business, and business should be conducted in a non-emotional manner.

Eat Your Spinach

It's not a personal insult when you take a loss. Ask brokers or advisors for the single biggest character flaw of their customers; they all say the same thing: "The customer would rather be right than make money."

You can't control the market. The only thing you can hope to control is yourself. If you become unhinged by your losses, you haven't built the right trading plan. You need to start over with different securities, different indicators, and/or a different win/loss ratio in your expectancy calculation.

Don't let a winning trade turn into a losing trade. You can have a fine trading system with excellent indicators properly backtested for the securities you're trading but still be a lousy trader if you don't have sensible trading rules. A good trader differentiates between indicators (which only indicate; see Chapter 4) and trading and money-management rules (which manage the risk; see Chapter 5).

Technical Stuff Never Goes out of Date

All through this book I name writers from the 1930s, concepts developed in the 1970s, or indicators invented in the 1990s. Nothing is ever discarded in technical analysis. Books written 70 years ago are still useful today. Technical thinking never goes out of date; the technical analysis crowd just keep adding to it. Thumb through the index of *Technical Analysis of Stocks and Commodities* magazine. You can find multiple reviews, updated nuances, and suggested uses for old-timey indicators and new candidates alike.

You've made a good decision to start your journey of technical discovery with this book. Start at point-and-figure or momentum and work back to moving averages. Start at candlesticks and move back to standard bars. Get a certain bare minimum of information under your belt before you start placing trades; the universe of technical analysis is flexible, and you can bend it in many different equally valid directions.

Although technical ideas never go out of date, they do go in and out of style. During the 1980s and enduring to today, Elliott Wave has been in style. In the 1990s, MACD was the fad of the moment. It's still a splendid indicator, but not front-page news. Today ichimoku is all the rage. You should care about fads in indicators because to some extent, the number of technical traders using the star indicator of the day are making its outcomes a self-fulfilling prophecy.

Diversify

Diversification reduces risk. The proof of the concept in financial math won its proponents the Nobel Prize, but the old adage has been around for centuries: "Don't put all your eggs in one basket." In technical trading, diversification applies in two places:

>> **Your choice of indicators:** You improve the probability of a buy/sell signal being correct when you use a second, noncorrelated indicator to confirm it. You don't get confirmation of a buy/sell signal when you consult a second indicator that works on the same principle as the first indicator. Momentum (see Chapter 13) doesn't confirm relative strength because it adds no new information.

>> **Your choice of securities:** You reduce risk when you trade two securities whose prices move independently from one another. If you trade a technology stock, you achieve no diversification at all by adding another technology stock. You'll get a better balance of risk by adding a stock from a different sector.

Swallow Hard and Accept Some Math

Appreciating the limitations imposed on trading by probabilities is one thing. Each indicator and each combination of indicators has a range of probable outcomes.

Say you've designed a good set of indicators that will likely generate a high return. But tweaks to your money management rules can double or triple that. Money management can be tricky and difficult, and it needs to be in a feedback loop with your indicator system. For example, should you increase your position in a winning trade? This is the position-sizing problem, and analysts are passionate about whether to do it or not.

Money management takes you into the realm of betting. In a nutshell, you have to know when to hold 'em and when to fold 'em. These decisions can be informed by your indicator probabilities, but the final decision is risk management in the face of other (non-indicator) factors that are unknown, known as the realm of *game theory*. Don't be surprised to discover that the first originator of the theory of games modelled it on . . . poker. Refer to the Appendix for additional reading on the subject.

REMEMBER

Money management is the central reason why it's usually a mistake to buy someone else's trading system, which was customized for the risk preferences of the designer — not you. To find your own risk preferences, you need to experiment with different money management rules. You can have a so-so system but magnify it into a splendid system with clever money management alone.

Chapter **20**

Ten Rules for Working with Indicators

Indicators measure market sentiment — bullish, bearish, and blah. Indicators are only patterns on a chart or arithmetic calculations whose value depends entirely on how *you* use them. You use indicators for many trading-related decisions, including identifying a trend, knowing when to stay out of a security that isn't trending, and knowing where to place a stop loss, to name just a few. This chapter offers a few tips and tools you need to maximize your use of technical analysis indicators.

Don't Jump the Gun

Figuring out technical analysis starts with bars, both standard bars and candlesticks. To use fancy indicators before you understand bars is to rush the learning process. Think of the bar as a miniature indicator. Besides, indicators are constructed by manipulating bar components arithmetically, and indicators will be easier to understand after you have mastered the bar and its components. And you can trade on bars alone without ever needing to dive into the intricacies of indicators. One example is trading on candlesticks alone. Many setup traders never look at indicators; they just look at bars.

Every bar tells a story about crowd behavior. Exceptional bars tell you more than ordinary bars, but try to listen to all bars. Floor traders complain that electronic trading lacks something valuable that being on the exchange floor offers — the noise of the crowd. As an individual trader, you can't hear the crowd, either, but as you look at bars, imagine the noise each bar must be sending out — shouts, hisses, groans. (See Chapter 6 for more on bar basics.)

Defeat Your Math Gremlins

You don't need to be good at math to use math-generated indicators. You may not understand how your microwave works, but you can still use it to reheat the soup. Don't give up too fast. If an indicator isn't immediately obvious, just observe it for a while.

If you put in the effort and still don't get it, don't worry — move on. The world is full of great indicators. You just need to find the ones that make sense to you. For example, I never did get the hang of average directional movement (ADM) indicators. Don't use an indicator because some self-styled expert says that it has a great track record. If you don't understand it, it won't work for you. Keep in mind that everything works. You just need to find what works for you.

Embrace Patterns

Patterns are indicators, too. Prices never move in a straight line, at least not for long, and patterns can help you identify the next price move. When you see a double bottom, you can feel confident that the right trade is to buy — and this principle is true well over half the time and normally returns a gain of 40 percent. Some patterns are easy to identify and exploit, whereas others may elude you. As always, if you can't see it, don't trade it. See Chapter 9 for the lowdown on patterns.

Pattern identification may be subjective, but it's a handy adjunct to math-based indicators, especially the candlestick patterns. They can save your bacon while your indicators are in the process of leading you astray.

Finally, you don't have to believe in elaborate theories about cycles or Fibonacci numbers to use a Fibonacci retracement pattern. Many experienced traders eschew math-based indicators and use only patterns, and for this reason alone, it pays to find out how to see patterns.

Use Support and Resistance

Support and resistance (see Chapter 10) are central concepts in all technical trading regimes. You can pinpoint support and resistance by using any number of techniques, including hand-drawn straight lines or bands and channels created out of statistical measures. Momentum and relative strength indicators can help estimate support and resistance, too. To preserve capital, always know the support level of your security and get out of Dodge when it's broken.

Follow the Breakout Principle

The breakout concept (which I cover in Chapters 10 through 12) is universally recognized and respected. A *breakout* tells you that the crowd is feeling a burst of energy. Whether you're entering a new trade or exiting an existing one, trading in the direction of the breakout usually pays. You'll still get zapped by failed breakouts — everyone does. The reason to study successful versus failed breakouts is to minimize those whipsaw losses. One of the key reasons to include ichimoku in your strategy is that it has a built-in whipsaw detector.

Watch for Convergence and Divergence

When your indicator diverges from the price, look out. Something's happening. You may or may not be able to find out why, but divergence often spells trouble. Convergence is usually, but not always, comforting. (This rule refers to convergence and divergence of indicators versus price, not the internal dynamics of indicators like the moving average convergence/divergence, or MACD.) For more on convergence and divergence, check out Chapter 12.

If your security is trending upward and the momentum indicator is pointing downward, you have a divergence. The uptrend is at risk of pausing, retracing, or even reversing. If you're averse to risks, exit. I know a trader who makes the buy/sell decision exclusively on convergence/divergence.

TIP

Look for divergence between price and volume, too. Logically, a rising price needs rising volume to be sustained. The most useful divergence is a paradoxical one, where the price is falling but by less than abnormally high volume would suggest. This divergence may mark the end of a major downtrend and is more reliable than the percentage retracement or round numbers touted by so-called market experts.

Backtest or Practice-Trade Honestly

Backtesting serves two purposes:

>> To get a better parameter for an indicator than the default setting that came packaged in your software or online service

>> To count your hypothetical trades with their gains and losses that arise from an indicator or set of indicators you chose to use in your trading

Experience shows that the standard technical analysis parameters are useful over large amounts of data and large numbers of securities — that's why their inventors chose them. For this reason, some traders never feel the need to perform their own backtests. They accept the standard parameters and put their effort into something else, like bar or pattern reading that is subjective and the very devil to track accurately and evaluate for effectiveness.

REMEMBER

But if you *are* going to backtest indicators to refine parameters, do it right. Use a large amount of price history when testing an indicator — and don't make the indicator fit history so perfectly that the minute you add fresh data, the indicator becomes worthless *(curve-fitting)*. Observing price behavior and estimating the range of sensible and reasonable parameters is better than finding the perfect number. The perfect number for the future doesn't exist.

While fiddling with indicator parameters is optional, backtesting to get gain/loss data and other information is not. You simply have to do it or else you'll be flying blind. You should never plunk down your money on a trade if you don't have an estimate ahead of time of how much you're likely to make and how much you're likely to lose and the percentage of times you can expect either outcome. In other words, you need positive expectancy to trade properly using technical analysis and the only way to get it is by some tiresome bookkeeping.

REMEMBER

Conditions are changing all the time in the technical analysis industry, but you won't find free online services that allow full backtesting where you supply your trading rules and indicators in deep detail. To do proper backtesting, you need your own software or one of the advanced brokerage platforms. Even then, it's a slog to master backtesting.

Accept That Your Indicators Will Fail

Indicators are only an approximation of market sentiment. Sentiment can turn on a dime, or the approximation can be just plain wrong. In fact, indicators are often wrong. Support lines break for only a day or two instead of signaling a new trend as a breakout is supposed to. Textbook-perfect confirmed double bottoms fail the very next day instead of delivering that delicious 40 percent profit. And moving averages generate whipsaw losses even after you've added every clever and refined filter known to man.

It's a fact of life — your indicator will fail, and you will take losses in technical trading. Don't take it personally. Indicators are only arithmetic, not magic. Console yourself with knowing that indicators reduce losses, and reducing losses helps you meet a primary goal — to preserve capital.

Get Over the Idea of Secret Indicators

Technical traders have devised thousands of patterns and math-based indicators. They can be combined in an infinite variety of ways over an infinite number of time frames with an infinite number of qualifying conditions. So the idea that somebody has discovered a superior combination of indicators is possible. But none of the indicators are secrets, and no indicator combo is going to be right all the time.

The secret of successful trading doesn't lie in indicators. Shut your ears to the guy trying to sell you an indicator that "never fails!" Of course it fails. If it never fails, why would he sell it to you? And why should you have to pay for an indicator in the first place? You don't. Every indicator ever invented is easily available in books, magazines, and on the Internet.

REMEMBER

The secret of trading success lies not in indicators, but rather in managing the trade. You can have a mediocre set of indicators but make very nice gains if your trade management is topnotch, which can include scaling in and out, allocation among securities, diversification, and the Big Kahuna — intelligent stops.

Open Your Mind

Indicators are addictive. You read about a new indicator that seems so logical and appropriate that it becomes your new darling. Suddenly you can apply it everywhere. It's good to be adaptive and flexible, but remember that the purpose of using indicators is to make money trading, not to get a new vision of how the world works. Always check that your new indicator plays well with your old indicators. You picked your favorite indicators for a good reason — they help you make profitable trading decisions. Keep discovering new indicators, but don't fall in love unless the new indicator meshes well with the old ones. A top reason to stay up-to-date on indicators is that their popularity waxes and wanes. Always take a new indicator out for a spin, if only to get a feel for what other traders are looking at. Remember, traders form a crowd and crowds move in conjoined ways.

Technical analysis never throws anything out. Ideas that were devised and written a hundred years ago are still valid and have been refined and improved over the years — and added to charting software on online charting. Don't close your mind to a concept because some old fuddy-duddy invented it in 1930. Equally, don't close your mind to something new. New things come along all the time, too. New things take two forms: modifications to core concepts and ideas from left field, like ichimoku. The best way to see modifications is in the pages of *Technical Analysis of Stocks and Commodities* magazine (see the Appendix). Chapter 18 discusses ichimoku in greater detail.

Appendix

Additional Resources

A first look at all the technical resources available today can be intimidating. Don't let yourself get overwhelmed. You don't need *all* this stuff; you just need enough to get started, and getting started really means knowing what topics to type into the search box of your browser. I believe that just about every key word in technical analysis appears in this book. Don't neglect YouTube; many technical analysts post short lessons on techniques.

You're welcome to find one technical trick and just use it over and over again, like Toby Crabel's opening gap tactic (see Chapter 16). In fact, the Crabel technique is one of the ones available on YouTube. Plenty of technical traders use a single technique to achieve their financial goals. I know one trader who made his first million after reading a single book, and a really old one, at that (Edwards and Magee — see the "Additional Reading" section later in the chapter). Others don't want to miss a trick and try all the ideas and methods.

You should spend time and money on research because you never know when you may come across an idea that strikes a resounding chord in you — the *Eureka!* moment when you say to yourself: I can do this. Don't forget — a workman needs good tools. Software, data feed, a few books, and a subscription to *Technical Analysis of Stocks and Commodities* magazine are all part of the beginner's toolbox.

If you're a beginner, you may choose a trial run with free online charting services. See an overview comparing online services with software by the American Association of Individual Traders at `www.aaii.com/journal/article/the-top-technical-analysis-charting-websites`. At that site you can read that online services are convenient, but don't offer the power or flexibility that you get from software and your own PC's operating system. Online charting just doesn't have the depth and breadth of features that software-based programs have. You can also find that online services usually have only a selection of indicators, not the full library.

The Bare Minimum

You could use price quotes from the newspaper, graph paper, and some colored pencils, but this is the computer age for a reason — efficiency. Here you can find information about charting software and other important online resources.

Charting software

Every major broker offers charting software today, including TradeStation (www.tradestation.com) and TD Ameritrade (www.tdameritrade) and its fancy platform Think or Swim (www.thinkorswim.com). If you prefer to get your own software and data instead of using what a broker offers, here are some ideas. *Disclosure:* I've been using Metastock by Equis (www.equis.com) since the early 1980s, and so to me it's the most user-friendly. It comes with preset indicators, user guide, and starter data.

Metastock is named year after year, along with TC2000 by Worden (www.worden.com) on the Top Ten lists available online. Good charting software is also available at eSignal.com, which offers a plug-in to link to more than 40 brokers. Other charting packages are

>> EnsignSoftware (www.ensignsoftware.com)

>> NinjaTrader (www.ninjatraderpro.com)

TIP

Conduct your own search online for software. If you're attracted to Elliott Wave, for example, type that into the search engine and check out the results.

REMEMBER

You should require the following from your software or online charting service:

>> Your charting software should allow you to switch time frames (from 3 minutes to monthly) and show bars in regular OHLC format, candlestick format, and point-and-figure.

>> It should allow you to draw an unlimited number of lines of different types, including standard error channels.

>> It should contain at least ten standard parameter indicators, including moving averages, moving average convergence/divergence (MACD), stochastic oscillator, Bollinger bands, and various momentum indicators, including RSI.

>> It should allow you to add your own indicators and to modify the parameters of the indicators included in the charting package.

>> It should allow you to backtest your own trading ideas by selecting start and end dates.

>> It should contain ichimoku charting, which most services now have.

Online resources

Become familiar with charting conventions you can find on websites such as www.stockcharts.com, www.stockchartwizard.com, www.finance.yahoo.com, www.chartadvisor.com, and other free sites. A dandy site that offers a lot of lessons, many free, is www.candlestickforum.com. In foreign exchange, www.fxstreet.com is useful.

You can easily find many excellent newsletters and blogs, but resist the temptation to start following them for education and entertainment. Until you get some technical work of your own under your belt, you just aren't qualified to evaluate the newsletter or blogger. If you find one that you can't resist, start keeping your own track record of the win/loss performance.

Aim for trading advice and tips from respectable sources. The websites www.seekingalpha.com/ and www.zerohedge.com/ often contain useful articles by advisors who also sell their main reports separately. You can research free blogs at https://tradingstrategyguides.com/top-10-trading-blogs/. When I checked this site, it named four of the blogs I follow. Other sites name top blogs. Judging whether a blogger is respectable or fly-by-night is sometimes difficult. Check the blogger's resume for education and for employment at top firms.

WARNING

Beware Twitter as a source of reliable trading ideas and advice. Free advice is worth exactly what you're paying for it. Plenty of perfectly respectable advisors use Twitter to promote their work, but unless you follow a single name for a long time — at least 6 months — and keep a detailed track record of the trades recommended, you're vulnerable to getting suckered into a pump-and-dump scam or some other error. On Twitter, people publish rumors as hard information and sometimes lie through their teeth.

TIP

Technical Analysis of Stocks and Commodities magazine (www.traders.com) offers annual reviews of all the charting software and system vendors. The magazine also contains excellent articles on new ideas (usually with formulas you can paste into your software), new combinations of old ideas, backtests, advice on how to manage trades, interviews with traders (I was interviewed for the December 2005 issue), and more. The subscription is $89.99 per year and worth every penny.

Additional Reading

I like books. Books are the medium through that other traders deliver new ideas and offer guidance on avoiding mistakes. I begin this section with a list of my favorites.

My favorites

Here are some of my favorites that I refer to on a regular basis:

>> *How I Made $2,000,000 in the Stock Market* by Nicholas Darvas (Lyle Stuart)

>> *How I Made $1,000,000 Trading Commodities Last Year* by Larry Williams (Windsor Books)

>> *Long-Term Secrets to Short-Term Trading* by Larry Williams (John Wiley & Sons, Inc.)

>> *Trader Vic — Methods of a Wall Street Master* by Victor Sperandeo (John Wiley & Sons, Inc.)

>> *Evidence-Based Technical Analysis* by David Aronson (John Wiley & Sons, Inc.)

>> *Candlestick and Pivot Point Trading Triggers* by John Person (John Wiley & Sons, Inc.)

>> *Profitable Candlestick Trading* by Stephen Bigalow (John Wiley & Sons, Inc.)

>> *Building Reliable Trading Systems* by Keith Fitschen (John Wiley & Sons, Inc.)

>> *Market Wizards: Interviews with Top Traders* by Jack Schwager (HarperBusiness)

Encyclopedias and reference guides

Sometimes you'll run into a term whose meaning you've forgotten or a concept you want to explore. You can look up just about anything in technical analysis if you have these on your bookshelf:

>> *Trading Systems and Methods* by Perry Kaufman (John Wiley & Sons, Inc.)

>> *Encyclopedia of Chart Patterns* by Thomas Bulkowski (John Wiley & Sons, Inc.)

>> *Encyclopedia of Candlestick Charts* by Thomas Bulkowski (John Wiley & Sons, Inc.)

>> *Encyclopedia of Technical Market Indicators,* 2nd Edition, by Robert Colby (McGraw-Hill)

>> *Technical Traders Guide to Computer Analysis of the Futures Market* by Charles LeBeau and David Lucas (McGraw-Hill)

Classics

Every trader should read these books:

- *Technical Analysis of Stock Trends* by Robert Edwards and John Magee (Saint Lucie Press)
- *Reminiscences of a Stock Operator* by Edwin Lefevre (John Wiley & Sons, Inc.)
- *Extraordinary Popular Delusions and the Madness of Crowds* by Charles Mackay (Harmony Books)

Special areas

To add more detail on specific indicators and techniques than I can cover in this book, check out this list:

- *The Definitive Guide to Point and Figure* by Jeremy du Plessis (Harriman House)
- *New Thinking in Technical Analysis: Trading Models from the Masters* by Rick Bensignor (Bloomberg Press)
- *Bollinger on Bollinger Bands* by John Bollinger (McGraw-Hill)
- *Beyond Technical Analysis* by Tushar Chande (John Wiley & Sons, Inc.)
- *Street Smarts* by Laurence A. Connors and Linda Bradford Raschke (M. Gordon Publishing Group)
- *PPS Trading System* by Curtis Arnold (Irwin)
- *The New Science of Technical Analysis* by Thomas DeMark (John Wiley & Sons, Inc.)
- *The Master Swing Trader* by Alan S. Farley (McGraw-Hill)
- *Elliott Wave Principle* by Robert Prechter and Alfred Frost (New Classics Library)
- *Martin Pring on Market Momentum* by Martin Pring (McGraw-Hill)
- *Ichimoku Charts* by Nicole Elliott (Harriman House)
- *Maximum Adverse Excursion* by John Sweeney (John Wiley & Sons, Inc.)

Money management

The technical mindset contains more than indicators — it also includes a form of disciplined trading that goes beyond obeying buy/sell indicators. Trading is more than a mechanical exercise because to succeed over a long period, you need to know your own risk preferences and risk management capabilities. Read these books:

>> *When Supertraders Meet Kryptonite* by Art Collins (Traders Press)

>> *Trading for a Living* by Alexander Elder (John Wiley & Sons, Inc.)

>> *How To Take a Chance* by Darrell Huff and Irving Geis (W. W. Norton & Company)

>> *Van Tharp's Definitive Guide to Position Sizing* by Van Tharp (International Institute of Trading Mastery)

>> *The Mathematics of Money Management* by Ralph Vince (John Wiley & Sons, Inc.)

Probability and statistics

You don't need to dive off a cliff into the deep waters of probability in order to gain a useful working knowledge of the subject. I selected the most entertaining and readable books on probability and statistics here — they each contain hardly any formulas.

>> *Thinking in Bets, Making Smarter Decisions When You Don't Have All the Facts* by Annie Duke (Portfolio/Penguin)

>> *Fortune's Formula, The Untold Story of the Scientific Betting System that Beat the Casinos and Wall Street* by William Poundstone (Hill and Wang)

>> *Probability For Dummies* by Deborah Rumsey (John Wiley & Sons, Inc.)

Index

Symbols

Numbers

A

B

backtesting, 74–77, 334, 342–343
Baltic Dry index, 46
bands
  applying stops with ATR, 263–264
  Bollinger, 261–263, 279
bandwagon effect, 34
bar charts, 113–115
bar scoring, 118–119
bar series, 113–114
bars, 10, 103–119
  black, 148
  building, 104–111
    closing price, 107–109
    the high, 109–111
    the low, 111
    opening price, 105–107
    price bar, 104–105
  candlestick bar, 103, 143
  down-days bars, 108, 113, 114
  Fitschen's simple bar-scoring, 119
  heiken ashi bar, 103
  identifying trends with, 111–113
  key reversal bar, 126
  placement, 148
  special bars, 121–140
    configurations, 121
    gaps, 127–135
    identifying, 123–125
    spikes, 125–127
    trader sentiment, 121–123
    trading range, 135–140
    uncommon, 125
  tick bars, 117
  time frames, 115–118
    daily data, 116
    higher time frames, 116
    shorter time frames, 116–118
  up-days bars, 108, 112, 114

base case, 116
bearish divergence, 248
bearish market sentiment, 7
bearish resistance line, 275
bears, 105
beat the market, 24–25
behavior, crowd, 34–35, 42–44
benchmark levels, indicators, 72
Bernard, Baruch, 180
best six months rule, 306
best-case expected gain, 90
Beyond Technical Analysis (Chande), 245
bias, 56–57
Bigalow, Steve, 141
big-picture theories, 308–309
Black, Fischer, 63
black bars, 148
black box algo trading systems, 19
black crows, 153–154
black real body, 143
blowout (blowoff) bottom, 201
blowout (blowoff) breakout, 193
blowout (blowoff) top, 201
Bollinger, John, 261
Bollinger bands, 261–263, 279
bottoms, double and triple, 276
box size, 271–273
breadth indicators, 49
breakaway gaps, 130–131
breakouts, 24, 70–71, 341
  distinguisng between false and true, 196–199
  false, 178–179
  projecting prices after, 276–278
  putting into context, 198–202
  retracements, 37–41
broken channel lines, 190
broker platforms, 267
Buffett, Warren, 22
Building Reliable Trading Systems (Fitschen), 118
Bulkowski, Tom, 156, 160, 166